THE NATURAL BORDER

THE NATURAL BORDER

Bounding Migrant Farmwork
in the Black Mediterranean

Timothy Raeymaekers

CORNELL UNIVERSITY PRESS   ITHACA AND LONDON

First published 2024 by Cornell University Press

Library of Congress Cataloging-in-Publication Data

Names: Raeymaekers, Timothy, author.
Title: The natural border : bounding migrant farmwork in the Black Mediterranean / Timothy Raeymaekers.
Description: Ithaca : Cornell University Press, 2024. | Includes bibliographical references and index.
Identifiers: LCCN 2023025144 (print) | LCCN 2023025145 (ebook) | ISBN 9781501773648 (hardcover) | ISBN 9781501773655 (epub) | ISBN 9781501773662 (pdf)
Subjects: LCSH: Agricultural laborers, Foreign—Italy, Southern—Economic conditions. | Agricultural laborers, Foreign—Italy, Southern—Social conditions. | Agricultural laborers, Foreign—Government policy—Italy, Southern. | Tomato industry—Social aspects—Italy, Southern. | Racism against Black people—Italy, Southern. | Italy, Southern—Race relations—Political aspects. | Italy, Southern—Emigration and immigration. | Africa, Sub-Saharan—Emigration and immigration. | Italy, Southern—Rural conditions. | Italy, Southern—Economic conditions.
Classification: LCC HD1536.I8 R44 2024 (print) | LCC HD1536.I8 (ebook) | DDC 305.5/630945—dc23/eng/20230901
LC record available at https://lccn.loc.gov/2023025144
LC ebook record available at https://lccn.loc.gov/2023025145

Contents

Acknowledgments

This book could not have come into being without the dedicated support of a great many people. I want to thank, first and foremost, my father-in-law, Franco, for passing on the love of his native region, Basilicata. It is through his spirit that I have felt, and continue to feel, the diaspora condition that reunites so many a migrant who has had to leave home and look for fortune elsewhere. Second, my wife, Silvana, and daughter, Viola, who have shared, and continue to share, this love with me. I feel that our many moments together in Basilicata have constructed our identity as a family. Third, my friend Paul, who, even though not there in person during my research, has continued to keep my connection to Africa alive in the Mediterranean—a fate we silently share as our lives continue. Fourth, Marco and Gervasio, who, in different ways, have been my guides and mentors in the research process that led to this book. Fifth, I want to deeply thank the many people in Basilicata who have delicately lent an insight into their passions, their desires, aspirations, and anxieties during and after my fieldwork—particularly at the Michele Mancino association, where I spent many months living and researching. I also remember with joy the many occasions I have been able to discuss my experiences, perplexities, and doubts with colleagues at the respective geography sections of the Universities of Zurich and Bologna, and with my friends at Cantieri Meticci, whom I all thank for their advice and patience, and who continue to remind me how precious it is to have such a constructive and collegial working environment in these difficult times characterized by neoliberal austerity and uneven distribution of academic resources. I want to thank Wissam Balays for his patient translation of the Arabic graffiti we discovered on Basilicata's ghetto walls. Last but not least, the summer school "at the edge of the state" with colleagues from Europe, Asia, and Africa also served as a regular collegial setting where I have been able to confront ideas with my peers in political ecology studies. A particular thanks to the people at Cornell University Press, who helped me smoothly through the editorial process, and to the two anonymous reviewers whose precious comments and suggestions I appreciated and took to heart. I want to dedicate a special mention, finally, to my colleagues at the Black Mediterranean Collective, in particular Camilla Hawthorne, with whom I have discussed many ideas present in this book. I hope the thoughts expressed here may inspire conversations among our generation and those to come.

THE NATURAL BORDER

INTRODUCTION

More than a concrete sign or place, the frontier is a feeling that creeps over me. It is a feeling of emptiness and abandonment, but also of imminent rupture, a stillness that is ready to explode at any moment. After making a right turn at the height of Candela, I enter a crossroads, which connects to the highway between Bari and Naples, in the heart of Italy's Meridione, or South. While the night sets in, the road gently bends toward the right, and a hilly landscape opens, covered with vast wheat fields. Far away mountain ridges reveal the shadows of a small village, an abandoned farmhouse, a lonely ruin standing still on the rough terrain. Then, suddenly, I smell the stench of burnt plastic. A minute later, I see small campfires on the side of the road, sex workers looking to warm themselves in the night. Another bend to the right, and I am surrounded by tomato fields. In the fading light, I discern the silhouettes of workers ripping the fruits from the soil, while I see tractors driving hectically back and forth to the large trailer trucks waiting to carry the produce away. As the sun sets, the dark sky makes way for the glow of smoldering wheat stubbles farmers leave to burn after the harvest.

This book summarizes five years of ethnographic inquiry in a turbulent territory of agrarian extraction. It discusses the way this territory is actively made from mobile infrastructures like temporary labor camps and informal migrant settlements, which mobilize, channel, and segregate the human and natural resources that enable the expansion of capitalist operations across space. At the same time, the book also highlights how such infrastructures remain a terrain of active struggle and contestation as they form the backbone of profound socio-ecological transformations that characterize the history of Mediterranean supply chain capitalism since the last century and a half. By highlighting the tension between the mobility and immobility, abandonment, and surveillance of migrant agricultural laborers in this deeply bordered space, I intend to highlight the paradox of extractive operations that actively transform the earth and human bodies into productive commodities but simultaneously destroy the very foundations of the life that sustains them—the main point being that, while these operations are often noted for their ability to include (non)citizens in the projects of high modernist development, they may also perform the function of structural exclusion, particularly of informal workers and racialized subjects who are deemed unworthy of modern "civil" integration. While erecting the edifices of modern urbanity and industrialization on one end, capitalist development—particularly in the domain of agrarian production—also actively continues to feed on its own counterimage, a "backward" and "uncivilized" outside space that is both actively marginalized and adversely incorporated into the ideal of formal, modern industrial progress.

The focal point of my inquiry is the South of Italy, more specifically the boundary between Puglia and Basilicata. This region has become an important site for industrial tomato production: a fruit that, like Mediterranean agriculture as a whole, progressively relies on the extraction of precarious migrant labor in the context of global retail supply chains. Taking these two factors, of "cheap labor" and "cheap commodities," as a starting point, I will explore what the deeper territorial processes are behind the production of this ostensibly "made in Italy" commodity of the industrial tomato: how political boundaries are drawn around the land and the resources needed to bring it to fruition, what technologies of exclusion and inclusion enable extractive operations to take place in this agrarian frontier, and which political mechanisms structure the allocation, use, and commodification of resources across space. Through these guiding questions I try to analyze how territories and the resources they are believed to contain are actively constructed through contested notions of identity and space. And I insist on the deep material-social entanglements that underlie and guide these processes of capitalist expansion and contraction through spatially complex dynamics of abandonment and valorization, expulsion, and incorporation.

In the following three sections, I will quickly introduce the main motivation for writing this book, before discussing my two main focuses of natural racialization and bordering infrastructures.

#RUINS

Initially, my decision to work in Basilicata appeared as a classical no-brainer. My wife's parents grew up in a small town at the foot of the Apennine Mountains on the Puglia-Basilicata border. For the last fifteen years, I spent most of my summers there, meeting my wife's friends and hanging around the parental house in the old part of town with my daughter, with the neighbors, and with the *emigrati* (emigrants) who cyclically returned to the village to meet each other and the kin they had left behind. Together with Marco, a photographer and architect, we used to wake up in the early morning hours to drive through the vast plains of the Alto Bradano area—a wide rectangle between Venosa, Lavello, Genzano, and Palazzo San Gervasio—to spontaneously explore the area of the *riforma agraria* (agricultural reform): boroughs and hamlets that once figured in the orbit of a vast land reform during the 1950s and 1960s. In a process that is frequently depicted as a development failure from the perspective of state reformers and agro-capitalist enterprises, the *riforma agraria*, which implied the expropriation and redistribution of around 600,000 to 800,000 hectares (about 1.5 to 2 million acres, or 2,300 to 3,000 square miles) of agricultural land, nevertheless generated a series of important transformations, though mostly indirectly: between the 1950s and 1960s, the Meridione's agricultural workforce dropped from 3.7 to 1.6 million; most peasants ended up working either in the industries in Northern Italy or emigrated abroad (Percoco 2018). Those who had access to the land reform's credit and infrastructures ended up setting up their own firms, which subsequently entered the global market competition. Each of the houses of the agro-towns spawned by the reform included a living space, a small stable for cattle, and a storage room for wheat and utensils. Other *borghi* (hamlets) consisted of a more complex urban organization: in Taccone, for instance, rows of terraced houses, a central square, a church, shops, and facilities for public services were constructed to gather inhabitants in a familiar setting. Subsequently afflicted by massive emigration, the municipality in later years offered free access to whoever would promise to transform one of these abandoned houses into a permanent residence. In the mid-2010s, the hamlet vacated for good, except for one of its warehouses, which kept functioning as a storage space for a local farmer.

While the ruins of the agricultural reform appear as lonely skeletons in the landscape, they also stand witness to a contentious Italian history of peasant revolts and state repression, of persistent socioeconomic inequalities and capital accumulation that runs like a red thread through the Meridione's post–World War II history. Next to this familiar Italian history, however, I was struck to find the traces of a not-so-distant past. In the area of Spinazzola, just across the Puglia border, for instance, boots, cutlery, and utensils lay around in the derelict buildings of an abandoned village as signs of a hasty eviction. On one of our journeys, we discovered an abandoned settlement that still contained the corpses of animals lying around the abandoned watering holes. Other hamlets were deliberately transformed: buildings covered with cardboard and plastic sheeting, used as storage rooms for mattresses and utensils, repurposed as open kitchens or dormitories. Some were permanently inhabited. On one cold winter night, we bumped into a Sudanese man hiding in the niche of what was once a wood oven of a singular house at Mulini Matinelle, close to Palazzo San Gervasio. The next weeks we stopped over to bring him sugar and canned food, until one day he was gone with the freezing wind.

Struck by these absent presences, I started to be more systematic in my travels through Basilicata as my attention gradually shifted toward the northeast, in the area around Palazzo San Gervasio. Here, the cultural heritage of the agricultural reform had gradually taken on a different aspect since the mid-1980s. Abandoned *borghi* were being reoccupied and repurposed by migrant agricultural workers who, when called in by local agri-food firms, came to be employed as "seasonal" laborers. As I quickly found out, though, "seasonal" was a euphemistic term for those workers who, despite their employment in agri-food jobs the entire year, were actively banned from accessing the most elementary public services of nutrition, health, and accommodation. Like the Sudanese man in Mulini Matinelle, these people did not count very much in the official historiography of the Italian land reform; on the contrary, during the next year and a half I spent in Basilicata I witnessed how they were actively reduced to a condition of those with no rights, subject to extortion and exploitation. Black African migrant workers—most of them of West African (Burkina Faso) origins—who make up the majority of the so-called seasonal laborers in Basilicata, continued to camp out in these makeshift ghettos: located amid the fields, built with whatever ready-to-hand materials (branches, sticks, straw, plastic sheeting, canvas, irrigation pipes) they could find, the crude shelters that partly coincided with the agricultural reform hamlets were a demonstration of the fact that agricultural workers had to use their own creativity and networks to fend for themselves in the absence of formal state support. As I was soon to find out, the regional administration's logistical approach to the "problem" of migrant labor, which consisted of the active destruction of migrant habitats combined with the haphazard construction of transitory reception centers or labor camps, contrasted sharply with the largely informal ways in which this agricultural workforce interacted with the rural economy and society.

As I was trying to make sense of the way rural capitalism in northern Basilicata accompanied a politics of inclusion and exclusion, yet another important layer added itself to these already complex dynamics. While authors like Anna Tsing, Dona Haraway, and Jason Moore rightly point at the detrimental socioecological consequences of the type of plantation agriculture I witnessed in Basilicata, I felt that something was missing from this debate. The missing link, in my view, concerned the flattening narrative about the relation between "man" and "nature." In its fundamentally color-blind conception of ecological extinction (Du Bois [1903] 2007; see also Davis et al. 2019), the narrative that tended to dominate public debate in Italy—but also globally—about plantation agriculture and its relation to the Anthropocene appeared to bolster, rather than resolve, the binary categories that had produced the foundations of rural capitalism in this context in the first place. On the other side of the Atlantic, this had not escaped the attention of critical race thinkers like Laura Pulido, who rightly criticized Anthropocene scholars for limiting the disparities produced by capitalist supply chains to the chasm between rich and poor, or "developed" and "developing" countries. Looking more closely, she notices, the problems we are facing today should also be viewed as an outcome of race-related practices, since the meta-processes that have contributed to the Anthropocene, such as industrialization, urbanization, and capitalism, are essentially the products of a racial politics of differentiation (Pulido 2017, 529).[1]

Building on a small but interesting Italian post-Marxist and antiracist literature—particularly in correspondence with the emerging concept of the Black Mediterranean—I grew gradually aware of the deeper history of Black struggle and the ways racial oppression shapes and is shaped by agri-food capitalism in the Italian context, but also of the deliberate marginalization of the *differentiated* life that inhabits contemporary agri-food supply chains but is both deliberately destroyed and restructured through such struggles and their wider political ramifications (McKittrick 2013; see also Black Mediterranean Collective 2021; Gilroy 2021; Hawthorne 2021a). This work has been key for me in developing a more diasporic perspective on the time-space of capitalism. More specifically, it has helped me to understand how the infrastructures of labor segregation that characterize contemporary agri-food chains across the Mediterranean reflect the racialization that has underpinned its birth and growth in this context. It has helped me to place the dynamics of racial differentiation within a longer history of internal and external colonialism (see also Chambers 2008). As I will review in detail in chapter 2, the consolidation of the geo-body of the Italian nation-state was not only significantly intertwined with a process of internal racialization—in the course of which citizens of the South acquired an inferior status as "less civilized" and "not yet" fully recognized citizens of the nascent modern nation-state—but this precarious national-racial identity also shaped Italy's relation with Africa, particularly the Italian colonies of Eritrea and Somalia, which unfolded alongside the process of national unification (Hawthorne 2021a). So, the aim of this book is also to place the history of contemporary Italian agribusiness into a more layered, geographically informed analysis of the Mediterranean as a cradle of modern capitalism, and of the Italian nation-state as one characterized by a constant tension around who can be regarded as a legitimate citizen and who can not.

Immersive Geographies

This book is not a stand-alone effort. My methodological starting point includes previous, detailed anthropological studies by, among others, Benoit Hazard and Hans Lucht, who narrate the attempts, particularly of West African migrants on the Italian peninsula, to reestablish connections between the desires and constraints of rural lifeworlds that have been significantly destabilized because of proceeding globalization and ecological destruction (Lucht 2012, xii; Hazard 2004). These studies accompany a longer interest, particularly in French African studies of the Burkinabè immigration to Europe, by among others Blion, Bagré, Zongo, Bredeloup, and Schmidt di Friedberg, on which this study gratefully builds (for a discussion see Bredeloup and Zongo 2005). The analytical lens of these authors is similar to mine as they describe how African migrants are taking daily jobs as construction workers, harvesters, and day laborers in the urban informal economy. Moving my lens from the urban periphery to the rural centers of industrialized agriculture, I look specifically for the traces that African migrants leave in the rural landscape, analyzing the signs of their segregation and exclusion, but also of their impermanent settlement in this agrarian frontier. The methodological innovations I bring to the fore in this context involve a more explicit sociomaterial outlook and multiscalar analysis of the phenomenon of agrarian change in this rhizomatic and interconnected landscape. Before moving to the discussion of this methodology, I need to say a few words about doing research in explicitly violent settings.

Even if this subject is only marginally addressed in geography as an issue of methodological concern,[2] the fact that I am dealing in this study with an explicitly violent phenomenon of illegalized labor intermediation requires separate attention. My engagement with capitalist labor exploitation in the context of the Mediterranean agri-food frontier—which involves explicitly violent modes of labor coercion, eviction, and destruction—has pushed me to further reflect on what it means to live with and make sense of uncertain and constantly changing conditions in the context of capitalist supply chains. Building on my previous experience (Raeymaekers 2014), I have decided to adopt what Teo Ballvé

(2020) calls an investigative ethnographic stance. Admitting the different onto-logical starting points of ethnography and investigative journalism, his method-ological outlook serves to move beyond the ethnographers' illusion with distant and lonely reflexivity, while grasping the ways certain practices are generated and given meaning as events in a given context. Contrary to overtly militant approaches to research, Ballvé associates himself with a research method that places the micropolitics of difference in the foreground to understand the sub-tleties and complexities of power relations in a postcolonial context (see also Gledhill 2000). In a field like this, it is mandatory to pay attention to daily life and lived experience. Ethnography indeed offers a unique method to immerse oneself into such experiences, critically reflect on one's positionality, and make space for interpretive iterations.

During my study, I combined a total of sixty recorded interviews with public administrators in Puglia and Basilicata at various levels of town and regional administrations, from population registries to town council members and regional migration offices, with labor union representatives and antiracist activ-ists, along with an uncounted number of unrecorded interviews with policy experts, journalists, and academics active in the domain of labor migration. Next to these interviews, I could rely on a detailed analysis of public records, specifically of newspaper articles and court cases about labor intermediation, in the region of Basilicata, thanks to my access to the database of the Associ-azione Michele Mancino in Palazzo San Gervasio. The association holds a vast archive of newspaper and court case clippings about migration, which it has been accumulating and storing since its inception in 1996. Furthermore, it has been an active participant in various contestations of human rights and labor rights violations. My connection with this association permitted me to secure further access to precious information in this regard: besides furnishing personal con-tacts, it allowed me to get hold of detailed reports and accounts of the history of labor migration in the Alto Bradano area of Basilicata, which gradually became the focal point of my inquiry. My research in Puglia, on the other hand, relies on shorter research I did on the site of Casa Sankara–Azienda Fortore, a former agricultural reform institution turned migrant reception center in 2014, close to San Severo (province of Foggia). Thanks to my connection to the project's main protagonists, whose story I tell in chapter 5, I could secure access to key political figures who supported the initiative. During my intermittent research visits to Casa Sankara (four in total) I carried out dozens of unrecorded interviews with migrant workers inhabiting the site, along with repeated, and partially recorded, interviews with the initiators of the project. These interviews accompanied a further snowball sampling of acquaintances and allies of the project's initiators, whom I also interviewed formally for this project.

Next to these formal inquiries, however, I felt I needed to spend more time to also foreground the lived experiences of the workers this book takes to heart. Beyond my short visits to the ghettos of Foggia (Grand Ghetto) and Cerignola (Tre Titoli, or Ghana House), where I interviewed inhabitants and activists from Radio Ghetto, CGIL, Caritas, and Emergency, I decided to focus my ethnographic inquiry on the Alto Bradano area, where, apart from the work of Domenico (Mimmo) Perrotta, there has been no systematic study of African labor migration. I spent a total of seven months in the ghettos and agrotowns of this area, hanging out regularly with African workers and with local youth. Methodologically, I build here on what Biao Xiang (2013) calls a "multiscalar" ethnographic method. Rather than an immersion exclusively in one social network or ethnic group, this method allows for more question-driven research, which explicitly follows through on multiple connections and leads. Multiscalar ethnography, as Xiang explains, is concerned with how social phenomena are constituted through actions at different scales. It follows the lead of multi-sited ethnography by tracing a series of empirically driven "tracking strategies" that follow commodities, people, or policies across interconnected geographic scales. At the same time, it seeks to understand how the constantly changing coordination of social networks across geographic scales actively transforms spaces. In my case, this method allowed me to note the increasing ethnic separation as well as the differentiated levels of social embeddedness of agricultural labor in the given context (for a discussion see Perrotta and Raeymaekers 2022). And it offered a way to conceptualize the active boundary work that different mediating figures fulfill while they contribute to changing norms and political subjectivities (compare Lindquist, Xiang, and Yeoh 2012; Lin et al. 2017).

Yet while such immersive methods do have the potential to reveal the quotidian dimension of extractive operations and the cultural and political meaning they acquire, they reveal only one part of the longer histories of racial oppression, colonization, and discrimination that today's experience of monocropping agriculture are embedded in. For these histories, I could only rely on existing literature. Chapter 1 tries to give an overview of that literature while bringing to the fore the missing links in what I call the color-blind perception that characterizes much of the Anthropocene literature. Finally, I need to emphasize that my personal inquiry has been at times a lonely exercise, but mostly, and fortunately, a constant collective reflection and conversation with others. People who have accompanied me on my tracks during the seven months I spent physically in Basilicata and Puglia between 2015 and 2019 during different agricultural seasons included my wife, a social psychologist; Marco, a photographer and architect; the theater director Pietro Floridia; and several students and colleagues.

One student, Marc-Antoine Frébutte, dedicated a master's study to an adjacent area, which resulted in a monograph (Frébutte 2021). A colleague with roots in Burkina Faso, Muriel Côte, stayed with me in the field for several weeks. With colleagues Ilaria Ippolito and Mimmo Perrotta, I also curated a couple of publications. These research collaborations did not emerge coincidentally but are also a way to demonstrate—*contra* the ideal of recording, lonely in the field, life as it is—that ethnography is and should always be a collective exercise, which involves joint reflections, strategies of inquiry, and adaptations to a constantly moving terrain.

It is evident that investigating violent economies, like the one I present here, also generates a more immediate problem of access—to people, sites, and information. The high stakes involved in my inquiries made the spaces I visited often polarized and politically charged. At a more rudimentary level, often people I talked to were extremely reluctant to share information. This reluctance concerned many stakeholders: from the day workers who were tired of intrusive media attention, to bureaucrats who were unhappy with outside interference, to NGO representatives who regarded research as ideologically laden. As Ballvé (2020) highlights, "The close-up study of economies of violence inevitably implies scholars' intrusion into high-stakes spaces that are dangerous, hyperpolarized, politically charged, socially opaque, and fraught with ethical dilemmas." Such intrusion inevitably results in moments when one must acknowledge one's proper limits. Despite my long experience in a protracted war zone like the east of the Democratic Republic of the Congo, I noticed sometimes during my fieldwork that I was not able to "cut it"—a feeling that sometimes left me desperately in doubt about the added value of ethnographic research in general (see also Billo and Hiemstra 2013; Coddington 2017).

One episode made these limits blatantly clear to me. While I was talking with a group of legal advisers in the ghetto of Ghana House in 2016, a young man in a pickup truck speeded perilously by, nearly running over my feet. "He's the son of the local boss," one of the legal advisers told me. "He just wants to show us who is in charge here." A moment later, a decrepit car screeched to a halt at the local bar in front of us. A tall man got out and went into the bar. We heard some noise inside. Not more than five minutes later, he stormed out again and speeded away in his car. Forty-five minutes later, an ambulance arrived. The driver said there had been a fight, and that someone had been wounded. Nobody seemed to care, not even the driver, who—after we indicated the bar in front of us— slowly parked his ambulance there, then helped carry out a heavily bleeding man moments later. Gathered around the trunk of another car a short distance away, a group of workers who were filling out forms with their Italian *capo* watched the scene with indifference.

While these events unfolded, a group of workers had joined us from their tents to get some legal advice. One told a member of the team that he had been expelled from a migrant reception center in Parma four months earlier. He said he had since been sleeping rough on the streets, first in Naples and then here, hoping to find some work. Another Ghanaian man said he arrived in Italy in 2011 from Libya. He didn't want to leave there, he said, because he had always worked there, was happy to earn his money, and had his own apartment. While we were commenting on Mediterranean geopolitics, another, considerably younger, boy joined us. He said, "You know why we don't learn Italian here? Because the only words they tell us are 'fuck,' 'fuck you,' and 'faster'!"[3] We all laughed. But at the same time, this short visit also revealed an intricate pattern of violence, which—as I wrote—was not easy to grasp, neither from a psychological nor from a political perspective. Twenty minutes later, while we were taking some pictures of a truck scale (a scale to weigh the content of truck trailers), a man walked toward Marco and me from a neighboring gate, asking us insistently what we were doing there. I protested, saying we were on a public road and he had no right to meddle in our business. Minutes later, a car stopped between us on the gravel pathway. The driver and the man at the gate told us again we should leave. Something snapped in me. Infuriated, I told them they should get lost. The driver called to Marco and told him that "your friend better calm down," showing him what looked very much like a pistol in his lap. Dragged away by Marco, I got into our car, and we drove off. I was still infuriated but—after Marco told me what he saw—happy to be safe from harm.

This episode brings together many of the acute challenges one faces when doing research in contested resource frontiers. Part of this challenge has to do with the difficulty of identifying who exactly is wielding power in such unstable environments—an opaqueness that, I will argue, is functional to the type of boundary I am describing here. But another part of my uneasiness, I felt, also had to do with the fact that I was doing ethnographic research "at home." To address these multiple challenges, I decided to adopt two complementary methods: triangulation and multi-sitedness. Concretely, triangulation involves a way of assuring the validity of research by using different kinds of data as well as methods of data collection. Mandatory for the nonmilitant researcher in such a context is to remain transparent about the fact that interviews will be held with as many stakeholders as possible. In my case public interviews involved humanitarian organizations, NGOs, local associations, local and regional administrators, labor union representatives, day workers, police, and activists. While this method may still raise suspicion—as I will indicate, humanitarian agencies remained surprisingly closed to any form of sharing information—it also opens doors that more militant research in this context would be unable to access. Besides interviewees sharing the official version of the region's political interventions, for example, I found some public administrators to be more open than they were with my Italian colleagues about the highly contested character of these interventions.

While openly activist research risks glossing over the inevitable discrepancies and internal struggles that accompany militant activism, a multi-stakeholder ethnography allows researchers to keep track of the five key questions that investigations of extractive operations in my view should hold dear: *who* is telling me *what*, for *what reason*, *where*, and *when*? I remain convinced that speaking out against the injustices and inequalities one inevitably encounters in the field does not require taking sides with one single perspective or group. A nonpartisan triangulation may help instead to take issue with the intricate patterns of inequality that typically have not one but many origins and are situated at different geographic scales. In Italy, there has been a tendency to blame one specific actor, or set of actors, as culprits in what appeared to me (but only after some time) to be much more systemic culpability of agri-business expansion in the given context. In this sense, I found it more instructive to spend some time with different participants in this informalized and marginalized economy, including such "bad guys" as the *caporali* (poorly translated as "gang masters") and their wider social networks, rather than a priori siding against them as either illegal outcasts or antistate rebels (see also Raeymaekers 2014). Knowing the motivations and interactions of *caporali* in Italian agri-business proved particularly helpful in understanding the reconfiguration of public authority in this domain; like spiders in an intricate web of connections, their role is often to ensure these connections while at the same time making their own role in this web opaque and indispensable. As Axelson et al. (2022, 594) have reiterated, it is important to regard regulatory spaces as being actively "made and remade through direct and indirect exchanges and interactions between intermediaries and state actors." Just as it is important to side with the workers, it is equally important to study the relative power of the differentiated actants that make up migrant labor assemblages, as well as the ways these are socially and materially entangled. In that sense, a nonpartisan, triangulated ethnography may prove indispensable for understanding the networks, practices, and social meanings that underpin not only the local proliferation of migrant labor assemblages but also their important global ramifications.

The Margin Is the Center of Change

This book is also embedded in a more personal engagement with the borders of the Mediterranean. Next to the ethnographic focus I described above, I have been progressively embroiled in a political process of living among events, dynamics, and alliances in ways that make it impossible to detach the story I write here from my personal experience. The entry point to this more embodied account was the cultural festival of Matera in 2019, the year in which this city, located in central Basilicata and supposedly one of the longest permanently inhabited urban settlements since the Neolithic period, won the title of European Cultural Capital. Together with the Associazione Michele Mancino, I was asked to give a contribution to this festival based on my ongoing research. At first, I decided to approach the subject with a certain detachment. My initial interest in Basilicata had grown out of curiosity with the spatial coincidence between what the medical emergency NGO Médecins sans Frontières (Medici Senza Frontiere, or Doctors Without Borders), in its 2016 study, had called the "informalization of refugee settlements" in Italy on the one hand, and the broader transformations of the country's rural landscape in this region on the other.[4] Since the downfall of Muammar Gadhafi and the subsequent NATO intervention in Libya around 2011 (which I will comment on in depth in chapter 3), a growing segment of migrant laborers in agri-food production of West African origin either had the status of refugee or were applying for asylum. With all this in mind, I imagined a more embodied approach to the issue of labor in this agrarian frontier. With a couple of friends, I co-instituted MIC|C—which stands for the Margin Is the Centre | of Change—at the time a yet anonymous group of activists, scholars, and migrant workers. One of the first actions of MIC|C was to occupy the main square of Matera with an intervention titled #RUINS. With this operation, MIC|C's intention was to expose the temporality of life as it had existed, like the ashes of a smoldering fire, or the remnants of a camp that had moved on.[5] By counterposing, on one end of the square, a pile of rubble taken from one of the destroyed agricultural reform hamlets, with the construction of a temporary ghetto shack on the other end, we wanted to highlight the visible tension we saw emerging between the active extraction of wealth from the earth and from laboring bodies, and the deliberate destruction of life that sustains this wealth.[6]

In the context of the inquiry that led to the writing of this book, MIC|C's operation thus could be interpreted as an initial, playful incursion into the terrain of this study—a kind of futuristic elegy with similar aesthetic dimensions as the Jinx Project's interventions in New York's underground and the Stalker project in Rome, for example (see Deyo and Leibowitz 2003; Wiley 2010; Elden 2013a). What appeared as playful and innocent at first, however, revealed a more serious questioning of the way ruined infrastructures in the Basilicata context coincided with a layered process of separation and segregation. MIC|C's subsequent project, Archaeology of a Frontier, in fact tried to document in a more systematic manner the kinds of impermanent settlements migrant workers in the northern Bradano area had built and inhabited. The interactive map and the objects displayed on the website had the main objective of documenting what it means to build a livelihood and organize one's life while being constantly on the brink of eviction. The objects MIC|C gathered in the abandoned ghettos were a demonstration of life as it existed—an abandoned shoe, a repurposed jerry can, a pay slip from a bus, a sachet of a painkiller. They showed the different components of an impermanent life, strained by extreme circumstances of displacement, marginalization, and exclusion. The map, in turn, contained the traces and connections of a much longer trajectory of forced displacements and resettlements in this interconnected landscape. By connecting the dots between the different ghettos and the agricultural economy they sustained, the map showed the functionality of reproducing ghettos as places that are both materially and discursively singled out as standing somehow "outside" the perimeters of civility, and migrant workers as "bodies out of place" in a political ecology that is charted along racial lines.

Social Reproduction

While discussing my material in subsequent workshops, conferences, and public events (including at the Black Mediterranean conference of the University of Palermo and the Development Studies program in Vienna), I initially joined the ranks of border archaeologists like Dan Hicks, Sara Mallet, and Jason De Léon, whose work demonstrates how today's bordering policies articulate the boundary between displaced and settled populations in the landscape. In their research on the forced eviction of the so-called Jungle of La Lande in Calais, France, for instance, Hicks and Mallet simultaneously foreground and criticize what they call a form of "environmental hostility": the official UK policy to deter migration across its territorial borders.[7] Through their archaeology, they show not only how identities are mapped into a landscape, but also how the limits and the protection of one are dependent on the limits and the protection of the other (Hicks and Mallet 2019, 19; Mould 2018). In a different context, of the US "Prevention through Deterrence" policy on the US-Mexico border, Jason De Léon foregrounds the role of contemporary archaeology in research on border processes and undocumented migration. His Undocumented Migration Project not only analyzes how the development of technologies to control and deter border crossings generates and intensifies illegal migration, but also how the deliberate weaponizing of the "natural" environment tends to normalize migrant deaths in the landscape of the Sonora Desert. Both works privilege a participatory ethnographic research method that uses archaeology as one of many tools we can use to study and document extensive border processes. As De Léon (2015, 51) writes,

"In my approach to clandestine migration, I see border crossers not as anonymous shadows crawling through the desert, but as real people who regularly live and die in this environment and whose voices and experiences we should privilege." During a brief encounter in Zurich, Mallet and I agreed on the necessity to overcome the disciplinary division of archaeology as a historical study of traces and geography as a science of separations and intersections while we were looking for the material entanglements between people and their environment in the context of hypermobility. While I was interested in showing not only how geography is used as a weapon in an active politics of displacement and unsettlement but also how life occurs and takes root in such apparently disturbing circumstances, Mallet shared her archaeological insights into the ways identities are actively mapped into a landscape, and how the limits and the protection of one are dependent on the limits and the protection of the other.

At a later stage, I came to realize that the experience of MIC|C enabled me to take the layerdness of contemporary supply chain capitalism seriously in my work. I saw this layerdness in contraposition to Anthropocene literature that continues to describe agrarian frontiers predominantly in terms of their commodification (Tsing 2005, 27; see also Moore 2015, 2016; Patel and Moore 2017; Steffen, Crutzen, and McNeill 2007; Chakrabarty 2009; Latour 2014; Haraway 2015). Building on the world systems analysis of Fernand Braudel and Immanuel Wallerstein, Jason Moore argues, for instance, how the plantation has become progressively rooted in a violent relationship with planetary webs of life. The terminology world ecologists like Moore adopt in this context is that of "cheap nature" and "cheap labor": through the commodification of the earth's (sub)soil as well as the human efforts in labor, they argue, the entire globe and its inhabitants have gradually taken on the semblance of an extractive frontier. For Moore,

> Cheap Nature is "cheap" in a historically specific sense, defined by the periodic, and radical, reduction in the socially necessary labor-time of these Big Four inputs: food, labor-power, energy, and raw materials. Cheap Nature, as an accumulation strategy, works by reducing the value composition—but increasing the technical composition—of capital as a whole; by opening new opportunities for the investment; and, in its qualitative dimension, by allowing technologies and new kinds of nature to transform extant structures of capital accumulation and world power.

For him, therefore, capitalist frontiers are nothing else than the closing in of capitalism on alternative ways of life: "In all this, commodity frontiers—frontiers of appropriation—are central. Thus, the tightly connective movements of 'internal' restructuring and geographical expansion that restore and reconfigure the Four Cheaps" (Moore 2015, 153–54).

While drawing inspiration from world systems analysis and world ecology, this book tends to take a different approach to the political ecology of capitalist supply chains. I invite the reader to consider a more dynamic approach to the way capitalist operations "hit the ground" in different contexts (see also Mezzadra and Neilson 2019, 2; McKay 2017). Rather than a straightforward process of capitalist machines rolling out their infrastructures and gobbling up previously disconnected ways of life in their abstract space, I see a much more fragmented process of articulating and disarticulating the foundations of these ways of life as "resources" that can be valorized in ways that feed, or do not feed, capital. As Gastón Gordillo (2014) notes on yet another agrarian frontier—that of the Argentinian Chaco—the ruptured multiplicity that characterizes these processes forces us to rethink not just what is destroyed but what is created by the apparently cyclical valorization and ruination of forms of life through capital's needs. And he invites us to move beyond this abstract homogenization that does not resonate with the sensuous texture of actual places and objects.[8] In this sense, I am much closer to Gordillo and Neil Smith, for instance. Smith argues that geographical space is not just a container in which relationships manifest themselves, but rather the opposite: it is through our actions and our relationships that we actively produce the space in which capitalist operations get grounded and unfold. The fundamental question about the specific spatial patterns that characterize capitalist society, Smith argues, and which I build on in this book, must be explicitly coupled to the *political* question of how these spatial configurations contribute to the survival and expansion of uneven capitalist development (Smith 2008, 3–4; emphasis added). Even if we can understand geographic space as the totality of relations that determine the mode of production globally, we must open our eyes to the uneven development of capitalism as the geographical expression of the tension that is inherent in its very expansion. As Smith (2008, 7) writes, "For not only does capital produce space in general, it produces real spatial scales that give uneven development its coherence." This focus on the production of scales enables us concretely to overcome what Doreen Massey calls a "Russian doll" perspective on space: a perspective that considers space as a flat surface on which time proceeds, in linear, progressive fashion. Instead, she writes, we need to reconceptualize time-space as being actively constructed out of "interrelations," as the "simultaneous coexistence and interactions at all spatial scales, from the most local level to the most global" (Massey 1992, 80). Space is not static, nor time spaceless. While we can analyze spatiality and temporality separately, neither can be conceptualized in the absence of the other.[9]

It is this production of spatial scales that I am interested in exploring further in the domain of agrarian capitalism in the Mediterranean. Two aspects of Smith's analysis will provide the foundations of my argument. The first regards the production of "nature": "What jars us so much about this production of nature," Smith writes, "is that it defies the conventional, sacrosanct, separation of nature and society. . . . We are used to conceiving of nature as external to society, pristine and pre-human, or else as a grand universal in which human beings are but small and simple cogs." But here, Smith warns us, our concepts have not caught up with the reality of the division of labor that capitalism has historically generated in our lifeworlds as "natural" human beings. Whereas Nature (with a big *N*) has increasingly become treated as a resource to be exploited for the betterment of humanity, the human efforts invested into this commodification are being valued subsequently as labor (for a discussion of labor as a commodity see chapter 1 and the conclusion). It is this process of the division of labor, as well as the subsequent spatial mechanisms that separate human labor from nature as a resource, that stands at the center of my argument. The focus of this inquiry will be the cyclical investment and disinvestment of capital through the spatial reorganization of the landscape that is inherent in the expansion of agrarian capitalism. On a conceptual level, this focus reflects Rosa Luxemburg's ([1951] 2003) observation that the process of original accumulation that Karl Marx wrote about is never quite completed, because as capitalism penetrates ever deeper into our lives, it tends to produce cyclical frontiers of intrusion and abandonment.[10] More specifically, I am interested here in analyzing and narrating the colonial efforts of claiming and repurposing the vast landscapes of Southern Italy and West Africa for the purposes of monocropping agriculture as a lived process (see also Mah 2010; Stalabrass 1996) that highlights their active rooting in complex memories and experiences.

The second aspect of my inquiry regards the reverse side of this argument, or the question of how, once "Nature" has been claimed as a resource, geographic spaces that are deemed as peripheral to capital accumulation are subsequently reframed as "natural" spaces (with a small *n*) that are depicted as simultaneously uncivilized and wild, distant, and threatening. Even if Neil Smith recognizes that, with the expansion of economic development, the material substratum we are used to call "nature" is more and more the product of a social production, and more specifically of the social relations of capitalist production (that is, the division of nature and society, and the division of labor between nature and humankind), he dedicates less thought to the social and material effects of this social production on those spaces that are not, or not yet, or not completely, encapsulated by the global division of labor. The point I want to make here is that, even if nature has become somehow a universal means of production in the sense that it becomes an appendage, an adjunct to the capitalist production process (what Smith calls "second nature"), there still remains a sphere of life that can be conceived of as "natural" in the sense that is not, or not yet, or not completely gobbled up in this capitalist production process. This is the sphere that political ecologists refer to as the sphere of reproduction.

In Stefania Barca's definition, the sphere (or what she calls forces) of reproduction comprises those "less-than-humanized (racialized, feminized, dispossessed) subjects who reproduce humanity by taking care of the biophysical environment that makes life itself possible": "they keep the world alive, yet their environmental agency goes largely unrecognized in mainstream narratives of that epoch of catastrophic earth-system changes that scientists have called the Anthropocene" (Barca 2020, 1). Building on Barca's definition, I pick up the invitation of political ecologists to think of the Anthropocene concept with "the obscene" (Swyngedouw and Ernstson 2018), that is, alongside and with those subjects who are deliberately removed from the official representation of Man's relationship with Nature, but also for that reason carry the possibility of repoliticizing that relationship via both struggle and alternative life practices (Armiero and De Angelis 2017). But as Barca and other eco-feminist scholars are quick to admit, this exclusion also involves an *adverse* type of inclusion: as capitalism subjects reproductive labor to increasing commodification and objectification, this generates a contradiction insofar as "reproductive labor becomes directly or indirectly incorporated within the money–commodity–money circuit of value" (Barca 2020, 6; see also Battacharya 2017; N. Phillips 2011, 2013).

In this book, I adopt a somewhat more restricted definition of social reproduction that focuses particularly on the racializing dynamics of this removal/reinsertion. I do this by focusing on those subjects who are simultaneously constructed as "less-than-human," "not yet fully human," or "not completely human" while the commodified value of their reproductive labor is actively integrated into the formal mechanisms of economic development from the edges of this naturalized, "outside space." I will call this process "natural racialization." Borrowing partly from Devon Carbado (2005), who talks about the legal naturalization process in the US as a form of racial naturalization, through which the figure of Blackness acquires a state of permanent nonbelonging (see also Merrill 2018), I look at the reverse process of "naturalizing" the space of Blackness as standing outside of European civilization based on the social and material—or sociomaterial—deployment of explicitly racial categories and distinctions (see also Hawthorne 2021a). The central question here is what happens if we privilege racism in the analysis of citizenship and the state. How might this perspective challenge the way we analyze the policing of the boundaries of who is categorized as a legitimate bodily presence in the contours of the national state and the national formal economy, and who is not? What emerges here is then not so much a story of exceptional exclusions and critical emergencies but a *longue durée* account of the intimate entanglement of racism and liberalism, of the institutional linkage between racism and the nation-state. Within this perspective, the term "natural racialization" specifically refers to the ways in which the experience of racism effectively *naturalizes* a group into belonging to the nation and to national citizenry through "inclusionary forms of exclusion" (Carbado 2005, 638). This notion thus cultivates the idea that racism, and racial nationalism in particular, do not represent some extreme aberration or deviation from the norm, but instead are foundational to the project of liberal nation-building and to the concept of the "national" labor force in particular. In short, the question of who is categorized as a legitimate territorial presence in the modern nation-state is repeatedly made intelligible through an overlaid spatial and cultural grid of racial differentiation, of "managing difference [through] spatial dispersal" (Hawthorne 2021a, 5).

A focus of my inquiry here thus concerns the racialized reproduction of labor power that functions simultaneously as a prerequisite for the social relations of capitalist production and acts as a source of capital accumulation, as Angela Davis wrote so brilliantly in her book *Women, Race and Class*.[11] Contra Davis, however, I do not agree that the capitalist employer in this context "is not concerned in the least about the way labor-power is produced and sustained, he is only concerned about its availability and its ability to generate profit. In other words, the capitalist production process presupposes the existence of a body of exploitable workers" (1983, 275). Rather, I follow Alessandra Mezzadri's call to consider the value-generating aspect of social reproduction, as she writes: "reproductive activities and realms play a key role in shaping [labor] relations and in the processes of surplus extraction they are embedded in, particularly (albeit not only), developing regions; that is, in the 'majority world'" (2019, 33). Like Mezzadri, I am interested here more specifically in the informal activities and spaces that form part of the reproduction of the Black African agrarian working class in Mediterranean agriculture and which, as Barca points out, carry the possibility of repoliticizing the global debate on the Anthropocene. In that sense, this study could be read as a double attempt to include the Mediterranean in "the majority world" and to take seriously the racial dynamics that underpin the adverse incorporation of reproductive activities in the realm of formal capitalist accumulation. Contra (or rather, complementing) Mezzadri, however, I place a stronger emphasis on the mechanisms of racial capitalism—in other words, on the assertion that race, as a social and cultural category that prefigures legal discrimination, has been a key political determinant for capitalism to take hold as a global economic system (see also Bhattacharyya 2018; Saldanha 2019; Eichen 2020).

The Black Mediterranean

As said, the entry point of my inquiry here is that of the Black Mediterranean. Cedric Robinson uses this term, mentioned in passing in his book *Black Marxism*, to signal the Mediterranean model upon which the advanced plantation systems of the Iberian Atlantic colonies would later be based (see also Best and Levitt 2009; Curtin 2012).[12] His point, as I will explain below, is therefore not to seek to reduce the question of capitalism or capitalist accumulation to a question of race, but rather to seek to explain the specific articulation of capitalist relations through dynamics of race.[13] As contemporary Black Marxists continue to argue (e.g., D. Thomas 2013; Pierre 2013; Oriji 2020), the way in which the Caribbean, American, and later African economy was integrated into the capitalist mode of production and accumulation through the slave trade, colonialism, and neocolonialism was through a particular set of racializing categorizations and appropriations that resembled very much the way Irish labor was integrated into the capitalist system in the seventeenth century. Marx appears to admit this in part, though is not ready to take his argument to full conclusion. Instead, I think we need to take seriously Robinson's claim that "capitalism was less a catastrophic revolution (negation) of feudal social order than the extension of these social relations into the larger tapestry of the modern world's political and economic relations" (Robinson ([1983] 2005, 42–43). For Robinson, "capital and racism did not break from the old order but rather evolved from it to produce a modern world system of 'racial capitalism' dependent on slavery, violence, imperialism, and genocide" (xiii). *Pace* Marx, though, Kelley (2017) and Robinson remind us that racial capitalism is not primarily about skin color identity but is a structure of power inherent in the capitalist mode of production and accumulation (Miapyen and Bozkurt 2022, 4).

I take up this argument about racial capitalism to apply it to how the neocolonial politics of exclusion in Africa and in Southern Europe today build on the construction of legal and social categories that identify who is deserving to become a citizen rather than a subject, who has the right to be attached to a particular location or territory and who has not, who has a right to be a "free" laborer and who not. Following Robinson, I find these categories—and the policies that they inspire—to constitute the basis on which the subsequent reproduction of capitalist accumulation can continue to take place across the globe. In sum, and despite the valuable critiques (Ralph and Singhal 2019), I consider Robinson's work a central precursor of my inquiry, as he has convincingly argued how capitalism as a system has been a key driver of differentially positioning human beings in relation not just to the state and the city, but to the profound geological and ecological transformations that are required for "modern" society to emerge and persist (see also Saldanha 2019; Dorries, Hugill, and Tomiak 2022). To make sense of the more recent deployments of extractive supply chains in the context I just described, I feel it is indeed important to think more carefully about what constitutes the underlying exception that has given birth and continues to reproduce capitalism as a global project. I argue, with Robinson, that any attempt to theorize capitalism without cornering the lived experiences of those who are precisely defined as not quite (or not yet) human, not quite (or not yet) modern and civilized, necessarily reenacts the racializing violence that makes capitalism thrive as a modernizing project (see also Saucier 2021). If, as Paul Gilroy writes, plantation labor represented "capitalism with its clothes off" (Gilroy 1983, 15), we need to advertise its nudity in the persistent, but differentiated, dispossession that continues to separate humanity into "worthy" citizens who may benefit from capital's gains and "unworthy" or "not yet" civilized subjects who remain simultaneously dispossessed and secluded by the means of capitalist production.

This focus on race—which, it needs to be emphasized, is not a matter of ontologically scaling differentiations of class, gender, and race on my part, but rather a matter of emphasis—will help me show how the mobile Black African agricultural laborers who form the protagonists of this study are not just a capitalist reserve army but an essentially segregated workforce whose partial placement outside the realm of formal development makes them simultaneously the subject of labor exploitation and a source of informal capital accumulation. Paraphrasing Robinson, the prevalence of such "feudal" racial habits in modern capitalism indeed makes the dichotomy of Europe versus the rest of the world less persuasive (Miapyen and Bozkurt 2022, 2). I use the concept of racial capitalism to define how capitalist accumulation operates by creating and reproducing inequality: in other words, how human beings and their activities are actively made distinct and reconfigured in ways that "feed capital" (Melamed 2015, 77–79). So, while the theory of racial capitalism clarifies the central place of race in profit maximization and capital accumulation, it also puts to the foreground how capitalist dispossession is never quite a complete process, but it relies on the constant valorization and revalorization of forms of life located on its edges (with regard to COVID and the circulation of capital see also Lawreniuk 2020; Wallace at al. 2020; Edwards 2021).

To summarize my reading, therefore, capitalist frontiers do not thin out, but rather "thicken" (Côte and Korf 2018, 478) political contestation over who has a right to benefit from certain "resources," what the terms of access are and on what legal and ethical foundations this access is based, and how activities and forms of life are being valorized as commodities ready to enter the webs of capital accumulation. In other words, resources and labor never are, but they need to be, actively constructed through notions of identity and space, which nevertheless remain contested, open to frictions and resistance. Such contestations may include the exact manner in which mechanisms of exclusion and inclusion that structure the allocation, use, and commodification of land and subsoils are being planned, implemented, purposed, and contested. But they also include the very terms on which boundaries get drawn around the "cheap" nature and around the "cheap" labor that are deemed central to produce "cheap" food commodities in any given context.

Under the broad umbrella of political ecology studies (see Peluso and Lund 2011; Hall, Hirsch, and Li 2011; T. M. Li 2014; Eilenberg and Cons 2019), I hope to point out the important reconfigurations of relations of property and citizenship, of territories and of natural resources, in the context of contemporary capitalist frontiers, providing Southern Italy in a strict sense, and the Black Mediterranean more widely, as a prime case study. I will use the next two sections to attach more flesh to the bone of this introductory outline.

Natural Racialization

A first key determinant in the dynamic of uneven capitalist development in agrarian frontiers, I said, is the way the earth's (sub)soil and human activity are being constructed as "resources" that can be valorized as capital. Rather than taking the commodities of "cheap labor" and "cheap nature" as a starting point of my analysis, I see these in a dynamic relation of articulation and disarticulation of capitalist relations in a specific context. One central source of inspiration is Stuart Hall's articulation approach—most notably his acknowledgment that capitalism can persist and thrive on articulation with noncapitalist modes of (re)production. Or, as he put it, market economies always represent some sort of "an articulation between different modes of production, structured in some relation of dominance" (Hall 1980, 320).[14] The key question here for me remains how capital simultaneously values certain activities (ways of life) and resources (sources of life) while devaluing others through concrete processes of articulation and disarticulation—and how it struggles to keep the tensions, frictions, and resistances these processes generate at bay.

The constant changes we are witnessing in global production networks today should be seen as a manifestation of a dynamic process of *differentiation*: as the (often adverse) incorporation of certain geographical areas, certain resources, and certain actors; these correspond at the same time with a disconnection and an expulsion of other areas, other actors, and other resources (see also Bair and Werner 2011). Taken together, this dynamic results in a constant tension between (dis-)articulations, (dis-)investments and (de-)valuations that leave their traces both in the ways of life and the spaces in which capitalist operations get grounded globally. In this sense, I see the ruined infrastructures and ghettos of Southern Italy's agrarian frontier not merely as derelict sites of devalued capital, left behind or dismissed as wasted lives, but rather as dynamic, layered spaces that articulate with the capitalist mode of agri-food production in intricate and often surprising ways. Located on the edges of formal industrial development, they are simultaneously sites of social reproduction and of rogue informal capital accumulation that end up being a systematic subsidy to capital.

The second factor I am interested in is the way the articulation of capitalist relations provides for the active stratification of humanity in ways that are beneficial to capital. One key element in this stratification process, I find, concerns the instrumentalization of "race." The articulation of capitalist relations of production and reproduction not only involves a process of differentiation but also of *stratification*. I use the concept of racial naturalization to highlight the ways in which the experience of racism effectively naturalizes and stratifies a racialized humanity into a stratigraphic order of "not yet," "not quite" and "nonbelonging" to the nation-state (Carbado 2005, 638; Hawthorne 2021a). More specifically, I am interested in the process through which the forces of agrarian reproduction are placed outside the confines of humanity following a racializing logic of separation, but the value of their agricultural labor is simultaneously commodified through the spatialization of their bodily presence as a "natural" resource that can be deployed at the will of capitalist firms and supply chains. Next to Stuart Hall, I am inspired here by scholarship on the Black Mediterranean, as that bordered, transcontinental space in which such stratification unfolds in the social and material relations that characterize diasporic Black lives across continents. Racial oppression in the Mediterranean today does not provide a state of exception, but rather a "state of repetition" of the subjection of Black life through apparatuses of surveillance, containment, captivity, displacement, forced labor, and dehumanization (Lombardi-Diop 2021, 5). It is exactly this state of repetition I want to highlight and explore further.

In the context of industrialized plantations, which have been rapidly expanding as the dominant mode of agricultural production across both shores of the Middle Sea since the late 1800s, the concept of the Black Mediterranean helps me to trace back how the unfree bodies of land laborers have been actively made distinct and reconfigured in ways that "feed capital" (Melamed 2015, 79), but also how this process has created a platform for tensions, resistances, and separations to arise and provide space for alternative ways of life that coexist in tension with the dominant mode of production. The central theme here concerns the way in which racial capitalism, as a specific articulation of capitalist relations, actively produces and reproduces "race" as a social category of distinction that reconfigures these relations in radical ways. In alliance with Black Mediterranean scholarship, and again in sharp contraposition to the Anthropocene literature and its color-blind vision of "Man" and its relation to "Nature," I ask myself how the instrumentalization of race actively contributes to drawing the boundary between what can and what cannot (or should not) be considered as "human" in the given context of agrarian development. One underlying premise of my argument, in fact, is that not labor exploitation per se, but the intricate relation between race and capitalism fosters the foundation of this persistent boundary. To quote Ruth Wilson Gilmore (2002a, 16),

> Racism is a practice of abstraction, a death-dealing displacement of difference into hierarchies that organize relations within and between the planet's sovereign political territories. Racism functions as a limiting force that pushes disproportionate costs of participating in an increasingly monetized and profit-driven world onto those who, due to the frictions of political distance, cannot reach the variable levers of power that might relieve them of those costs. Indeed, the process of abstraction that signifies racism produces effects at the most intimately "sovereign" scale, insofar as particular kinds of bodies, one by one, are materially (if not always visibly) configured by racism into a hierarchy of human and inhuman persons that in sum form the category "human being."

Following Gilmore, I say it is not an absence of state control but rather the active construction and manipulation, by multiple actants and agencies, of racial inferiority that forms the basis of the dispossession, abandonment, and displacement of racialized capitalist laborers and producers. In this regard, I agree with Pulido (2017, 529) when she writes that the production of racial segregation is not an aberration or the result of market failures. Rather, it is evidence of the "normal, routine, functioning of capitalist economies" that actively maintain and reproduce social and environmental inequalities supported by the nation-state.

Bordering Infrastructures

Exploring more in-depth this "normal, routine, functioning of capitalist economies" (Pulido 2017, 529) in the context of the Mediterranean agri-food plantation, I became gradually more interested in what Alexandre G. Weheliye (2014, 79, 202), in a different context, calls the "racializing juridical assemblages" that are responsible for the construction of race as a set of sociomaterial processes that discipline humanity into full humans, not-quite-humans, and nonhumans in ways that feed capital. These concepts, of racializing assemblages and natural racialization, help me explain more specifically the actual relations of production and reproduction that unfold in the context of the Black Mediterranean plantation. Moving beyond the depiction of Black labor as a mere expression of unfreedom, and of migrant ghettos as the sites of state abandonment, the inquiry that has driven this book centers on the way this stratified, racialized boundary has been and still is actively mapped into the landscape while reconfiguring social relations in ways that feed capital in a process that is never quite attained.

The terminology I use in this contest is that of bordering infrastructures (Dijstelbloem 2021). Put simply, infrastructures are physical networks that facilitate and direct flows. They are material in that they are "matter that enable the movement of other matter" (Larkin 2013, 329). But they are also defined by their social relations, as infrastructures necessarily emerge through social arrangements and processes (Simone 2004; for a discussion see Elyachar 2010; Larkin 2013; Lin et al. 2017; Anand, Gupta, and Appel 2018; Lemanski 2020; K. A. Thomas 2021). To some extent, the discussion on infrastructures refers to Michael Mann and his attempt to set apart the state as an arena that reflects "the condensation, the crystallization, the summation of social relations within its territories" (1984, 63). In the context of the Black Mediterranean plantation, however, I have been inclined to push this conceptualization a bit further. With regard to the bounding of migrant labor, the multiplicity of bordering processes I have been confronted with in this agrarian frontier—and of which the current Mediterranean "crisis of migration" forms a central example—has led me to acknowledge that borders do not just embody territorial differentiations, but they actively create those differences. Indeed, the technologies of separating, disciplining, and coercing migrant labor increasingly act as filters that separate "the desirable from the undesirable, the genuine from the bogus, the deserving from the undeserving" (Gargiulo 2021, 15). A focal point in this analysis concerns the gang masters, *caporali*, or labor brokers whose function it is to simultaneously make migrating workers fit for flexible employment while outsourcing the cost of the protection, care, and social reproduction of labor power directly onto the networks of racialized and sexualized workers. In line with infrastructure-of-migration scholars like Xiang Biao and Johan Lindquist, I regard informal labor intermediation not merely as a criminal feature of an otherwise "normal, routine" market economy but rather as an essential bordering infrastructure, whose function it is to link the value of "informal" work to the "formal" economic systems and circuits of capital (for a discussion see chapter 1).

In that sense, my work effectively links up with what has been termed an "infrastructural turn" in the study of labor migration.[15] Following some more recent contributions in this arena, I insist on the sociomateriality of such bordering infrastructures, in a sense that the technologies that bound migrant labor to the territory of agricultural production and reproduction comprise a wide variety of agents, platforms, and architectures through which such labor is actively connected and disconnected from global value chains. What matter to me in this context are not so much what are referred to as the social forces of production in an orthodox, Marxian sense, but more broadly speaking the material-discursive "cuts" (Barad 2003, 816) that actively co-constitute the agrarian frontier as an assemblage of intra-acting physical and social forces.[16] The terminology of bordering infrastructures serves exactly this end of taking seriously the *political ecology* of agri-food production as a constantly shifting ensemble of human, nonhuman, and more-than-human entanglements.

As I hope to make clear, the spatialization of nature that has historically enabled, and continues to enable, plantation economies to thrive and be productive, goes hand in hand with a naturalization of space that simultaneously allows for this economy's reproduction in sites and locales that are deliberately placed "outside" the formal domains of capitalist development. I see a direct logical connection between the ways in which yesterday's peasant communities and today's migrant workers are being constructed as belonging to a "not yet civilized" and threatening "outside world" that is material-discursively placed on the edges of the state and of formal economic enterprise. The racializing work that so-called nonstate infrastructures like the illegalized gang-master intermediaries effectuate alongside other, more state-centered material-discursive interventions in the domain of migration management tends to reinforce the nature/human divide on which the cyclical accumulation of capital is ontologically founded. Polly Pallister-Wilkins (2022) makes exactly this point by highlighting the explicitly racist premises on which contemporary bordering infrastructures are founded. By perpetuating dualist ontologies of nature/culture and nature/human by which illegalized migrants are linked to the natural (read premodern) world, and by producing illegalized migrants as "bodies-out-of-place" in a political ecology that is concomitantly (re)produced as a whitescape, the infrastructures of border and migration management reproduce a fundamentally racist stratification and hierarchy that is functional to both state territoriality and to the accumulation of capital.

As a counterpoint to Wilkins's analysis, I take as an entry point the "black spaces" that characterize migrant preclusion and stratification in the EU-Africa borderland—whereby the term "black space" acquires a wider significance as that space in which the struggle over territorial belonging literally comes "to matter" (see also F. Li 2013, 400; Reeves 2014; Emmenegger 2021). At a broader level, therefore, the terminology of bordering infrastructures helps me regard the spatialization of nature and the naturalization of space in the Mediterranean agrarian frontier as two sides of the same process. Indeed, what makes the articulation of capitalist relations here so distinct, I argue, is the way in which the instrumentalization of race, as a category of capitalist differentiation and distinction, allows capitalist firms to systematically act as predators on the forces of reproduction. Recalling Stefania Barca's definition, these comprise exactly those "less-than-humanized (racialized, feminized, dispossessed) subjects who reproduce humanity by taking care of the biophysical environment that makes life itself possible" (Barca 2020, 1). To overcome the color-blind and male-centered conception of the Anthropocene, therefore, we need to also take account of the often violent and exploitative ways in which capitalist labor—and specifically, agricultural labor—is reproduced as a commodity through the informalized, marginalized, and inherently sexualized and racialized wageless work that goes on beyond its formal limits. This acknowledgment automatically requires an intersectional research agenda as, especially in the domain of agricultural and plantation labor, such work typically includes the reproduction of life in the barracks and the ghetto that is not accounted for in the official books of capital accumulation, such as the manual upkeep of workers' habitat, the planting, care, and harvesting of food including livestock, mutual care between workers, sex work, and the social networks in which they are embedded.

I am interested in showing how the unwaged, informal work concentrated in the Black workers' ghetto becomes the subject of surplus extraction as, in the long run, in those places the distinction between work and reproductive time becomes blurred, and, perhaps even more importantly, "non-waged time" becomes fundamental to the production of compliant laboring subjects. Alessandra Mezzadri, who adopts a similar position in her inquiry of the Indian sweatshop industry, calls this process the externalization of the cost of social reproduction. It is the process through which the household, the village, the community, as well as non-capitalist activities, are progressively deployed as a systematic subsidy to capital. Rather than being a cheap commodity ready to exploit, therefore, the migrant ghetto fulfils a central role in the reproduction of this labor, as in these locations activities that are deliberately placed outside the sphere of agricultural production, such as the care, accommodation, and feeding of workers, in fact become a hidden subsidy for the formal agricultural enterprises that reap the profits from this exclusion.

At the same time, though, I contend that migrant networks do not just generate "informal capital" that is accumulated elsewhere. They also reproduce the conditions of their own exploitation by commodifying such unwaged work within their social networks. In the migrant ghettos I visited, bars, restaurants, and brothels, transport back and forth from the workplace, water provision, waste management, as well as the precarious accommodation that migrants build for their shelter, all become sites for accumulation for the various intermediaries (gang masters, humanitarian organizations, state agencies) involved in reproducing such settlements as areas situated outside the formal market economy. The fact that these activities take place in the marginalized, informal sphere does not mean that these are valueless. On the contrary, life in the ghetto frequently involves conspicuous spending, and gang masters, capitalist firms, and state regulators gain tremendously from such reproductive activities. So, paying attention to the "interlocking systems of domination" (Federici 2020, 29; see also Federici 2004, 2018) that determine the simultaneous destruction and uneven incorporation of such wageless work into market enterprise becomes a necessary premise to simultaneously demystifying and untangling the apparent contradictions built into the social relations of capitalism.

Chapter Outline

In chapter 1, I will outline the wider theoretical and empirical objectives of this book. Building further on the political ecology scholarship introduced in this chapter, I share the observation that, as processes of infrastructural ruination unfold, these also inherently create the conditions for a new object, a reconfiguration to emerge in the debris of the old and, therefore, I am interested in the more profound transformation that involves both the social and material infrastructures of ruined infrastructures and those who are using them. My inquiry links up with a larger body of political ecology scholarship that explores the variety of competing claims about how environments have been and should be used in the context of contemporary capitalism. At the same time I highlight the transformative effects of expanding commodity frontiers such as the monocropping plantation agriculture that has taken root in the South of Italy since the early 1980s. I build on the works of Rosa Luxemburg and Walter Benjamin—but even more so on radical political ecology and critical race studies—to inquire how, as capitalism penetrates ever deeper into our lives, it tends to produce cyclical frontiers of intrusion and abandonment, and in so doing solidifies social and environmental inequalities. More specifically, I highlight the importance of race, and of racism, as a central element of this infrastructural transformation. In the process of territorializing claims to infrastructures of capital and labor in the agricultural frontier, infrastructural ruination and abandonment do not represent a form of state incapacity, but such processes form a cyclical, material expression of the politics of racialized exclusion that historically underpins the social relations of production in this agrarian mode of production. In the Italian Meridione, state policies have historically produced and maintained the infrastructures of exploitation that assist and support racial capitalism.

Chapter 2 details the historical trajectories that have converged into the contemporary, racialized plantation labor we now see taking root across the maritime boundary of the Mediterranean. I further explore a central element of debate around today's agri-food commodity chains: the relation between mobile labor, capital, and public state intervention. While once more highlighting the importance of race, and of racial technologies, in understanding how state interventions have historically sought to institutionalize boundaries, and to differentiate populations with regard to their right to national citizenship and economic wealth, I highlight how geography comes to matter in contemporary agrarian supply chains. More specifically, I explore the converging manners in which state policies across Mediterranean borderlands have in fact generated important links between different territories of agricultural extraction.

In chapter 3, I concentrate on more recent efforts to "territorialize" the mobile labor employed in Southern Italy's plantation agriculture—notably through state efforts to formalize migrant labor infrastructures. In the context of the Mediterranean "migration crisis" that state governments have been trying to address with increasingly repressive means since 2011, I notice a tendency toward the securitization of labor in agricultural supply chains, in the sense that the new intersections between migration and border policy in this period are producing new convergences between border security, humanitarian aid, and labor coercion. I highlight once again the importance of race, and particular of the spatial politics of race, when it comes to upholding and reproducing the boundaries between different categories of agricultural laborers. And I explain how the ruined infrastructure of the migrant ghetto constitutes an outside space that serves national economic wealth but is deliberately located off limits, beyond the protective realm of official state infrastructures.

Chapter 4 takes a complementary look into migrant ghettos as emerging rural labor infrastructures. Building further on my previously introduced notion of bordering infrastructures, I inquire into how the ghetto's relations to rural society become embedded into a differentiated social and cultural identity. Considering rural ghetto infrastructures as social and material space, in my view, opens a possible frame for understanding the tension between the persistent criminalization of informalized spaces and their adverse incorporation into the political ecology of agrarian production and reproduction. The chapter also highlights the intricate ways in which the relation between capital, labor, and public authority reconfigures notions of citizenship, belonging, and identity in this highly contested space.

In the fifth and last chapter, I explore how racial differences become gradually "naturalized" in the context of migrant labor formalization in the South of Italy. Building on a specific case—of the eviction of the Grand Ghetto of Rignano

Garganico in Puglia and its replacement by alternative forms of migrant reception in neighboring San Severo, I highlight the intricate ways in which racialized bodies become adversely incorporated into Italy's national state territory. Through the example of Casa Sankara–Azienda Fortore, I explore how racial hierarchies have become part and parcel of a national teleology of integration that simultaneously segregates and connects subjects who are differentially positioned in relation to the country's "racializing juridical assemblages" (Weheliye 2014, 79, 202).

COMMODITY FRONTIERS

That day we set out to go back to Santa Maria, an abandoned warehouse in the vicinity of Borgo San Nicola.[1] Two days before, I had visited the place with Karim and Youssouf. Santa Maria represented an important node in our trajectory as we were trying to map the network of migrant settlements in the area. During our visit, Karim and Youssouf told me about their experience of being displaced there in the winter of 2009. They sheltered temporarily in Santa Maria after they had been expelled from the reception center for seasonal laborers located in the vicinity of the town. While they recalled the experience of their displacement and resettlement with me, both men talked about the deliberate evictions and destructions of their homes, here, in this border zone on the edge of Puglia and Basilicata. While recalling their permanent mobility since the early 2000s, Karim said, "We just *had* to live in these abandoned houses [*case abbandonate*]. It was that or nothing." Pointing at the rubble of a destroyed building, he suddenly added, "You see there, we were the very last, the last last last last! We left because they started breaking down the houses there. My gas cooker is still there." He added, while climbing up the pile of rubble and sifting through the waste, "The gas cooker, the dishes, even my electric generator—they are all there, right below the rubble." Later, he remembered the winter of 2009 in that place, when, while the first snowflakes started to fall, he finally drove away from Santa Maria in the car of a local volunteer.

After returning to Borgo San Nicola, I wanted to know more about this place, Santa Maria, which had appeared so central in the lives of these West African workers. While we had been there, evaluating their losses, both men had been vividly debating the next planting season on the phone, with their bosses from Borgo, discussing prices and negotiating wages. Now it was a few days before the start of the planting season, and I had just spent several days traveling across the fields and between abandoned hamlets and settlements. So, one day I set out for Santa Maria again with a worker from Youssouf's team, Abou, and Marco, a photographer and architect I had traveled with to Basilicata several times before. We stopped on the side of the dirt track to take some pictures from the destroyed building where Karim used to live with his companions. While Abou paused for a moment, Marco shot a picture of his silhouette from the back. Then we slowly descended to the abandoned site. Abou and I climbed up the rocks that had been placed in front of the doorway to prevent people from entering. I told Abou to look down. He pointed the flashlight of his phone into the darkness, and a pile of polystyrene boxes appeared. I said people used to sleep on those (I remembered that from the picture in the newspaper). We could make out some pieces of clothing in the dirt. The place smelled moldy and moist. I asked Abou if he knew about this place. He said no, he didn't. We climbed down toward the adjacent warehouse where Marco was busy taking pictures. While we walked through the rooms, we smelled the remnants of a fire—a sign that someone had stayed here not so long ago. The walls were blackened and covered with writings in different languages. The place was littered with utensils and clothes. Abou started scavenging through the stuff that lay scattered across the floor. At some point he lifted up a piece of charcoal, and he wrote his phone number on the wall. Next to it appeared a phrase in Arabic: "Respect and you will be respected, Niamey Niger 27.8.02."

The Corporate Food Regime

For some time now, Italy has been known as the world's third-largest producer of tomatoes, after China and California. Like other Mediterranean intense agrifood production areas—for instance, southern Turkey (Adana Province), Greece (Kalamata), and Spain (Andalucía)—the country has become a main supplier of fresh and canned food for global supermarket chains—with radical consequences for the social relations of production and reproduction in food-producing areas (for a discussion see Rye and Scott 2018; Pelek 2020; Perrotta and Raeymaekers 2022). The country grows five million tons of tomatoes every year, representing 50 percent of the European and 14 percent of the world's volume. Tomato fields cover a total land surface of 70,000 hectares (about 173,000 acres, or 270 square miles) in Italy. Part of this land is in Emilia Romagna and Lombardy, where planting and harvesting have been rendered almost fully automatic. In the Capitanata plains, in Foggia Province, Puglia, as well as the northern section of Basilicata known as the Alto Bradano, however, agricultural plots are decisively smaller and apparently unsuitable for mechanization, which is part of the reason for a preponderance of manual labor. Here, approximately 3,500 companies occupy around 33,000 hectares (about 81,000 acres, or 127 square miles) of tomato land in this area. Another fruit cultivation area has emerged more recently in the southern coastal and interior plains: in Lavello (Basilicata), a diversified horticulture produces fruits and vegetables for European supermarkets practically all year round. Another important horticultural district is Metaponto, home to the typical "made in Italy" Candonga strawberries. Between 2018 and 2019 the land surface dedicated to strawberry culture rose by 13 percent in this area, to approximately 1,000 hectares (almost 2,500 acres, or 4 square miles), representing an annual turnover of about 120 million euros for this trademark produce. Besides strawberries, Metaponto also hosts 15,000 hectares (37,000 acres, or 57 square miles) of fruit trees and 10,000 hectares (25,000 acres, or 39 square miles) of horticultural land, which altogether produce a total of 70,000 tons for European markets annually (altogether, Greece, Spain, and France produce around 350,000 tons annually)—according to the farmer's association Coldiretti. Notwithstanding its relatively small productive capacity, therefore, Basilicata has become increasingly defined as a prominent agrarian frontier and an area that, owing to its constant expansion every year, has been progressively integrated in the vertical agri-food supply chains known as the "new food regime." In a famous article, Harriet Friedmann defined a food regime as "the rule-governed structure of the production and consumption of food on a world scale" (1993, 31). The regime sets the standards and conditions that direct the production, distribution, and consumption of food. The principles and ideology of the food regime organize what and where food is produced and consumed, and by whom. The regime forges a link between food—a fundamental human need—and hegemonic political and economic power. In a subsequent article, Friedmann and McMichael (1989) framed two food regimes: the colonial-settler regime (1870–1914) and the postwar food regime (1947–1970). McMichael subsequently identified a third food regime commencing in the 1980s, which marked the beginning of corporate-led agriculture (2005). This is the corporate food regime in which we find ourselves today.

For many observers, the years 2008–2009 constituted a rupture moment in this rapid transformation of the global food regime. The initial causes of this crisis were several severe droughts in grain-producing countries, coupled with rising oil prices. Yet while the media focused predominantly on the social unrest that ensued after the dramatic increase in food prices in 2007 and the first and second quarters of 2008, the reasons for these price spikes were more complex.

Oil price rises had caused an escalation in the costs of fertilizers, food transportation, and industrial agriculture—a clear sign of the growing dependence on large-scale, industrialized food production on a global scale. An additional factor of this global crisis was the rising demand for biofuel, which placed pressure on subsistence agriculture as a major source of food production, particularly in the global South. There was also a rising concern with the growing importance of financializing food production through hedge funds, futures markets, and commodity index funds. In 2010, the UN Food and Agricultural Organization (FAO) raised concerns about the growing role of hedge funds' speculating on prices, which led (and continues to lead) to major instability of food prices.

Of greater interest for this study are the effects of this global food crisis. At least two misconceptions around these effects need analytical readjustment. The first of these concerns is the influence of the global land grab on Mediterranean agri-food production. Broadly speaking, the global land grab literature links the 2008 global food crises with a growing accumulation and concentration of agricultural land properties on a world scale. Land grabbing is seen to emerge out of the need to secure food supplies in a period marked by huge price fluctuations and price hikes in international food markets. Or, as one observer notes, "The food crisis coupled with the broader financial crisis has turned control over land into an important new magnet for private investors. We're not talking about typical transnational agribusiness operations, where Cargill might invest in a soya bean crushing plant in Mato Grosso in Brazil. We're talking about a new interest in acquiring control over farmland itself. There are two main players here: the food industry and, much more significantly, the finance industry" (GRAIN 2008, 7). This is the main reason why the ramifications of the 2008–2009 "food crisis" require a global rather than a national analysis. The general idea that drives this thesis is that the global land grab progressively pushes small farmers from the land, thus providing the backdrop for massive emigration of unskilled laborers who are easily exploited.

Yet while I agree with this sensitivity to the global scale, neither Italy nor West Africa—from where most of Italy's seasonal laborers originate—appears to confirm this trend. Overall, the rapid reconfiguration of agricultural production in West Africa over the last thirty years has been predominantly driven by the rapid concentration of transnational agribusiness interests (see Dolan and Humphrey 2000; Losch 2002; Young 2004; Gibbon and Ponte 2005). But this does not mean the region has been confronted with a global land *grab*. The dominant players in global food markets today are large supermarket retailers, which avoid direct involvement in production. Instead, they prefer to specialize in controlling marketing and supply chains. Being virtually monopsonic (the sole buyer) by default, they tend to outsource production to diversify risks and impose control over quality, while investing predominantly in branding and logistics. Rather than engaging in land grabs, which would be seen as counterproductive, global supermarket chains develop strategies to impose their conditions of production and distribution on farmers and suppliers. Being able to access supplies from a variety of locations at different moments, they subsequently force suppliers to absorb the cost of price-cutting competition. This competition has in turn generated what can be defined as a "dispossession from below" (Amanor 2011, 27), in which the pressure of market competitiveness gradually fosters a concentration of farm property in the hands of commercial smallholders. In West Africa, these smallholders—which comprise a variety of actors, from retired bureaucrats to private entrepreneurs—have been able to tie in their production with global agribusiness with the help of government market reforms and investment opportunities. This concentration of capital has led in turn to the exit from farm production of the rural poor, whose livelihoods are increasingly ruined by the combination of liberalizing policies and demographic pressures. Important to keep in mind here is that most smallholders continue to operate in local and regional markets, but the combination of dispossessions from below and global liberalization has been putting such territorial systems increasingly at risk.

In Italy—where the share of agricultural supplies to supermarket retailers grew from 44 percent in 1996 to 75 percent in 2013 (AGCM 2013)—a similar trend of "supermarketization" can be noticed (on the term "marketization" see Callon 1998; Berndt and Boeckler 2009; Çaliskan and Callon 2009; and Çaliskan 2010; specifically regarding tomatoes see Boeckler and Berndt 2014). Through their rising buyer power, a small oligopoly of retail corporations (the ten largest of which are concentrated in four countries: the UK, France, Germany, and the US) has increasingly been acquiring control over the production and distribution of food, thereby not only determining the production costs, standards, distribution, and processing of food, but also the way we buy and consume it. Like in West Africa, the growing competition fostered by retailer firms has increased pressures on smallholder firms, which causes their dispossession "from below." This term indicates at once the growing authority of retail networks in setting the standards and conditions for food production, distribution, and consumption, as well as their progressive externalization of the risks associated with agricultural production to ever bigger firms, who consequently push out the small fish from the market. In Italy, this is shown, for example, in the reduction of the number of agricultural firms, which at the same time have grown exponentially in size.[2] National and international legislation has furthermore bolstered this trend toward market monopsony. On the waves of the 2008–2009 food crisis, the WTO's General Agreement on Trade and Tariffs as well as European policy have been known to systematically favor supermarket investments as well as the liberalization of retail distribution markets (Douwe Van der Ploeg 2008). The rising challenges of global food production, including, increasingly, the effects of global climate change, are thus progressively pushing the small, family-owned enterprises that characterize the agricultural sector into systematic self-exploitation and economic marginality. One farmer I interviewed in 2016 summed up his situation to me like this: "[Farming] is a bit like playing cards: you wait for the right hand" (è come gioccare le carte: aspetti la mano buona).[3] In other words, farming increasingly becomes a gamble played at the mercy of global food corporations who dictate the terms of agricultural production, distribution, and even the consumption of our food.[4]

Next to this "dispossession from below," another important effect of the corporate food regime in West Africa and Southern Europe has been the rapid replacement of import-substituting industries with new export-oriented agricultural industries that benefit from their major integration into transnational food chains. One prominent example here is Ghana. Since the gold boom of the 1880s, the country has been attracting migrant workers from neighboring territories like the southeast Boulgou Province in Burkina Faso, among others, to work in its expanding tomato sector.[5] Succumbing to the pressures of the International Monetary Fund (IMF) in the early 2000s, the Ghanaian government finally reduced customs duties on imports, which immediately generated a flood of foreign products in local markets—particularly of tomato paste. Ironically, this changed Ghana from a main regional exporter to being the largest importer of tomato concentrate in Africa, of over one hundred thousand tons per year from Italy and China.[6] This irony becomes even more acrid if one considers that a large segment of the migrant workers from Burkina Faso and Ghana who used to operate as seasonal land laborers in West Africa now end up as day laborers in Italy's tomato fields (see also Auvillain and Liberti 2016).[7]

In Italy, the effects of the corporate food regime have been a major market concentration of food processing and distribution in a few, vertically integrated enterprises. To remain with tomato production: the sectoral reorganization following the 2008 "food crisis" has contributed to a major concentration of capital in a few processing plants. Historically, the production and processing of industrial, *salsa* tomatoes—the most famous of which is the oblong San Marzano variety—has been concentrated in the region of Salerno and the Piana del Sele. Until 2005, the only large southern cannery located outside Campania was near Lavello, in Basilicata, a plant that had been built with public funds in the late 1970s. After the operation was bought up in 2005 by one of Campania's largest canning groups (Antonino Russo, the most important and powerful Campania tomato industrialist), the company built a large new cannery near Foggia (Puglia) in 2009, which subsequently was purchased by a British and Japanese industrial giant. While this cannery has the potential to process around 20 percent of the entire tomato production of Puglia and Basilicata, most produce continues to traverse the Apennines toward Salerno, where the largest processing plants of the South continue to be based. As Domenico Perrotta (2014, 18) argues, this history shows the extent to which Southern Italian agri-food production has been suffering the effects of market concentration. In Emilia-Romagna, by contrast, where agricultural cooperatives provide a stronghold against the expanding powers of the big retailers, the latter are cited as the main reason why the southern supply chain is "under pressure." One of the major outcomes of the corporate food regime, in fact, is precisely the growth and the oligopolistic position occupied by the major players in organized distribution.[8]

As these two introductory notes on Southern European and West African tomato production over the past fifteen years show, the analysis of the effects of the food crisis on a global scale should equally involve a multiscalar analysis of global food supply chains that takes seriously the intersection of local decision-making processes with national and regional institutions, while contextualizing the conjunctures of socioeconomic, ecological, and political transformations and their effects on rural livelihoods from an intersectional perspective (see also Gray and Dowd-Uribe 2013). The new linkages, flows, and circulations generated by the corporate food regime—including those driving and produced by international migration and land investments—do not produce a leveled playing field at all (Zoomers 2018). I share the call of agrarian sociologists like Rye and Scott (2018, 932), therefore, for us to investigate the "specific historic roots and present-day particularities" of agri-food production networks. Next to the general observation that global changes are also producing variegated effects on rural societies, contemporary forms of rural mobilities may also generate novel socio-spatial divides that clearly transgress the local scale. In this context, the infrastructures of agricultural labor emerge as an important topic of investigation, especially at a time when the exploitation of labor appears to be one of the primary factors in the restructuring of global agri-food production. Of particular interest here is the growing interconnection between globalized commodity chains and informal migrant labor, a connection that, as I will show in the next section, allows for the vertical integration of agri-food farms in retailer-driven agri-food supply chains, but also generates a ground for continued dispossession of rural producers in the context of the global food regime (see also Colloca and Corrado 2013, 205; Gertel and Sippel 2014; Corrado, De Castro, and Perrotta 2016; Pelek 2020; Perrotta and Raeymaekers 2022).

A final issue of concern involves the effects of the global "land grab" on migration. New scholarship on the nexus between rural livelihoods and migration asks for major sensitivity to our understanding of the effects of global changes on "local" conditions. "Local" livelihoods in fact involves a contradiction in terms because, for centuries, what West African and Mediterranean farmers have been experiencing is a circular labor migration from and to the home region. Though it is fair to say that labor migration has been, and remains today, the main constant to counter the multiple challenges of rural communities, current mobility patterns in West Africa should indeed be seen as building upon older patterns of migration. Usually, rural communities' livelihoods rely on a combination of regional migration, which is mostly circular and short term (often, this migration is linked to the search for labor opportunities in the dry season, with people returning to their fields when the rainy season starts) and outward emigration, which involves migration trajectories of many years. While multiple factors have contributed to the intensification of the latter over the past fifteen years—including the crisis in Libya starting in 2011—it is important to keep in mind the intersectional dimension of such migration patterns on rural societies.

One example I will return to repeatedly is that of Béguedo, a rural town in the province of Boulgou in southeastern Burkina Faso. Nicknamed the "town of women" by a BBC report because of the circular migration of male migrants to Italy (Adjovi 2015), the town has become a synonym with such racialized and gendered migration patterns. But Béguedo is not unique, in the sense that the large majority of labor migrants from West Africa today are young male members of extended households. Their journeys are a way to supplement the incomes not just of destitute and poor farmers, but also of richer, middle-class households with the desire to strengthen their socioeconomic position in a rural context that has become characterized by an increasing competition for arable land. An important element I will emphasize in this study is the active reinvention of rural lifeworlds that results from this circular migration, as social networks of migrant workers remain important to acquire access to labor abroad and secure land ownership at home—a factor that effectively continues to exclude the younger generation from livelihood opportunities even after embarking on an often perilous and exhausting stay abroad (Kaag et al. 2019, 68).

Similar patterns of gendered and racialized migration afflict the South of Italy, too. According to the European statistics bureau (quoted in Quintano, Mazzocchi, and Rocca 2018), Italy is the European country with the most NEETs (young adults between fifteen and thirty-four who are "not in education, employment, or training"). Important here is the distinction between young men and women: while 33.2 percent of young women and 22.5 of young men can be defined as NEETs, Southern Italy counts almost one in two young people between eighteen and twenty-nine years as officially unemployed and inactive (41.4 percent of men, 43.5 percent of women). As I will explain in the next chapter, the main reason for this social and economic exclusion continues to be the historical marginalization of Italy's Meridione, where the lack of employment opportunities accompanies a generalized lack of state support and intervention in the promotion of economic integration. That this phenomenon affects women more than men is usually ascribed to the difficult reconciliation between work and family: to start with, the mentioned numbers also include women who, by choice or by obligation, dedicate themselves exclusively to the family (this partly explains why between twenty-five and thirty-four years of age the percentage of "inactive" women rises to 55.1 percent). The result of these familial obligations explains why, in the southern Mediterranean, a much larger segment of young men travels to look for jobs than do women. Besides (and often against) their personal will, Southern Italian youngsters thus appear to bolster the trend of racialized and gendered migration that has characterized the expansion of capitalist development in the Meridione in the postwar period.

New Slaves?

A key premise of this book is the observation that the racialized body of the informal migrant worker does not represent the limit of the commodification of labor, but it stands as capitalism's very center. The conceptual starting point for this premise concerns a famous passage in *Capital*, where Karl Marx identifies the two major conditions that underpin the sale of labor power. He says, "Labor power can appear on the market only as a commodity [and] only if, and in so far as, its possessor . . . offers it for sale or sells it as a commodity." For this to occur, the person who sells this labor power to the market must not only be "the free proprietor of his [or her] own labor-capacity, hence of his person," but "he [or she], must rather be compelled to offer for sale as a commodity that very labor power which exists only in his [or her] living body." Marx's main objective of course is to unravel the conditions of inequality and exploitation that underpin the seemingly speckless domain of market exchange where commodities are apparently traded freely ([1885] 1973, 279–80). Starting form this observation, of the commodification of labor, Marxian political economy recognizes the centrality of waged labor to the capitalist mode of production (Weeks 2016; Tyner 2019).

A century and a half after its publication, however, two important corrections need to be made to Marx's groundbreaking analysis. The first one regards the centrality of labor: if we consider that today most jobs include a range of "informal" arrangements that do not involve wage labor strictly defined as the sale of labor power, it is indeed urgent to consider work more broadly, as the "productive cooperation organized around, but not necessarily confined to, the privileged model of waged labor" (Weeks 2016, 14; Denning 2010; Ferguson and Li 2018). One immensely important factor in this respect concerns the proceeding informalization of labor as work: what global institutions still euphemistically refer to as "informal economic activity" now statistically accounts for 61 percent of global employment, rising to 70 percent in the global South and 86 percent in Africa (ILO 2018, 15; World Bank 2019).[9] But what does effectively count as formal and informal labor/work? My reliance on Black Marxism helps me to untangle this question not from a legal perspective but from a perspective of Black oppression and struggle. As Yousuf Al-Bulushi (2020, 258) suggests, Black radicalism explicitly "breaks from a reliance upon the law as the only mechanism for pursuing justice, and instead embraces the necessity for forms of marronage that flee established polities and embrace communities of mutual aid bound by non-political ties." Rather than "formal" and "informal" work, a more convincing terminology to me is that of proletarization and deproletarization. As Tom Brass argues, the increasing proletarization of the agricultural workforce effectively pushes agro-capitalists and state regulators to use a growing set of extraeconomic means in order to cheapen, coerce, and discipline their workforce (Brass 2014, 571; see also Brass and Bernstein 1992; Bernstein 2010). As a result of these measures, workers thus become constrained to offer their labor power "at the will" of agro-capitalist firms.[10]

Moving beyond a purely legalistic interpretation of "formal labor" and "informal work" allows me to broaden the question of how the work invested in both agricultural production and in the reproduction of its labor force is being valorized as labor, and also the question how workers who are nominally free but disposed of the means of subsistence figure differently in a commodified form of capitalist exploitation. Let me address these one by one. To start with the second question, I argue that the reduction of the difference between "free" and "unfree" labor to a simple dichotomy risks bypassing the complex arrangements and diversifications on which today's labor markets are organized at multiple scales. As Orlando Patterson (1982, vii, 35, 13)—a central scholar on historical forms of slavery—observes, even the violent relation between slave and master on the plantation cannot be divorced from the distribution of power throughout the wider society in which both master and slave find themselves, as "even at this most elementary level of personal relations it should be clear that we are dealing not with a static entity but with a complex interactional process, one laden with tension and contradiction in the dynamics of each of its constituent elements." Slavery, therefore, should never be reduced to the mere imposition of force and the right over life and death over unfree humans, but, more importantly, it involves a form of *social death*—a form of permanent liminality from where there is little escape.[11] What makes the slave status unique is that the slave is treated as a nonperson, a nonhuman. In that sense, slaves are the extreme expression of human unfreedom, a form of bare life that can be killed but not sacrificed. They represent the institutional destruction of the very possibility of political and symbolic subjectivity (Ziarek 2008).

Though it is undeniable that contemporary migrant workers have a history and a future, it makes sense considering their social death from a different perspective. Patterson argues that we should consider even the crudest form of unfreedom in the context of the active politization of labor because, in essence, the nonsubjectivity of the slave forms the specter against which *all* abstract labor is ideologically and materially placed. Second, and related to this, one should consider the social death of unfree workers not merely as a function of slavery, but more widely as a function of capitalist relations: the political liminality of unfree workers—in terms of their territorial nonbelonging and their adverse incorporation into the dominant mode of production, stripped as they are of recognition and deliberately placed in the margins—is inherent in the way contemporary capitalism thrives and survives as a system (see also Kasmir and Carbonella 2014).

The other question concerns the valorization of work as labor. In orthodox Marxist analysis, this distinction is usually addressed through the terminology of the "reserve army." As Pradella and Cillo (2021) point out, this terminology serves to understand how unfree labor can very much be a component of capitalist relations—contrary to "slavery," which orthodox Marxism defines as entirely belonging to the feudal sphere. It is exactly this difference, between slavery and unfree labor, that determines the role of what Marx calls a relative surplus population. Indeed, it is capital accumulation as such—with its tendency toward technological progress, and the concentration and centralization of capital—that generates at once a redundancy of formalized (proletarian) laborers and the growth of a population of underemployed, unemployed, and displaced workers as well as direct producers. This population, which is far from superfluous, is necessary to the process of capital accumulation because it simultaneously puts pressure on employed workers by limiting their claims and resistance, and by allowing capital to increase exploitation and sustain profitability. At first sight, migrant workers do fulfill this role in Italy. As elsewhere, the growing "supermarketization" of Italian agriculture has indeed coincided with a process of internationalization, segmentation, and precarization of the agricultural workforce, with conditions of unfree labor particularly affecting undocumented workers in irregular employment, EU immigrants, and especially women (Martin 2017).

But here lies exactly the issue: what are the factors that determine who is regarded as relative surplus and who not? And where lies the difference between unfree labor and slavery if not in the denial of personhood and *social death*?

Once again, a focus on the Black Mediterranean enables me to develop a more pronounced political focus based on the recognition that the distinction between free and unfree, waged and unwaged labor, slavery and freedom, always is the result of a political process, of the active making of capitalist subjectivities (Kasmir and Carbonella 2014; Thompson 1963). Two related questions arise in the current context: what are the grounds for precarious workers' mobilizations in the context of their growing fragmentation and exploitation by oligopolist capital; and second, how do enterprises, the state, and social factors more generally contribute to widen the rift between such relative, or differentially, included populations? Rather than categorizing slavery as either a matter of the past or a mere issue of human rights violations, I will bring the issue of slavery to the fore as a *political* possibility emerging in the midst of Black struggle, by building explicitly on the "human experience from which the rebellion [rises]" (Robinson [1983] 2005, 238). To summarize my argument, I agree that state operations have been and continue to be divisive in their association of labor and migration management. But in the context of extractive agri-food chains, which involve a continuous movement of contraction and expansion, investment and abandonment, I feel the need to investigate the articulation and disarticulation of agricultural workers' *relative* inclusion and exclusion from formal capitalist development. In this context, it remains important to analyze the process of racialization that continues to take place, and which, in my view, reflects a dynamic of racial stratification and reorganization, of managing difference through spatial dispersal, but also of outright resistance and struggle (Hawthorne 2021a, 5). In this section I will discuss more in depth the effects of the corporate food regime on mobile agricultural labor, while in the book's last chapter I will focus empirically on the meaning of slavery in contemporary Black struggles.

Italy is no exception to the trend of growing segmentation and segregation of migrant labor that is indeed characteristic of the "global factory." In the family-run agro-enterprises that dominate the agricultural sector in Italy, family members are typically employed all year round, while the planting, weeding, and harvesting of cash crops is left almost entirely to the wage workers of non-Italian origin who occupy an increasingly permanent place in the daily life of the enterprise. At the same time, though, the number of migrant workers has increased tremendously over the past three decades. In 1989, the CREA (Consiglio per la ricerca in agricoltura e l'analisi dell'economia agraria) estimated the number of foreign workers in Italian agriculture to be around 23,000. In 2010 this number had grown to 318,000. By 2017 the number of "foreign" agro-workers had reached 364,000 (CREA 2019). In 2020, the Placido Rizzotto Observatory estimated the number of foreign workers in agriculture to be around 400,000—representing a third of the regularly employed agricultural labor force (Osservatorio Placido

Rizzotto 2020). The main nationalities of these workers are Romanian, Indian, Moroccan, Tunisian, and—for what is mostly considered the "reserve army" of seasonal harvesters—sub-Saharan Africans, predominantly from West African countries like Senegal, Côte d'Ivoire, Burkina Faso, Mali, Gambia, and Ghana. It is those mobile workers, and not the family enterprise, who face growing levels of labor exploitation in the agricultural sector.

The labor unions usually limit the definition of labor exploitation to the absence of "formal" contractual obligations. According to the Placido Rizzotto Observatory, which represents the largest farmworkers' union, FLAI-CGIL, most migrant farmworkers are employed either without or only partially through formal contracts and on a piecework basis. And they suffer exclusion from social benefits because of this discrimination. On top of this legal discrimination stands the competition between migrants of different nationalities, as well as the sheer impossibility of finding employment without the intermediation of the gang masters, or *caporali*. The labor unions see in this phenomenon a clear indication of migrant workers' legal discrimination in terms of irregular employment, which according to these criteria has risen from 100,000 to as many as 180,000–200,000 workers between 2014 and 2020 (Osservatorio Placido Rizzotto 2014, 15; 2020, 188).[12] Characteristic of these workers' living condition, according to the major labor unions, is their concentration in rural ghettos. Described by Francesco Caruso as the zones of confinement of the Mediterranean subaltern workforce (Caruso 2015), these places have come to symbolize the growing discrimination of socially and politically oppressed workers who occupy the bottom scale of contemporary supply-chain capitalism in the field of agri-food business since the early 1990s. These ghettos have not only become a growing thorn in the eye of public representatives and state institutions, but they have also become the major target of state interventions that seek to eradicate and resettle rural migrant workers—often through explicitly violent means.

At a larger scale, the legal campaigns of labor unions and governments have tended to support a new abolitionist narrative that has become the discursive foundation of a politics of humanitarian security. Discursively, the new abolitionism can be summarized like this: since "seasonal workers" in retail agriculture are the new slaves, an abolition of these new forms of slavery needs to address the root causes of their exploitation, which are the criminal gang masters and human traffickers and their acolytes. One protagonist of this discourse has been the former Italian prime minister Matteo Renzi, who in the context of the rising death tolls in the Mediterranean post-2011 called the networks responsible for carrying migrants to its shores the "slave drivers of the twenty-first century."[13] On the Right, the imagery of the migrant slave worker has instead bolstered a narrative that promotes national food sovereignty as a form of economic protectionism.[14]

Political protagonists like Matteo Salvini, who has actively pursued the repressive border policies introduced by the governments of Matteo Renzi (2014–2016) and Paolo Gentiloni (2016–2018), continue to insist on the *Italianness* of local agri-food production against what they consider a rampant global invasion of imported commodities and laborers (Iocco, Lo Cascio, and Perrotta 2020; see also Scoones et al. 2019). In this frame, the trope of the migrant slave worker thus explicitly serves the end of purifying Italian food production from the "alien" elements of criminal human trafficking and slave labor.

In Italy, the new abolitionism has carried forward two main decision-making processes, in the domains of anti-racketeering legislation and the securitization of labor. Since 2011, the Italian parliament has introduced a series of anti-gangmaster legislation with the official aim of protecting labor rights but practically resulting in a new form of humanitarian labor management. Following the protests of Nardò (see below), the law decree 138 of August 13, 2011, changed illegal labor intermediation (or *caporalato*) from a simple administrative offense into one punishable by a prison sentence (Perrotta 2014). Law 199/2016 furthermore extended the responsibility of illegal hiring from the *caporale* labor intermediary to agricultural firms, thus making more explicit the offense of labor exploitation by the employer. A second policy assemblage concerns the securitization of labor, which, as I will cover in more detail in chapter 3, concerns the progressive encapsulation of the question of labor into a humanitarian-security logic. This narrative and material intervention is founded on a strict reading of abolitionism that associates migrant labor conditions as the sole and unique consequence of gang masters in the ghetto. The main effects of this policy can be read in the rural landscape today: it consists of the systematic and forceful eviction of migrants from their living spaces to capture their labor power and channel their mobility toward the official reception centers operated by humanitarian agencies.

Other observers are not so convinced of this policy frame, however. By holding criminal networks responsible for the persistent labor exploitation in Italy's agri-business, critics on the Left continue to neglect the systematic racist surveillance, discrimination, and segregation that have become key elements of the mode of production in Southern Italian agricultural districts. While criminal infiltrations are undeniable, the exclusive focus on organized criminality and illegal labor intermediation risks diverting attention from the equally important issues of capital concentration and overaccumulation, and of racialized labor infrastructures that determine the social relations of production in significant ways. In a similar manner, right-wing discourses that try to narrow down the argument about food sovereignty to a question of protected national borders have also increasingly bumped into difficulties: when in the spring of 2020 thousands of Romanian and Bulgarian workers did not reach Italian soil because of anti-COVID restrictions, it suddenly became clear to everyone how important migrant workers' contributions are to the Italian economy.

The insistent discourse on contemporary migrant slavery as a form of labor exploitation reflects widespread refusal in Italy and Europe to grapple with the structural racism that has historically become part and parcel of global supply chains. Retail-driven agriculture today thrives on racial differentiation for extracting capital from bodies that produce value and generate wealth outside the formalized mode of production (see also Ippolito, Perrotta, and Raeymaekers 2021). The widespread concern with criminality as a cause of premature migrant death in fact prevents us from asking the more pressing question of whether it is still sufficient to consider the sovereign right to make life, take life, or let die as a matter of a bio-political state of exception of sorts, or must we instead confront the bio-economic issue of how one's precarious life and premature death is conditioned by one's position in capitalism (Tyner 2019, x).

More concretely, two problems arise within the new abolitionist frame. First, the major difficulty with antiracketeering legislation is that it excludes most factors leading to labor exploitation from the legal terminology. The central judicial instrument introduced by these measures has been the crime of enslavement (*riduzione in schiavitù*)—a condition that comprises the restriction of personal freedom through imprisonment or personal and financial blackmailing. Given that accusations of slavery require an active denunciation of the presumed tormentor, however, it is very rare that victims of serious labor exploitation gather the courage to denounce their own state of oppression and illegality. Some legal activists have therefore called for a more systemic approach toward labor exploitation as a form of social unfreedom. The main deficiency of the legal approach toward slavery, they argue, has been its incapacity to also tackle the structural causes of labor exploitation. To differentiate these conditions of unfreedom from what is quite narrowly described as a condition of slavery indeed forms one of the main gaps that neither legislators nor scholarly experts have been able to bridge so far (for a discussion see Marks 2010; Skrivankova 2010; Rigo 2015).

A second point of critique concerns the securitization of migrant mobility, which has tended to reinforce rather than diminish their vulnerability in terms of labor exploitation. Particularly since 2011, when NATO ships started patrolling Mediterranean waters, the policy narrative around migration has completely shifted. The direct result of this shift has not only been a recurrent association of economic migration with "bogus" refugees, profiteerism, and illegitimate demands. But it also means that labor migration has been completely eclipsed from the state's legislative and policy concern a trend Dines and Rigo (2015) earlier identified as the "refugeeization" of the agricultural labor force.[15] But while this transformation may look like a self-fulfilling prophecy that underscores the growth of "bogus" economic migration, it reflects a discriminatory differentiation of the labor market, which serves both state and employers' ends—thus signaling what Neil Smith ([1984] 2008) calls a politics of scale, or the active production of geographic scales in order to differentiate flows and their speed and penetration at different levels of capitalist globalization.

So, whenever terms like "inhumane" and "slavery" determine the public debate and the political interventions that stem from it in the domain of labor exploitation, this should be a reason for reflection rather than uncritical acceptance, critics seem to argue. Treating migrants as victims to be saved on the one hand, and as a security risk on the other, risks producing a vicious circle of constant displacement and peripheralization of workers who are at the same time central to the survival of formal capitalist development. State interventions in this domain thus tend to exacerbate an enclave economy, which facilitates workers' precarity, while reinforcing their illegality and exclusion from society (Cuppini and Peano 2019). While the racialized segmentation of the labor market is not exclusively tied to agriculture, it remains important to note the differences, in terms of the social relations of production, between agri-food and industrial supply chains. These differences, I argue, have very much to do with the way the construction of race and nature are coupled in a mutually reinforcing dynamic. It is this dynamic I will now turn to.

Black Struggles

A different perspective on the racial dynamics that underpin the reproduction of migrant labor in the plantation economy of the Mediterranean potentially brings to the fore the undoubtedly complex and multifold Black struggles that are both given shape and giving shape to this economy. As said, I use the terminology of natural racialization to highlight those processes of racialization that allocate Black lives in contemporary agri-food chains to a kind of prehuman, "natural state" located outside the perimeters of modern and civilized humanity. In this sense, African migrant ghettos acquire a different meaning both as fugitive sites and as locales of political renewal. As Harney and Moten suggest (2013, 5), "fugitive planning and black study" are mostly about reaching out to find connection in a world that is characterized by brokenness. Black fugitive sites emerge in this context as new economies of giving, taking, and being with. Examples include the communities that emerged in the context of flight from slavery, like the Brazilian *quilombos* and the South American maroons, and which, next to open resistance, also developed a series of ambivalent economic and political relations with the colonial powers. Black fugitive sites thus express the double desire, as

Grada Kilomba (2008) writes, to oppose that place of Otherness in which Black life is cast in the domain of modernity, and the desire to invent oneself anew. As I will argue more in detail in chapter 5, recent years have seen the ghetto emerge both as a site of capitalist reproduction and as a locale of active, anticapitalist resistance. Whereas the latter dynamic has been widely recognized in the context of Italy's antiracist movement over the past twenty-five years, the former still requires a deeper reflection because it is exactly in this reinvention that relations between fugitives and the social relations of production tend to become more ambivalent. The engagement with Black studies and with Black Marxism offers the possibility to conceive of these same sites as open frontiers, where the law is not the only reference when it comes to defining the boundaries of sovereignty, citizenship, and political subjectivity.

Several crucial moments can be remembered here. A first shock wave concerned the uprising of African workers in Villa Literno after the fatal shooting of Jerry Essan Masslo on August 24, 1989. The South African national and anti-apartheid activist was shot during a robbery by a band of local Camorra youth in his temporary habitat close to the town: an abandoned warehouse where he stayed with hundreds of other seasonal workers, mainly of West African origin, and which had become the center of Italy's first migrant ghetto. The memorialization of his death simultaneously gave rise to the Italian antiracist movement and to the first immigration decree, which was ratified the next year (see also chapter 2). A famous Naples-based dub band, Almamegretta, dedicated a song to the place in their album *Figli d'Annibale* (Sons of Hannibal)—remembering the journey of Hannibal as the African roots of the Mediterranean. Such marginal gestures aside, the area where Masslo was killed kept being determined by a violent exclusion of Black Africans from local society. In 1994, a local Camorra clan set fire to the ghetto of Villa Literno, thus activating a mass eviction of predominantly West African seasonal land laborers toward Puglia, Calabria, and the rest of the Meridione (at its peak, Villa Literno had hosted over fifteen hundred workers). Several activists remember that moment as a crucial eye-opener that racism had taken on another face in the Mediterranean at the end of the Cold War.[16]

While it is impossible to provide an exhaustive list of abuses and protests here, it remains intriguing how the reactions of Italy's government and main labor unions continue to be characterized by a denial of this structural racism and instead insist on the criminal nature of these abuses—thus carrying forward the thesis that migrant labor abuse is a feature of the "backward" and "uncivilized" segments of southern agrarian society dominated by Mafia, 'Ndrangheta, and Camorra clans.[17] Contrary to this paradigm, a small group of antiracist scholars insists instead on the systemic quality of these abuses and on the necessity to interpret migrant protests as "events characterized by a disruptive resistance and protest against a system which, while denying the most elementary needs and all dignity to workers in the fields, denies life or admits it only as a mere presence, a mere being-alive" (Borretti 2010, 521). The revolt of Castel Volturno in 2008 erupted after a local gang sprayed gunfire at six African migrants, leaving one seriously wounded. Sick and tired of the systematic discriminations against them, workers spontaneously took to the streets and protested for days—pushing local antiracist associations to run to their support and spurring the government to deploy four hundred security forces to the area and expel all "irregulars."[18] In December that year, a spontaneous uprising erupted in Rosarno, Calabria, after two Ivorian workers were wounded by gunfire. But the real wakeup call was the protest that erupted in January 2010 in the same town, after a gang of local Italians opened fired on three African workers.[19] In a mass revolt that lasted for days, Ghanaian and Burkinabè workers demonstrated in front of the town hall, shouting "We are not animals" and carrying signs saying, "Italians here are racist." In the spate of anger—during which cars were set on fire, garbage cans thrown over, and windows smashed—one protester wrote on the wall of a migrant squat: "Avoid shooting blacks. We will be remember" (*sic*). The protests risked escalating into urban warfare when they were followed by an assiduous manhunt in which local youth chased African workers through Rosarno's streets—causing a national outcry as well as a prompt state intervention. Typical of the structurally racist undertone of state interventions in that period, the interior minister Roberto Maroni called on the government to take immediate action, saying that the tensions were a result of "too much tolerance toward clandestine immigration."[20]

Many more protests would follow. The events of Rosarno in 2010 and subsequently the strike of African laborers in Nardò, in Salento, in the summer of 2011 stimulated the commitment of many organizations—collectives, peasant organizations, trade unions, NGOs, community-supported agriculture initiatives, religious groups, and so on—all of whom spent their energy, time, and resources toward a betterment of the conditions of agricultural workers in the South. Commitments such as these have forced national and local public institutions to intervene on the issue. Various laws have been enacted, including the two laws against illegal hiring and labor exploitation, in 2011 and 2016. So, the situation cannot be said to have remained unchanged over the past decade. However, no action has fundamentally changed the structural causes of the dramatically woeful working and housing conditions of the migrants who populate the countryside, not only in Southern Italy but in the Mediterranean (see Perrotta 2020). That is why further research and action is needed on the fundamentally racist causes that have historically underpinned, and continue to underpin, rural capitalism in this region.

To push forward the discussion on the racialization of migrant labor and struggles, I insist on foregrounding Black epistemologies in the struggle against the persistent oppression of racial capitalism. More explicitly, I build on a small but interesting post-Marxist literature in Italian (Dal Lago 1999; Basso and Perocco 2003; Basso 2010; and particularly Borretti 2010). The combination of these two literatures serves to place the Italian antiracist movement into a larger ongoing debate about racial capitalism and the place therein of the Mediterranean; but it also deepens our understanding of the factors that contribute to the reproduction of the social and spatial boundaries that keep the corporate food regime in the Mediterranean so dangerously intact. Over the last twenty years, two milestone studies have been those of Pietro Basso and Fabio Perocco of 2003 and Pietro Basso of 2010. Particularly the latter stands out for its original thesis about the racial state, not just in Italy but across Europe and the US, as the key facilitator of labor exploitation at a time of capitalist crisis (see also Goldberg 2002). Basso insists on the *top-down* dimension of racism, as the institutional translation in terms of legal provisions, government, policing and surveillance practices, of racial categories that have the direct purpose of feeding capital and dividing the labor force. The main point he and other contributors to his volume make is that liberal democracies in Europe have become *organically* racist: institutional racism has become "a weapon firms, the market, and global capital use against globalized wage labor to divide it deeply and appropriate its vital lymph" (Basso 2010, 10). For him, as for me, racism is therefore not a mere matter of cultural prejudice, but a *systemic* quality of the way global capitalism penetrates our lives through the agency of the state. More concretely, Basso writes, the last thirty years of neoliberal policy have been characterized by a constant and violent imposition of policies *against migrants*, policies that are characterized by a series of discriminatory, racially inspired measures.[21] Migration policies in Italy have actively built and consolidated the legal and social categories that identify who is deserving to become a citizen rather than a subject, who has the right to be attached to a particular location or territory and who has not, who has a right to be a "free" laborer and who has not.

To answer the question of how racism is articulated in contemporary rural capitalist relations, two associated issues need to be addressed. One of these concerns the predominant informality that characterizes these relations. While it should be said that the informalization of migrant labor is not unique to agriculture but that this dynamic characterizes the differential inclusion—or rather, adverse incorporation—of mobile workers under conditions of "extractive" capitalism (for a discussion see N. Phillips 2013; Mezzadra and Neilson 2011, 2013; Svampa 2012; Arboleda 2020), rural capitalist labor relations are specific in that they involve the deliberate whitening of waged labor in contrast to the informal work that goes into the reproduction of this labor (and which is being creamed off twice, as a subsidy to capital and as a source of informal accumulation). In Italian, this shift is known as the change from *lavoro nero* ("black labor") to *lavoro grigio* ("gray labor"), or labor that *only partially* occurs outside the realm of officially sanctioned channels (see also ILO 2001). Rather than resolving the problem of illegal employment, this shift in fact reflects the emergence of a widening gray zone where the social relations of production are deliberately destabilized. Globally speaking, this shift has been the topic of global value network analysis, which in fact has enhanced our understanding of the ways the contemporary industrial growth model has led to a growing outsourcing of production—a phenomenon scholars also refer to as the "global factory." In the Italian context, the net result of this "Russian doll" model of capitalist accumulation, as well as the neoliberal labor policies that support it, has been a concentration of low-paid, semiskilled and unskilled jobs in the lower ends of industrial supply chains, where immigrant workers usually perform the most precarious, unhealthy, and dangerous jobs.[22] What makes "gray labor" specific in this realm, I will argue, is the deliberate "blackening" of the space of social reproduction; in other words, gray labor is the space where "white" waged labor is creamed off from the naturalized "black" space of the African migrant ghetto where the reproduction of that labor takes place and is taken care of.

Second, and in line with the former, it should be emphasized that the intent of the state has never been, as often wrongfully assumed, to halt international migration. As a matter of fact, the large majority of those people applying for territorial residency permits in Italy are already present in Italy at the time of their application.[23] The objective is rather to simultaneously lower the value of global "living labor" while withdrawing support from—or, increasingly, directing violence against—those who fall victim to the state's persistent neoliberal reforms. Robinson's Black Marxist perspective thus dovetails nicely with Basso's and Perocco's observation that the deliberate manipulation of the terminology of the "clandestine migrant," not just in Italy, but across the globe, has triggered a steady normalization of state and nonstate violence against those segments of the migrant working population that are considered unworthy, or not yet fit for integration in the formal frame of development. The political drive to formalize migrant labor through the instruments of territorial residency and other security measures can be redefined as a form of state racket, a legalized blackmail that serves not to stop the arrival of so-called illegal migrants but to coerce their labor and exercise power over them.

Based on these findings, we can conclude that what makes the state's role so central in advancing capital accumulation these last thirty years has been its aggressive facilitation not only of market oligopolies but also of the progressive manipulation of global "living labor" through its insistence on the boundary between "irregular" and "regular" migrants. At the heart of this distinction lies the conflation of "irregular" migrant status with "informal" employment, and of "regular" migrant status with "formal" employment. As Rossana Cillo (2010) argues, the combination of these two factors in contemporary state policy in Italy, especially since the 1990s, has laid the foundation for a simultaneous segmentation and segregation of the workforce not just in national but in global terms. In other words, states act directly toward the creation of an ultraprecarious and ultraflexible workforce whose integration in the national labor market is increasingly dependent on a form of differential inclusion based on racial categories and provisions. Central here remains the state's legal interpretation of economic informality as the absence of an employment contract, the cost of which, as we have seen, is being entirely poured onto the "foreign worker": no contract means no residency, means no right to basic health and social welfare under the conditions stipulated by contemporary immigration policy. In a situation of predominant informality, however (which, as we have also seen, is becoming the norm rather than the exception in certain economic sectors, like agriculture), this places such state policies in a somewhat perverse position, as they simultaneously exclude "irregular" migrants from enjoying basic human rights under the permanent specter of deportability, while they exclusively tie their integration as "regular" immigrant workers to the decision of capitalist enterprise.

We can indeed reframe the increasingly restrictive migration policies that characterize liberal democracies within the ongoing erosion of the welfare state that runs parallel to the increasing concentration of capital on a global scale. Italy forms no exception in this regard—in fact it exhibits a long tradition of market liberalizations that have entirely worked toward the division and fragmentation of the national labor force, starting with Silvio Berlusconi's welfare reductions and redimensioning of the collective bargaining process, to Mario Monti's attack on Article 18 (which defines the scope of unfair dismissal). The peak of this interconnection could be noticed from 2008 onward, not surprisingly the period of galloping capital crisis. One measure concerned the so-called *pacchetto sicurezza* ("Security Package": Law 94/2009), which introduced the penal crime of "illegal stay," thus enhancing an already ongoing process of criminalization of immigrants (a law that was even reinforced with the introduction of a penal crime in 2009). A second measure (both were introduced by Prime Minister Matteo Renzi) concerned the Jobs Act, which consolidated the abdication of the Italian state from its historical mediating role between state and capital. In the domain of agriculture, these two measures were detrimental for migrant workers because now they not only risked being legally punished for their "illegal" stay in case they were caught living in informal rural settlements, but the Jobs Act also entirely coupled their fate as workers to their agricultural employer. Technically, the Jobs Act introduced the *centri per l'impiego* (CPI), which function as official registration centers in the agricultural districts under the authority of the regional administration. In practice, however, the CPI simply register employment demands forwarded by agricultural firms through their sectoral organizations (the so-called CAF, *centro di assistenza fiscale*). From 2008 onward, therefore, one can speak of a growing *securitization of labor*, which signifies its "flexploitative" dimension on the one hand (forcing "free workers" to be recruited at the will of the employer: see also Peck and Theodore 2001; Jessop 2002) and, on the other, its circumscription within the limits of "regular"—state-sanctioned—contracts under the specter of deportability (in case of an absence of contract or a verified "irregular stay").

What is at stake here is not so much a discrimination that can be expressed exclusively in legal terms, but rather a process of racial and gendered stratification of the global workforce, which reproduces the conditions for their segmentation and segregation while it reaps the benefits from this very exclusion by giving free space to the operation of informal, intermediary institutions that link these separated constituencies to the circuits of capital accumulation. What makes agrarian capitalism specific in this regard, therefore, is not its reliance on an informalized and legally discriminated-against workforce, but rather the intricate ways in which the sources of life that sustain the reproduction of this workforce are explicitly separated and made available for extraction. The mechanisms of separation underpinning this process comprise, as I said, a series of spatial reorganizations that simultaneously reframe these sources of life as resources that can be extracted while reframing the forms of life that they sustain as "natural" spaces that continue to be situated outside the realm of formal development.

COVID and the Crisis of Labor Reproduction

While the 2008–2009 "food crisis" definitely laid bare the internal contradictions that characterize the agricultural labor market and agri-food markets more broadly, the SARS-CoV-2 (or simply, COVID) pandemic made these even sharper. Like in 2007, when the world faced rising food prices because of reduced grain outputs and rising oil prices, the effects of government restrictions on labor mobility and on food exports caused a ripple effect across the globe. Rather than investing in more resilient food systems based on short supply chains, however, international institutions, particularly the World Trade Organization and the European Union, ensured that national government measures did not detrimentally impact global food supply chains (Bello 2020). One acute aspect of the global "food crisis" in 2019–2020 in fact concerned the apparent lack of "manpower" in the countryside. Because of restrictions on human mobility, many Eastern European farmworkers, for example, decided to return to their countries of origin or found themselves unable to travel to the West for the start of their working seasons. Other workers who resided in Italy but did not have a residency permit or an employment contract at the time of the COVID outbreak were forbidden to move. This situation of being displaced-in-place was especially relevant for African workers, who found it difficult to go from their places of residence to the fields, but also to move between regions. A report of the NGO Doctors for Human Rights (MEDU) on the Plain of Gioia Tauro (Calabria) said the following:

> The limits on national and local mobility imposed by the government prevented the movement of laborers to other regions to seek employment in seasonal crops (strawberry picking in Campania, tomatoes in Puglia, etc.). Even ordinary forms of mobility that allow laborers to reach workplaces have been banned, despite agriculture being one of the production sectors deemed essential by the [national decrees on COVID containment]. Cases of laborers who received administrative sanctions were not uncommon because they were stopped by the police while trying to reach workplaces in neighboring municipalities. In several cases, the police asked detained laborers in addition to their self-certification [which demonstrates the necessity to travel under the given restrictions][24] for their employment contract. (MEDU 2022: my translation)

MEDU's study shows the extent to which the climate of alarmism with which employers' organizations in Europe faced the shortage of manpower favored a corporate, rather than human, interest in solving the pandemic crisis. Deliberately inflating the numbers at hand, for instance, the Italian farmers' association Coldiretti estimated a labor shortage of 370,000 workers.[25] Shortly afterward, Confagricoltura (another farmers' association) spoke of a shortage of 200,000 agricultural workers, while calling for urgent measures to facilitate the mobility of workers from Eastern Europe. Their reactions reflected the overall anxiety of agricultural corporations, and of governments, toward the shortage of labor supplies across the globe. The British Farmers Association, for example, launched an appeal to establish a "Land Army" to support agricultural production. In many countries, farmers tried to recruit students and pensioners to harvest vegetables to replace foreign laborers, while organizing private flights and online platforms for their workers' temporary employment (or so-called "green corridors"). Meanwhile, governments and international institutions introduced various emergency measures to regularize the employment of migrant workers without a residency permit—with the European Union once more taking the lead with its introduction of the category of the "essential worker," which, significantly, includes mobile agro-workers (Lodovici et al. 2020). Emblematic of these efforts in Italy was the introduction of a "sanatory law" (*sanatoria*) to formalize the "nonregular" component of the agricultural workforce at the time of the pandemic, which served to further associate the right to territorial residency with the right to formal employment.[26]

To put it plainly, the subsequent "food crises" of 2008–2009 and 2019–2020 have shown that global agri-food production has no labor shortage but rather a shortage of workers willing to work under conditions that go beyond the accepted perception of the humane. The "inhumane" circumstances of these workers who are generally excluded from enjoying even the most basic human rights as they camp out in makeshift ghettos and are exploited to the bone are rather a reflection of the expanding boundary that separates this workforce from what are considered the limits of civilized humanity. It is in this context, of an increasing dehumanization and natural racialization of the migrant workers' living space, that I place the major effects of this global crisis. In parallel to the extractive wealth that characterizes the corporate food regime more broadly, it is this double dynamic, of naturalized racial segregation coupled to the monetized valorization of a steadily informalized and deregulated workforce, that perhaps makes agri-food production in the Italian context, and particularly in Southern Italy, so specific. In the next chapter, I will turn to the historical origins of this dialectical relationship before discussing the more acute forms of labor securitization and segregation that characterize the contemporary plantation economy in the Mediterranean.

PLANTATION ASSEMBLAGES

This chapter focuses on the deep transformations that have characterized the social ecology of Mediterranean and sub-Saharan monocropping plantations since the late nineteenth century until today. My main geographic focus will be the growing connection between the central Mediterranean and the Sahel—two socioecological systems that have become increasingly interconnected in the last four decades. From a global perspective, the mode of production of the plantation has undergone considerable changes since it was first introduced in the Mediterranean in the premodern era. While forced slavery has been gradually replaced by different forms of labor exploitation, and the capitalist supply chains responsible for commodifying labor and the produce of the land have progressively taken on a more networked form, the composition of labor and capital has also changed considerably over time. One of these changes concerns the different paths of mobility of agricultural laborers who are constantly moving between different places and forms of livelihood. In our current globalized market economy, agricultural capital input also appears to move constantly while firms and investors deliberately move assets between spaces of production and nodes of accumulation. Though these trends are by no means confined to the Mediterranean, I choose this focus for reasons I explained in the previous chapter: at the center of my inquiry remains the question of how the contemporary crisis of the Mediterranean—which has been explained foremost in geopolitical and humanitarian terms affects relations between labor, capital, and public authority in the context of supply chain agriculture, which remains a dominant mode of production in the area. In the present chapter, I will inquire how the growing mobility—of capital, and of labor, more specifically—is paired with an equally important immobility and containment of laboring subjects through the territorial infrastructures and spatial politics of the liberal nation-state.

The terminology I employ to grasp this tension is that of a plantation assemblage. This term highlights the way corporations, communities, and political authorities actively negotiate the ways in which supply chain agriculture hits the ground in specific places and environments (Hennings 2018; Thaler, Viana, and Toni 2019; Mezzadra and Neilson 2019). I pick up the notion of the assemblage from Gilles Deleuze and Félix Guattari. In their book *A Thousand Plateaus* they describe an assemblage as "the increase in the dimensions of a multiplicity that necessarily changes its nature as it expands its connections" ([1987] 2014, 7). Reconnecting to this definition, Tomas Nail defines an *agencement* (the original French term Deleuze and Guattari used in their book) as an "arrangement or layout of heterogeneous elements" whereby what counts most is not the terms or the elements but what is "between" them, the in-between, a set of relations that are inseparable from each other (Deleuze and Parnet 1987, viii; Nail 2017, 22–23). This terminology in my view facilitates a more sophisticated understanding of the ways capital and labor flow through interconnected hierarchies and how territories of extraction fold together in place. My approach starts from the premise that capital, labor, and regulatory interventions do not simply "hop" from place to place, but they intersect in a multidimensional space that is actively molded by the heterogeneous elements that constitute such assemblages—including the corporations, governments, and nongovernmental and community organizations who play an active role in negotiating the commodification of labor as economic value. At the same time, I find, the active negotiation over value in capitalist frontiers constantly invokes new questions about who has the right to wealth, and who can be considered a legitimate subject in the making of capitalist production and reproduction. This negotiation constitutes the subject of this chapter.

In the first section, I will pick up the discussion about plantation agriculture and its consolidation as a dominant mode of production across the Mediterranean and Sahelian space since the late 1800s. It is in fact no coincidence, I will argue, that at the turn of the twentieth century, lands that were once despised for being "backward" and "uncivilized" became the foundation of a vast commercial plantation economy for cereals and cash crops in these regions. In my view, this development has much to do with the way the liberal nation-state unfolded its agenda of territorial development: reformers, planners, and administrators saw themselves as part of a civilizing mission that was to generate value from these vast territories, which they considered at once "empty" but "full" of potential (Regassa, Hizekiel, and Korf 2019, 935; see also Tsing 2005; Eilenberg and Cons

2019; T. M. Li 2014). Both in the Sahelian and northern Mediterranean, the proceeding colonization of agricultural and common lands in this period significantly transformed the geography of existing social ecologies as it simultaneously introduced new boundaries and connections.

After forcibly claiming new agricultural estates from the forest and the agricultural commons in the newly independent Italian state, liberal entrepreneurs introduced a geographic division that would determine the future of Southern Italian agriculture for a century to come. Next to destroying the moral basis of the *latifundia*—the large land estates that had historically dominated Southern Italian rural society—state development policy introduced a new boundary between the mountains and the plain areas, the forest and the cultivated lands. The continuous resistance against these tentative reforms would eventually inspire decision makers to impose a series of state interventions in the sphere of agricultural development, technology, and urbanization that were to simultaneously colonize the supposedly "empty" lands of the South and make peasant populations malleable to capitalist labor. While introducing new technologies and infrastructures, these policies would also open a vast labor reserve of mobile, marginalized, migrant workers, who continued to straddle the boundaries of state-led capitalist development. This tension, in my view, lies at the heart of the modern liberal frontier: the tendency to simultaneously incorporate and refute, extract, and expel subaltern lands and peoples who thus end up forming a constitutive outside of formal capitalism and the benefits of modern civilization (see also Sanyal 2013).

In Northern Africa and the Horn of Africa to the east, the promise of modernity acquired an even more overtly violent character. Italian colonialists in their newly occupied lands not only extirpated local communities but also introduced a colonial economy based on extensive production and crop exports. South of the Sahara, French and English colonial state administrations in the meantime fostered a drastic reconfiguration of mobility patterns between what were once considered as oscillating ecological frontiers—thus liberating a vast labor reserve for the modern plantations of Senegal, Guinea, and Côte d'Ivoire. Internal migration would further reinforce these mobility patterns until the early 1980s, when the first cracks started to appear in West African plantation economies because of growing land conflicts generated by accelerating globalization (Chauveau and Dozon 1985; Richards and Chauveau 2007) and West African labor pools became more closely attracted to expanding Mediterranean agri-business.

In hindsight, it is safe to say that European agrarian policies initiated during the early twentieth century formed the backdrop of the persistent inequalities that still characterize the connections between states, capital, and labor across the Mediterranean today. The fundamentally racist stereotypes that historically drove the colonization of rural societies, based on tropes of backwardness, of racial inferiority and of underdevelopment, underpin the unfair ways in which their contemporary heirs continue to be linked up to global projects. To understand these tensions, we need to go back to the early period of agrarian colonization, when both sub-Saharan Africa and Southern Europe were subjected to a profound, and to many effects destabilizing, transformation of the lands, of the geography and the agrarian landscapes that underwent these vast territorial interventions. These tensions and connections will be the subject of the next section of this chapter.

In the subsequent section, I will concentrate on the forms of urbanity that connect agricultural labor to the factors of production across this vast geographic space. My focus here is not the modern metropoles and their promise of modern progress and civility, but the rural infrastructures that unfolded in their global peripheries. These infrastructures, I will argue, have become a key facet of a planetary form of urbanization that has enabled the emergence of vast networks of exchange in the context of the contemporary plantation economy. I will build on the double example of Italian and Burkinabè rural-urban migration to show how urban infrastructures continue to underpin the social relations of production in the context of cash-crop-oriented commercial agriculture. Considering important qualitative differences, I notice how marginalized agricultural laborers continue to settle into mobility, while at the same time producing and maintaining a sense of connectedness in this constantly moving ecological and geopolitical frontier.

Urbanizing "Nature"

Since its inception, the Italian nation-state has been characterized by a deep-seated fragmentation between the economically "developed" industrialized North and the decisively more rural and "underdeveloped" South (Agnew 2002). In his book *Darkest Italy: The Nation and Stereotypes of the Mezzogiorno*, John Dickie (1999) sketches the cultural dynamics that underpinned the colonization of the Italian South during the mid-nineteenth century. Italian nationalists in the South were convinced that modernity would pave the way for the civilization of what they regarded as a large, backward territory left behind by the preceding Bourbon kingdom. Leopoldo Franchetti, who in the 1870s undertook a parliamentary inquiry in the Mezzogiorno, repeatedly uses the terminology of "savagery," "barbarism," and "primitivism" to account for the South's presumed lack of economic development (Franchetti 1875). In the same context, Enrico Cialdini, lieutenant of the new Italian king Vittorio Emmanuele, famously said on his arrival in Naples, "This is Africa! Other than Italy! The Bedouins, in comparison to these peasants, are like milk and honey!" (Del Boca 2020, 55). These statements were emblematic of the way in which, in the aftermath of the Italian Risorgimento, liberal nationalists continued viewing the Mezzogiorno as a "nonsociety"—as Dickie observes (1999, 171), a society that not only lagged seriously behind in economic development but also lacked the very fabric of civilization.

In hindsight, it is no coincidence that these racist stereotypes emerged exactly at a time of liberal expeditions in Italy's southern backwaters. These stereotypes and depictions of the Other—nonindustrialized peasant societies—served both to capture and control what were predominantly interpreted as "not yet" developed humans and territories. The predominant vision of the Italian South as a *terra ferma*, an immobile territory characterized by desolation and abandonment, became an important trope through which exponents of the Italian ruling class confronted the multiple causes of the South's continuing impoverishment (Alliegro 2019, 13). Despite their diametrically opposed political views, parliamentarians like Francesco Saverio Nitti (socialist) and Eugenio Azimonti (liberal) proposed a rapid and systematic colonization of pastures and common agricultural lands to confront the miserable existence of the southern peasantry. In their reports, they harshly condemned the aristocratic landlords, who continued to rule southern territories from their residences in Naples and Taranto through a public administration that remained marked by clientelist rivalries. The main causes of underdevelopment, they insisted, were the lack of technical progress and the absence of infrastructures of rural development. The rural South not only lacked paved roads but was also characterized by persistent land erosion and overpopulated townships. Peasants lived together in crowded villages characterized by what liberal reformists saw as a promiscuous cohabitation of people and animals. Peasants spent their time between subsistence farming and working on the extensive landholdings of the absentee landlords of the latifundia, which had remained the dominant mode of production throughout the Mediterranean since Roman times. No wonder that many people continued to leave the region. Between 1869 and 1912, for example, Francesco Saverio Nitti estimated that more than 250,000 people emigrated from Basilicata to Northern Italy or elsewhere in Europe, or to the Americas. Nitti—quite visionary for his era—highlighted as the main cause of this rural exodus the *political* condition of oppression lived by the peasantry, which was not determined by an excess of population, he thought, but by the dominance of the landowning class (Nitti 1888).

Socialists and liberals of the Italian First Republic proposed the modernization of what they considered Italy's rural backwaters through a combination of administrative and commercial reforms. Their main purpose was to break the power of the latifundia. One of the early protagonists of this historical rupture was the Lombardy-born Eugenio Azimonti. In the early 1900s, he descended from his native town close to Milan to establish a private farm in the vicinity of Pedali (the current Val d'Agri). Taking over the directorship of a regional agrarian institute, he experimented with different agrarian techniques. His memoires, *Tentativi di colonizzazioni in Basilicata* (Attempts of colonization in Basilicata), were published in 1929. In the meantime, in Lavello, Giustino Fortunato and his brother Ernesto launched what was soon to become the most competitive agricultural enterprise on the boundary of the Vulture and Capitanata plains. In a region that counted an average of fifteen hundred malaria-related deaths per year, the brothers not only succeeded in drying the common pasturelands but also introduced a complex irrigation system that was celebrated for its technological innovation at the time (Saitta 1967, 13). Quite significantly, in fact, Francesco Saverio Nitti dedicated his book about southern emigration to Giustino Fortunato, who continues to be considered an agrarian revolutionary for his successful attempts at colonizing Basilicata's marshes.

The question remains: at what price? What gets often eclipsed from historical accounts of Italy's postindependence years is the huge deforestation that accompanied this technological advancement of the countryside. In the late 1800s, the Italian *Meridione* suffered the loss of hundreds of thousands of hectares of woods and forests to create new pastures for the herds, but above all to make room for the cultivation of wheat, rye, and corn in the lowlands. Throughout the end of the eighteenth century and the first half of the nineteenth century this process had a profound effect on what had hitherto been a fluid, oscillating frontier of agro-pastoral activity: next to subsistence farming, peasant communities held in common large pastoral lands they used for the transhumance (seasonal movement of livestock); and they used the forest to hunt game, pick fruits, and collect wood for heating and construction. Contesting the enclosures of these common lands, peasants in fact did not cease to revolt against what they saw as an illegitimate intrusion into their rights of passage through the common woodlands and pastures that were now taken up, destroyed, and repurposed for commercial farming.[1] Furthermore, this massive destruction also had a deteriorating effect on villages and roads, as they now lacked the necessary protection against landslides and rockslides that continued to hurt the local peasantry and farm owners alike. So rather than a cause, land erosion was a consequence of the expansion of large commercial landholdings.

Climate scientists in fact agree that Mediterranean deforestation was an early example of the relentless ruination we define today as the Anthropocene. During this period of intense modernization in the early twentieth century, between seventeen thousand and two hundred thousand hectares (about 65 to 772 square miles) of forest subsequently disappeared in Basilicata, Abruzzo, Molise, and

Calabria. There is a scientific consensus now that this deforestation formed the start of an important climate shift in the Mediterranean toward radically drier conditions (Hoerling et al. 2012; Cook et al. 2016). On the one hand, Mediterranean communities have been experiencing exponential levels of drought exactly at a time of rapid agricultural expansion: over a period of a hundred years, half the land surface of South Europe, the Balkans, Northern Africa, and parts of the Middle East have become devoted to agriculture. On the other hand, there is consistent evidence for anthropogenically forced drying in the region, which has both indirect causes (like rising sea temperatures) and direct causes, related to human economic activity. While the main culprits of contemporary climate discussions today remain greenhouse gas and carbon aerosol particles emitted by various types of human activity, another important factor has been water consumption. Considering that agriculture consumes 60–80 percent of freshwater supplies in the Mediterranean today, it is no surprise that scientists have become increasingly worried about the threats of industrialized agriculture to the region's food security (Nelson et al. 2009; FAO 2020). The seeds of this problem were sown in the beginning of the 1900s with the progressive colonization of lands that were considered "marginal," "abandoned," and "undeveloped."

From the 1920s onward, the Fascist government in Italy continued, with varying success, to dry the marshes and pastures of the southern coastal plains through the introduction of new rural infrastructures. Their reforms pointed at the demographic colonization of what its protagonists perceived as an irrational, unplanned, and wasted "nature." One emblematic project in this regard concerned the so-called *città di fondazione*: rural new towns that had the double objective of emphasizing Fascism's utopian, nationalist ideal while simultaneously introducing a modern rationalized agriculture in those areas where commercial enterprise was deemed lucrative (Ipsen 1996; Caprotti 2007). Underpinned by a teleology of modern rationality, these public interventions had the objective of creating a new social class of small sharecroppers and agricultural landowners who, in their disconnection from industry and the dynamics of urbanization, would become the carriers of a new corporatist society concentrated around Fascism.

Combining technological knowledge, technical expertise, and colonizing rationality in these new towns, the new architecture of Fascism was to represent the glory of its modern ideals while making the rural masses fit for modern progress (for a wider discussion see also Kaika and Swyngedouw 2000; Swyngedouw 2004; Giglioli and Swyngedouw 2008). Toward this purpose, the rural infrastructures of the *città di fondazione* typically combined a linear, celebratory architecture, concentrated around a conglomerate of public institutions in a town's center (church, hospital, town hall, militia barracks, schools, and certain commercial activities), with a modern irrigation system that associated these rural settlements to their hinterlands.² The most frequent type of rural urbanization in this period corresponded to a service center located within a wider area of agricultural settlements, in which rural dwellings were placed directly on the agricultural plot assigned to the farmhouse family. These individual plots then remained attached to the new town through a concentric system of plots and roads.

As part of Mussolini's larger ambition to reclaim the marshlands of the peninsula through a series of large public works, these agricultural new towns thus maintained a specific rural character that was not assimilable, both in size and design, to an urban center. An important aesthetic expression of Fascism's rural conquest, in fact, were the numerous reservoirs placed along these irrigation infrastructures, as well as the aqueducts of the Agri and Bradano Rivers,³ which thus inserted a rationalization of "nature" to the end of monocropping agriculture. Despite the thin historiography dedicated to the Fascist new towns and their rural hinterlands, they had quite a determining impact on the way agriculture production expanded throughout the South of Italy, and in Basilicata in particular, as the irrigation infrastructures and rural settlements introduced during Fascism gradually became the center of a modern, export-oriented horticultural industry. In the postwar period, exactly these sites and infrastructures would become the nodes of the retail revolution in agrarian supply chain capitalism. Before turning to these developments, however, I feel the need to insist on the rather neglected passage of this rural urbanization in the Terre d'Oltremare (Overseas territories), on the other side of the Mediterranean, where Italian and other imperial forces were radically transforming the African landscape and the people living on it.

In colonial Africa during the 1920s and '30s, Italian administrators continued to reinforce the same ideological and technological instruments they had developed to appease and civilize the Meridione since the early 1900s. Pushed forward by an ideology of Mediterraneanism—the project of Mare Nostrum (Our sea) as a living space of Imperial Italy heralded a central place in Fascism's geopolitical ambitions—Mussolini's objective was to transform Northern Africa and the Horn into an extension of Italy's *Lebensraum* (literally: living space), notably through the erection of grand infrastructural works (Antonsich 2009).⁴ Important to note here is that, rather than representing an aberration or exception, this ambition was founded on the same ideals that had driven early liberal reformists' beliefs, namely the capacity of man to overcome any natural obstacles by the force of his will. This idea of voluntarism (*volontarismo*), which was best rendered by one of Mussolini's slogans ("It is the spirit which tames and bends the material"), indeed helped shape the specific character of a masculinist Italian geopolitics that proclaimed itself the geographical doctrine of Fascism, Antonsich (2009, 269) writes.

Yet while these ideas and policies were fundamentally misogynous and racist,[5] they also were transformational in the way they legitimated the active molding of peoples and nature into industrial instruments serving the needs of the superior colonial powers. In Eritrea and Somalia, the prestige and strategic potential of a large colony on the Indian Ocean continued to far outweigh any revenue that could cover the colony's material costs. In Libya and Ethiopia, the liberal, and later the Fascist, government actively encouraged the settlement of so-called soldiers of work—traders, artisans, farmers, and workers—to demographically engineer these colonies' political economy of agricultural production. Through this demographic engineering, the colonization of the North African countryside took the form of a forceful occupation of the land. Through colonial schemes that were based on wholesale expropriation of cultivable lands, the "new builders of Empire" tried to forge—mostly without success—a lasting bond between the colonial authorities and the settler populations.

In synchrony with the demographic colonization of rural South Italy, colonial administrators thus started to assign key responsibilities to the same architects, urban planners, and institutions that were simultaneously employed in the efforts to dry the Pontine marshes. Notably, the ONC (Organizzazione Nazionale Combattenti) became responsible for managing the colonial *terre demaniali*: the state-owned lands confiscated from anticolonial forces or simply deemed uncultivated and thus "unitlized." Such land reclamations, which happened on a large scale in Libya and Eritrea (Santoianni 2008), also became a notable decompression valve for Italy's rural South: the many dispossessed and impoverished farmers that Italian reformists had left in their tracks in the Meridione now would ideally find employment as agricultural laborers in the colonized lands south of the Mediterranean Sea. Despite its practical failure, however—most Italian emigrants left Africa quickly for other destinations—the predominant idea of an expanding agrarian frontier in the service of modernity kept tantalizing Italian colonialists until their final defeat by the Allied forces in the Second World War. In that sense, Italian efforts in Africa did not represent an exception to, nor a more benevolent case of, colonial imperialism.[6] As Labanca (2018, 128) concludes, "Even though the Italian government, like all its imperialist peers, insisted on the uniqueness of its African conquests, the history of Italian colonialism shared common traits with the history of European colonialism of the time. For example, while Eritrea was, in some respects, a typical colonial trading entrepôt, Somalia was more characteristic of other tropical African colonies, and Libya and

Ethiopia evinced patterns of racial stratification common to white settlement colonies such as Algeria and Rhodesia."

Constructive Colonialism

When read through the lens of racial capitalism and the urbanization of "nature," the European scramble south of the Sahara indeed followed spatial trajectories quite similar to Italy's attempts to demographically colonize North Africa and the Horn. Two parallels are worth discussing here: the growth of rural capitalism and the mobilization of rural labor.

With regard to rural capitalism, Meillassoux has argued convincingly that Western African colonialism radically transformed the social relations of production through the promotion of a new type of rural capital accumulation. In contrast to Eastern Africa, where British colonial administrators expropriated many of the best lands for large-scale, plantation-style production, and local communities were forcibly coerced to work on large plantations, West Africa was prone to a different type of rural accumulation based on the promotion of small cash-crop production (for a discussion see Gray and Dowd-Uribe 2013). This resulted in a growing land hunger among smallholder entrepreneurs and a large sector of the rural poor who depended on work as hired, migrant labor to supplement their incomes gained by farming on small, individual plots (Meillassoux 1973). The reality for most small-scale farmers in French Western Africa, therefore, was a more subtle process of "dispossession from below" through competition over customary and private land systems.[7] The British Colonial Office lacked the capacity to implement a system of direct control over land, so it depended on the support of chiefs who demanded rights to control and sell land under their jurisdiction through so-called indirect rule. This resulted in British firms buying directly from African producers through a network of commissioned buyers rather than investing in plantation development.

The failure to control land markets directly led colonial powers in West Africa to engage in a form of "constructive imperialism" (Amanor 2011, 5) associated with the building of a modern infrastructure. The French and the British turned their colonial efforts toward the building of roads, railways, and other infrastructural interventions aimed at undergirding the circulation of free wage labor and the opening of new land markets foundational to a truly modern capitalist development. Significant interventions in the French territories, for example, included the administrative division of the Upper Volta into Côte d'Ivoire, Soudan (now Mali), and Niger, as well as the construction of a long railway line between

Abidjan and Bobo-Dioulasso, which opened more of the Voltaic labor force to work in the cocoa and coffee plantations in Côte d'Ivoire.

As Immanual Wallerstein (1967) highlighted, however, labor remained relatively scarce in the West African colonies until at least the late 1920s. Because the mines, plantations, and cash-crop farms were concentrated in the coastal regions and coastal forest areas, and social systems remained intimately tied to land tenure, few men were prepared to leave their place in traditional society and their rights over land. Given these conditions, the possibility of working for short periods outside the village often remained the most attractive option and stimulus to release a voluntary labor supply from the savannas and draw it toward the coastal regions. To confront the persistent problem of finding migrant labor for their cash crop productions, the French colonial administration sought to incorporate and regroup African farmers outside of export crop production and into intensive cash crop plantations through its policy of *colonisation indigène* during the 1920s and '30s. *Colonisation indigène* called for the resettlement of African farmers in areas that Europeans considered ideal for agricultural development. These relocated farmers worked their own plots and were required to follow expert European advice on farming, including the use of agricultural technology, intensive cultivation, and specific crop rotations. In *colonisation indigène*, therefore, the French combined their belief in the importance of high population density with their convictions regarding the superiority of intensive agriculture and the centrality of private property and the nuclear family to a developed agricultural system. Undergirding *colonisation indigène*—similarly to Fabian socialism promoted in the British colonies—was a social evolutionary model of change in which all human societies would evolve along a similar, European pathway.[8] As a policy seeking simultaneous change on several fronts, *colonisation indigène* has been considered one of the first comprehensive approaches to inducing social and economic change in colonial Africa (Van Beusekom 1997).

There is a consensus, however, that the massive resettlement schemes planned in this context—among others through the Office du Niger—in the French Soudan (including today's Mali and Burkina Faso) continued to be confronted with a consistent flight and other forms of resistance by indigenous farm laborers. These farmworkers remained reluctant to be marshaled into development schemes that did not meet their needs and were based on poorly planned state strategies to "capture" the peasantry (Van Beusekom 1997, 304; see also Grischow 2006; Cowen and Shenton 1991). In the savannas of the Upper Volta, for example, French colonialists had to face an unremitting exodus of people it wanted to employ as laborers. In striking parallel to the political discussions in Italy at the time, in fact a sharp controversy existed between those administrators who associated migrations to the weight of colonial constraints (like taxes, compulsory

labor, public works, and military conscription) and others who saw these migrations as a sign of a gradual transformation of the peasantry due to rising socioeconomic inequalities (Hazard 2010, 508). In the early 1960s, J. M. Hunter (1963)
recorded that the near totality (98.6 percent) of land in the old cocoa pioneer
district of New Suhum (in today's Ghana) was cultivated by migrants (see also
Fairhead and Leach 1996).

Capturing the Peasantry

Building on the existing literature, it is fair to say that labor migration remains
the main constant in efforts to counter the multiple challenges of rural communities in West Africa. In fact, the same difficulties of capturing rural farm
labor continued to afflict West African states even after colonial independence
(see, e.g., Wouterse and Van den Bergh 2011, as well as the historical studies by
Arthur [1991], Findley [1997], and Adepoju 2007). While the demographically
low-density areas of Burkina Faso, Mali, and Niger remained important sources
of migration labor for cash crop production in Côte d'Ivoire and Senegal, mining, agricultural, and industrial concessions in Ghana and Nigeria in the 1970s
(Blion and Bredeloup 1996; Devillard, Bacchi, and Noack 2015) saw a growing
influence of international institutions such as the World Bank, which, through
its smallholder approach, sought to promote contract farming. In West Africa,
the World Bank started to fund resettlement schemes in conjunction with African state interventions that sought to integrate smallholder peasant production
with modern agriculture technical and service industries. The result was that by
the 1980s, a growing horticulture and agricultural exports industry conglomerated around smallholder contract farming in many West African countries. These
developments raised new demands for available lands, which were subsequently
reconfigured in such new commercial cash-cropping schemes.[9]

The only exception to this grip of liberalization appeared to be Burkina Faso.
The revolutionary government of Thomas Sankara initiated a series of important public works as well as a massive reforestation program. Furthermore, Sankara introduced a vertically integrated organization for the country's cotton
production operated by village-level cooperatives. Increasing pressures from the
World Bank and the IMF, however, forced the country to adopt reforms directed
toward the liberalization of land and agricultural markets (Kevane and Englebert
1998; Gray and Dowd-Uribe 2013; Harsch 2014). This led to a growing presence of private investors, civil servants, and commercial entrepreneurs becoming
engaged in land markets and land speculation, resulting in an increasing conver-
sion of traditional or communal land rights to private tenure, the enclosure of

traditional grazing areas, deforestation, and the facilitation of agricultural land acquisitions by outside commercial interests (Cotula 2013). In the Boulgou area in southeast Burkina Faso, where land is generally overexploited and degraded, a more strained relation developed between customarily held land and emerging commercial interests. The double allocation of local plots led to a bloody land conflict in 1982, which even needed the army's intervention and left a deep rift between two neighboring communities that is still felt today (Reyna 1987; Breusers 1998; Brasselle, Gaspart, and Platteau 2002; Kaag et al. 2019; Wouterse and Van Den Bergh 2011). In the following years, the nexus of rising levels of food imports, an unstable climate to produce staple crops, and a growing population density in the country's dry plains created an increasing dependency on food imports. This shows how the attempts to counter the detrimental effects of globalizing agri-food production—in this case by boosting national food production through import substitution—is never simply the sum of a local process of global marketization. It is also an example of how a country like Burkina Faso actively engages with its own position in a food production system through several regional and local strategies.

From the early 1990s onward, the growing monopolization of agri-business led to a rapid reconfiguration of agricultural production in West Africa. To give one prominent example, the global food trader Cargill became one of the three major cocoa grinding processors in the world during the 1990s through the acquisition of private-sector and state grinding facilities, including within the main cocoa-producing countries of Côte d'Ivoire and Ghana (Losch 2002). As I argued in chapter 1, though, the dominant players in global food markets remain large supermarket retailers, who avoid direct involvement in production and instead specialize in controlling marketing and supply chains. The result of this reorganization in West Africa has been a gradual displacement of import-substituting industries with new, export-oriented agro-industries whose rapid integration in transnational food chains forces states to engage in liberalizing market regulations. So, while international financial institutions keep pushing agricultural restructuring with the objective of creating markets more favorable to the poor and alleviating poverty, the liberalization of markets has frequently undermined the stability of traditional export crops in the region, thus eroding the power of both governments and noncommercial smallholder farmers who remain trapped in the bargain.[10] In some cases, this has led to increased competition over land in previously unexplored areas. The expansion of cash crop growing has increasingly made way for small and intensive cultivations. In Côte d'Ivoire, where cocoa output multiplied sixfold between 1950 and 2000, the government tried to bend its dependency on cocoa by adopting an ambiguous discourse on land rights that increasingly marginalized these immigrant farmers, up to a point of massively expelling Burkinabè migrants—some of whom had been living in Côte d'Ivoire for generations. These events were ultimately to unravel into the ethnic divisiveness that was to result in civil war (for a discussion see Richards and Chauveau 2007). Despite these multiple changes, therefore, it is fair to say that intracontinental mobility remains the dominant pattern of West African livelihood diversification nearly sixty years after colonial independence.

Two elements are worth emphasizing here in conclusion. First, scholars insist that current mobility patterns should indeed be seen as both building on, and extending, older patterns and politics of migration. Though the armed crisis of Côte d'Ivoire has definitely pushed migrant laborers to undertake longer journeys toward Northern Africa and Europe, most migration is still inter-regional, with Côte d'Ivoire, Ghana, Gabon, Nigeria, and later also Libya as the main destinations (Kaag et al. 2019). Particularly the interior savannas and desert areas of Burkina Faso, Mali, and Niger remain important sources of migration labor for domestic cash crop producers in Côte d'Ivoire and Senegal, mineral mining regions, agricultural estates, and industrial hubs of Ghana and—to a lesser extent—Nigeria (Cross and Cliffe 2017; Devillard, Bacchi, and Noack 2015). Over time, these circular migrations also expanded toward North Africa, particularly Libya, where hundreds of thousands of—predominantly male—Africans were able to find employment in the country's extractive industries and construction sector. During his forty-year dictatorship (1969–2011), Muammar Gadhafi continued to use this substantial African migration to Libya as a diplomatic instrument to pressure the international community, and the European Union in particular, to soften their stance on his repressive regime. During his ideological trajectory from pan-Africanism to pan-Sahelism in the 1970s and 1990s, he pushed active recruitment programs to import cheap labor for his state projects linked to the gas and carbon economy, before engaging in the massive expulsion of sub-Saharan African immigrants in the early 2000s in the attempt to gather support to lift the international embargo against his country. Many agree, in fact, that the politics of Gadhafi's pan-African engagement during this period contrasted sharply with his active discrimination against people of sub-Saharan descent. From the early 2000s, his quest for international recognition further intensified this discrimination, as the price for bettering diplomatic relations with the West was the imposition of a more repressive border regime.

Yet, while the European Union and international organizations like UNHCR and the International Organization for Migration persistently define Libya as a transit country for migrants coming from Western and Eastern Africa, the Libyan experience of many sub-Saharan African youth during these past four decades forces us to take seriously these South-South itineraries and dynamics, which continue to impact on and interconnect with transcontinental flows. For almost four decades Libya functioned as a kind of safety valve that supplemented both African livelihoods at times of drought, conflict, and economic regression, and European border policies to temper African immigration at a time of growing political anxiety and economic crisis. Notwithstanding the strong racism and marginalization that characterized Libyan society, Libya continued to be an appealing country for hundreds of thousands of migrants from regions south of the Sahara—especially young African men looking for work and some level of personal autonomy. Attracted by economic opportunities and a favorable political climate, they continued to engage in circular mobilities to work, earn money, and accumulate capital within the Saharan-Sahelian space.

Second, these circular migration patterns have fostered the emergence of a transient, if largely informal and marginalized, form of urbanity that simultaneously provides for the undergirding of modern transnational societies and comprises the architecture for its circulation (Larkin 2013, 328). The constantly shifting migration policies, not just of Libya but also of other African states,[11] forced African migrants to engage in clandestine routes that connected their home regions through a system of largely informal but fundamental infrastructures. The journey from West Africa to Libya, for example, usually passed through Niger or Algeria, where Tuareg smugglers facilitated the passage into Libyan territory. On these journeys, relatives and friends of West African travelers acted as "drop points" (Timera 2011) while settling their kin in the ghetto (or *foyer*). In the fluctuating space of Sahelian-Saharan migration, the ghetto functioned basically as a gathering space—an apartment, room, or improvised shelter—where migrants shared information, as well as a "sensation of being part of the same common destiny," as Bredeloup and Pliez (2005) observe.[12] In this sense, it provided a response toward both a necessity to move and to (temporarily) settle. Initially, the ghettos were organized predominantly along lines of kinship and common (national or ethnic) descent, and therefore they also signaled the racialized condition of Black Africans in Northern Africa.[13] Subsequently, the space of the ghetto acquired a more criminal connotation as Libyan and other African states on the Sahelian-Saharan trajectory started their crackdown on "illegal migration." The Treaty of Friendship signed between Libya and Italy in 2003 can be seen as a rupture point in this regard.[14] On the one hand, it signaled an encroachment on African territory of the European agenda to channel and filter migration flows considered as "irregular." This externalization of the European border occurred through various cross-border collaborations and technologies that were intended to freeze the fluctuating space of the Sahel-Sahara as a zone of transit, capture, and repatriation. On the other hand, the progressive closures of legal pathways to Europe, along with an unfolding border security response across the Sahel-Sahara Desert and Mediterranean Sea, contributed to the transformation of migration routes from smuggling toward human trafficking. This distinction, indicated by Sarah Pierce, refers to the preponderance of threat, coercion, and fraud for the purpose of exploitation of mobile individuals in the practice of human trafficking. In contrast to smuggling, which may raise a connotation of licit, or legitimate, contravention of state policies that are considered inadequate or repressive, human trafficking can be understood as an "inherently exploitative" practice, she writes (Pierce 2014).[15]

In the wider space of African South-South migration, however, it is worth noting the expansion of this transient migrant spaces as a form of connecting through mobility (Kaag et al. 2019). As Danny Hoffman writes in the context of Sierra Leone (2007: 401), the double narrative of African urbanism has always been that of a crumbling infrastructure and a failed governance on the one hand, with the particular "worlding" of African cities (Simone 2001) on the other, in which urban Africa becomes a staging post for opportunities beyond its own borders. What is lacking from this narrative, however, is the way in which African citizens are making sense of their own circulations across—or rather their constant straddling between—these borders, as well as the boundaries of rural and urban lifeworlds (see also Roitman 2005; Vigh 2009; Bjarnesen and Turner 2018). One prominent example I already mentioned is the "Little Italy" of Béguedo, where three-quarters of young people between the ages of twenty and thirty-five have one experience of migration, and 90 percent of families have at least one migrant son. As I will detail below, Little Italy emerged because of Béguedo's circular migration to Southern and Northern Italy, where (predominantly male) members of the town's extended kin ended up working in horticulture around Naples, and, later, as factory workers in the Italian industries of Brescia and Bergamo. As Benoit Hazard indicates, however, this intensifying circulation between two such apparently different environments has not entailed a disappearance but rather an active reinvention of rurality in the context of transcontinental migration. Whereas in the Italian context the migrant ghetto became a site where immigrants were allowed to negotiate a place to survive in their migratory circulation, as I will explain in the next chapter, the construction of Little Italy as a separate urban space in Béguedo has opened the possibility for its inhabitants to diversify their activities and foster independence in terms both of landownership and of their autonomy from extended kin. This dynamic shows, in fact, that transnational migration entails not a disappearance but a reconfiguration of rural relationships at multiple scales. In the years following the Libyan regime collapse and the subsequent development of an increasingly repressive border regime on both shores of the Mediterranean, these reconfigurations would become increasingly determined by the politics of securitization that characterized government's approaches to the question of migrant labor.

I have argued that the division between mountains and plains, forests, and savannas we are used to seeing as "natural" divisions in the rural landscape are the direct result of the profoundly dualist ideology that since the early twentieth century has characterized, and continues to characterize, modern agricultural "development" in the spaces of colonial Africa and the Mediterranean. Liberal reformers and colonial administrators envisioned their interventions in these landscapes as the transformation of a seemingly "empty" space that was, however, "full" of potential, either to produce resources directly or to produce labor that could be employed elsewhere. In so doing, they transformed existing mobility patterns along with the administrative and logistical infrastructures required to move workers, capital, and state resources from one corner of the empire to the other. While this did not of course result in a singlehanded success, the political and economic differentiation that arose from these colonial interventions produced a fragmented territorialization of rural societies, which became increasingly settled both in and through mobility: while on the one hand, the new political borders and administrative divisions introduced in this period had the obvious effect of separating territories, they also contributed to an important labor migration that sustained the economies of scale of plantations, mines, and industrialized farm enterprises, and thus of mobile livelihoods, across borders. Even more importantly, these new geographic divisions gradually fostered the emergence of a transient form of urbanization, comprising a jigsaw of urban concessions, villages, and temporary migrant settlements that spread rapidly throughout this agrarian frontier and would thus form the backbone of contemporary agrarian labor circulation in the current corporate food regime. It is this dynamic development I will now turn to.

Agricultural Reform

The idea of modern development in the Mediterranean and in sub-Saharan Africa has been carried forward by a disruptive imaginary of a "backward" and "uncivilized" peasant society that needed to be freed from the shackles of its feudal past for it to gain its autonomy and freedom. This ideology, which circumscribed one set of human subjects to the domain of freedoms and obligations related to a common public good, and the other set, considered as the not, not-yet, or less-than-human, to a permanent ontological and geographic margin (see also Holland 2000; Weheliye 2014; Broeck 2018; Warren 2018), runs like a common thread through the history of modern capitalism, as the same logic of liberating the peasantry continued to characterize the rural development approach of the World Bank and the international financial institutions in Africa even after the end of colonialism. The same can be said to be true for postwar Italy, where twenty years of Fascist attempts to rationalize Italian agricultural production and society had not been able to break the power of the latifundia. In Basilicata, agricultural enterprises of over two hundred hectares (a little more than three-quarters of a square mile) in 1945 still owned close to 50 percent of the land in Matera Province; in Potenza Province these corresponded to 34.5 percent. Official government statistics estimated agriculture to remain the predominant occupation in the same provinces, engaging 73 percent of workers, compared to industry (8.3 percent) and the tertiary sector (18.7 percent).[16]

At first, it appeared as if peasant revolution would finally break these links with the past. Exhausted by hunger and despair, rural families across the Metaponto and the Alto Bradano area occupied several large-scale latifundia farms during the mid-1940s and early 1950s in reaction to the structural inequalities that determined their fate. Not coincidentally, these protests took place where a modernist agrarian transformation had already partly taken root. While women often took the lead in these illegal occupations, local administrations typically responded with harsh repressions. Aware of the public threat that southern rural uprisings could potentially cause during this period of difficult economic recovery, the Italian postwar government launched a series of public initiatives to redistribute property, promote agricultural development, and put pressure on the peasantry to leave the occupied lands in favor of a more commercial, entrepreneurial type of farming.[17]

Financed through the American Marshall Plan, the agricultural reform involved a significant restructuring of land property, which left the peasants subsequently "free" to buy or sell their land with the support of the national credit institution Cassa del Mezzogiorno (Percoco 2018). Implemented in 1950–1951, the reform formally expropriated and redistributed around six hundred thousand to eight hundred thousand hectares of land (roughly 2,300 to 3,000 square miles). Percoco (2018), who charts the change in the distribution of landownership in Puglia–Basilicata–Molise during this period, indicates quite clearly the substantial reduction of the share of large holdings with a subsequent increase of small-to-medium plots. To further this objective of reconverting peasants into rural capitalists, the *ente della riforma* (reform institution) also engaged in an active reeducation of the peasantry: next to literacy classes (considering that a large majority of the beneficiaries were illiterate), experts descended on the countryside to teach specialized techniques in irrigation, orchard pruning, and livestock husbandry.

To complete its modernization of the rural South, the Italian government subsequently sent its urban planners and architects to build a series of new agrotowns in the middle of these newly claimed lands—partly building on their

Fascist predecessors. A famous example was La Martella. This modern agropolis was to provide an up-to-date replacement for the infamous *Sassi* (caves) of Matera, which postwar reformers continued to designate as a national "shame." According to a famous passage in Carlo Levi's book *Cristo si è fermato ad Eboli* (*Christ Stopped at Eboli*), which was subsequently re-evoked by the Communist Party leader Palmiro Togliatti during a visit to Matera in 1948,[18] the city represented what both men described as a metaphorical stain on Italy's modern history (see also Potrandolfi 2002). Though Matera's living conditions were in fact not that remarkable compared to the rest of the country's miserable rurality, they appeared to reinforce the predominant, distorted imagery of an archaic and backward rural society, as Tenzon (2018, 499) writes. Basilicata's peasant urbanity represented a form of social reproduction and cultural intimacy that, to paraphrase Michael Herzfeld (1984, 1985, 2005), did not correspond to the right version of peasant culture (see also Byrne 2011).

Driven by the perception of anticommunitarianism and antimodernity that characterized Matera, urban planners and architects subsequently organized the eviction and resettlement of the city's cave population using the well-known templates, planning models, and architectural aesthetics introduced by their Fascist predecessors.[19] In contrast with the prewar-year efforts, though, the aesthetic functions of Italian architecture came closer to the modern ideal of individualism. Designed and planned by Adriano Olivetti, whose social entrepreneurship symbolized a period of economic prosperity for Italy (and who was also a strong supporter of Fabian socialism), the implementation of La Martella followed the lead of Ludovico Quaroni and Mario Ridolfi, who were famous for their stylized and abstract architecture. The new agro-towns that were built in this period indeed followed a more individualistic model: single homesteads were connected through a branched network of roads and individual landholdings, but which all together reflected a geometric integrity and aesthetic ideal. In close cooperation with the United Nations habitat program, the architects built these agricultural new towns according to what the sociologist employed on the project defined as a communitarian neighborhood model (translated in Italian as *unità residenziale* or *unità di vicinato*) that was to generate the architectural foundation of a booming and integrated rural community.

In the years after the eviction of Matera's *Sassi* to La Martella, other new agro-towns would arise in the Alto Bradano area, in Boreano, Gaudiano, Monteserico, Poggorsini, and Santa Maria d'Irsi, in addition the *borghi* that had already been erected in the Metaponto area by the Fascist regime during the 1920s and '30s. As Tenzon (2018) observes, however, this architectural model was based on a dramatically outdated notion of social aggregation. In fact, only few of the evicted families of Matera expressed the desire to live closely together in a context that had generated considerable social tensions in the past. Furthermore, they also felt the consequences of massive outward migration, which had significantly fragmented their sense of community. Notwithstanding these critiques, the nostalgic vision that had inspired La Martella as a revolution of peasant society would continue to drive Italy's postwar politics of rural development in the years to come.

The aim of La Martella was exactly to break up a layout consisting of what the rural planners involved in the project considered as overpopulated and spaced-out settlements to work toward a "maximum efficiency" of auxiliary centers and isolated houses according to the well-established schematic of the Pontine marshes (De Dominicis 2019, 4). In the years following Matera's forceful eviction, the Bradano Valley and Metaponto Consortia continued to build on these rural development plans, including the construction of two huge dams as part of a network of artificial irrigation reservoirs and the initiation of other major hydraulic works intended for irrigation of agricultural estates. The plan was as ambitious as it was political: according to the first ten-year plan issued by the Cassa per il Mezzogiorno (but which was never brought to completion), fifty-one aqueducts and around three thousand kilometers (almost nineteen hundred miles) of roads would provide the necessary infrastructure to rehouse millions of farmers, while 139 new settlements and 46,450 isolated houses would result from the new subdivision of land. Much of the funding was tapped from the US Marshall Plan, while newly established local authorities were entrusted with the handling of the technical aspects concerning land reclamation and resettlement.

Postwar reformist government in Italy did not in any way represent a break from Fascist corporatism—quite the contrary. In fact, the residential model on which La Martella and the other postwar *borghi* was based continued to conceal the twofold purpose of keeping the rural masses locked in a status quo while preventing them from fostering any sort of social and cultural connections that might be conducive to revolution against the control over the means of production. Through the planned institution of territorial boundaries, of laws, policy, and bureaucracy, including the implementation of census categorizations, demographic registries, and other governmental technologies, the postwar modern state thus defined its power to exclude and include, to categorize hierarchically, and to administer racially ordered populations. And it did so by following a clear logic of racial naturalism, or the fixing of racially conceived populations in an environment that is both bounded and connected by a specific set of development infrastructures (see also Goldberg 2002; Lentin 2007; Kurtz 2009). The agricultural reform reflected exactly this ambivalent rural development agenda, verging on but never really emancipating rural communities that were regarded simultaneously as an expression of a nostalgic past, as a kind of autonomous, closed ensemble in which social, economic, and environmental values had been preserved from the passing of time, and as an emblem of amoral backwardness and underdevelopment. In that sense, the description of Matera's *Sassi* as the "shame" of Italy captured quite well the country's historical treatment of the rural Mediterranean as an absence, a gap that needed to be filled with modern infrastructure and provisions.

I tend to disagree with the historical interpretation of the agricultural reform as a development "failure," and for two main reasons. First, the land reforms straightened the path toward rural capitalism in an area that had been traditionally dominated by the landed aristocracy: though it did not result in a shift of ownership of the land toward the rural peasantry, the small-to-medium plots that were redistributed through the *ente della riforma* quickly acquired the function of land property, which, if accumulated, provided the basis for capitalist accumulation. Second, the radical dispossession and displacement of small-scale farmers liberated a massive labor pool of precarious and mobile workers who could now be employed at the will of the industrial class in the cities of the North. In the thirty years after the war's end, this rural exodus acquired an ever more staggering dimension. It has been estimated, for example, that between 1951 and 1976 the Mezzogiorno lost more than half its agricultural labor force. Between 1950 and 1960, agricultural employment dropped from eight million workers to five million: the majority of these originated from the South. Between 1950 and 1970, furthermore, twenty-five million Italians changed their initial residence to move elsewhere, usually between regions. Next to the unknown long-term effects on the peninsula's social demography, the broader question raised by this massive rural exodus was how the apparent consensus of a population driven by the desire to change their destiny in the context of modern industrialization could redeem the historical inequality between Northern and Southern Italians, or possibly just reproduce it "in a different manner" (Alasia and Montaldi [1960] 2010, 24).

One domain in which these contradictions became especially apparent in this period was that of informal urbanization. A couple of fundamental studies placed the finger on this paradox at the time. One of these was "Milano, Corea," a social examination of the infrastructures of urban immigration in the periphery of Lombardy's capital. Between 1951 and 1971, the population of the province of Milan grew by 26 percent, adding over six hundred thousand people. These new inhabitants invariably ended up in the city's suburban areas and in dilapidated and abandoned farmsteads. Initially, workers took refuge in the ruined *cascine* (farmhouses) left behind by peasant families who had gone likewise to the city. With salvaged bricks, wood, and metal roofing, some started adding small shacks and semipermanent houses to rent out to fellow workers. Gradually, these informal quarters acquired the name of "Koreas" (*Coree*)—after the shocking images shown on television of the Korea War. In 1965, an estimated one hundred thousand people dwelled in such *Coree* in Milan's periphery.

Strikingly, the appearance of such modern ghettos amid Italy's economic miracle did not receive much attention at the time, apart from the occasional journalistic inquiry (emblematic was the title of an *Espresso* article, "Africa in casa," which pretended to explain the reasons for this rural "exodus" in 1959). Crainz ([1960] 2010) and Quiligotti ([1960] 2010) see three main reasons for this lack of interest. First, the left-leaning postwar governments still widely read the southern question through a lens of backwardness and underdevelopment: optimistic that industrialization would ultimately lift the rural masses from their misery, they publicly hoped for a trickle-down effect of national wealth. Of course, this never happened, as northern industries benefited both from the massive availability of workers and from their relation to international markets, so that the historical division between North and South became even more entrenched. Second, the hegemonic vision, which equated the urban periphery with extreme poverty and marginalization, precluded a more in-depth analysis of the highly complex nature of these neighborhoods, which became a kind of informal city in the absence of official state planning and infrastructures. While the *Coree* initially arose in the vicinity of existing rural structures, they quickly acquired an urban morphology that became encapsulated in the city's infrastructure. Thanks to this self-propelled growth—often stimulated through strong "ethnic" social networks—the *Coree* could reproduce a sense of community built on bonds of solidarity and relationships transmitted from and to the workplace (Foot 2005). In that sense, "Milano, Corea" did raise a precise indictment against the illusion of the Italian economic miracle at the time, by arguing what no one else dared to say out loud: that the country's celebrated modernization took shape through new exclusions and marginalization. With his remarkable vision, Danilo Montaldi concluded there is a type of marginality that is not backwardness but is fully part of capitalist development.

Even more remarkable is the fact that in the industries of the North, nonresident laborers found themselves in a condition of illegality owing to the denial of their citizenship rights. Because of the persistence of Fascist legislation (the "Provvedimenti contro l'urbanesimo" of 1939), rural migrants could not take on an urban residence because the law prohibited their inscription into the demographic administration in the absence of an official labor contract. Despite rising judicial and constitutional pressures, subsequent Italian governments continued to apply this legal framework to maintain control over the national labor market. Local administrations demonstrated a passive reluctance to grant residence to rural citizens who came to the city in search of work. Under these conditions, therefore, the new generation of urban immigrants, as illegal citizens in their own country, needed to find alternative means to stabilize their condition. That is why a growing number of fake cooperatives emerged to grant often fake employment contracts to fellow citizens, often from the same social background and located in the same neighborhood, and provide an alternative foundation for social organization in the margins of formal modern urbanity.

The analysis of postwar agrarian reforms in Italy makes clear that, even if they distanced themselves ideologically from their Fascist predecessors, postwar Italian state administrations firmly built on the former's normative and material foundations to control and manage rural landscapes and populations. This continuity became particularly apparent in the context of rural urbanization. Whether it concerned the forced eviction of Matera's "shameful" caves, or the active discrimination against rural citizens in the industrialized cities of the North, the means through which postwar administrators and planners addressed Italy's rural question basically remained embedded in the same racial politics of exclusion that had been introduced in the late 1800s. In that sense, the celebration of Italy's modern miracle indeed involved a continuous internal refusal, a form of persistent refoulement of those citizens who were deemed unfit and unwilling to perform the country's modern ideals but whose labor was desperately needed to make things work in a crude material and physical sense (Alasia and Montaldi 2010, 30). This refoulement took shape through the political technology of territory, or the techniques of separation and the wider ideology through which the "spatial order of things" comes to be normalized and perpetuated (Elden 2013b, 16).

While the technique of territorial residence functioned very much like a mechanism of exclusion, or an "invisible border" (Gargiulo 2021) in the domain of social stratification and differential labor inclusion, the fundamentally racist divisions that kept driving territorial administration of Italy's rural areas showed the discretionary form of sovereign power that kept underpinning Italy's capitalist development. Then, as now, racism functioned as a "limiting force," in that it continued to "push the disproportionate costs of participating in an increasingly monetized and profit-driven world onto those who, due to the frictions of political distance, could not reach the levers of power" that were not of their own making (Gilmore 2002a, 16). In that sense, I see the systematic seclusion of migrant workers in the postcolonial economies of both the global North and South not as a developmental failure, but as part of an active project of state building that reproduced this racist abstraction from the most intimate to the sovereign scale. It is this double dynamic, of racial segregation and labor market stratification, that I will now turn to.

The Rise of the Ghetto

During the 1980s and '90s, the combined logics of labor market stratification and racial segregation would contribute to freeing up the labor force of agricultural wage workers who appeared both "too free" to be able to negotiate their place in transnational labor markets and "not free enough" to negotiate the terms of their adverse incorporation in the increasingly globalized value chains of retail agriculture. In the Southern Italian districts of the Alto Bradano and Metaponto, in Basilicata, this stratification of the labor force was made possible by the confluence of two distinct migration trajectories, one cross-regional and the other transnational. Farmers from neighboring Puglia, who had already started their specialization of fresh food production for national and European markets in the 1970s and '80s, started looking for new lands to expand their productive base. Initially, agricultural firms turned to the area around Lavello, where early Italian reformers had introduced a well-functioning and sophisticated irrigation system in the early twentieth century. To benefit from this integration of market forces, farmers from the Alto Bradano progressively joined the dominant Organizzazione Produttiva (Agricultural producers association) of neighboring Foggia, which possessed the necessary expertise and cooperative capital. The result is that of the around 150 agricultural enterprises operative in the triangle between Palazzo, Venosa, and Lavello, close to one-quarter officially reside in Puglia today. The evolution of farming enterprises over this period in fact confirms a strong capital concentration that has been typical for the oligopoly of retail distribution networks: by controlling prices and channeling produce logistically, supermarket chains have generated a siphoning effect that pays off to the industry and weakens the position of small-to-medium farmers (see also Perrotta 2014). Benefiting from their privileged access to European markets, processing companies located around Salerno and Foggia could not only start dictating the terms of the production process, but also, and progressively, buy up productive land across the regional boundaries that had historically determined the means of production.

As to the second, transnational, trajectory, migrants from West Africa started arriving in Basilicata in the early 1990s through their initial circulations from Naples and Castel Volturno. As I wrote in a previous section, Sahelian plantation economies were undergoing a deep crisis at that time because of the eruption of the Ivorian civil war, as well as a growing "dispossession from below" of poor small-croppers and agro-pastoralist communities. Ironically, one could say that central Mediterranean agriculture in Southern Italy experienced a rapid boom exactly at a time of rapid economic decline in West Africa. At second sight, it is of course clear that these phenomena are closely related: while destructive droughts and a plantation economy in crisis effectively freed migrant labor on the one end of the Mediterranean, the concentration of capital and resources along subsidized supply chains on the other generated a significant pull factor for seasonal agricultural workers that was difficult to meet locally—also because Italy's industrialization miracle had basically left rural families bereft of their livelihood (see also Bonifazi and Livi Bracci 2014; Corrado, De Castro, and Perrotta 2016; Avallone 2017). Like many other Sahelian migrants, workers from the south of Burkina Faso who were already used to a transient livelihood in Ghana and Côte d'Ivoire started to progressively widen their circular journeys, first to the north of Africa (particularly Libya) and later to Southern Europe (particularly Italy, Spain, and France). Southern Europe represented an increasingly attractive destination for sub-Saharan migrants at the time because of its employment opportunities in agriculture, construction, and services, as well as the possibility of gaining legal status through regularization processes in these countries (Molinero Gerbeau and Avallone 2016).

But although this trend could generate once more an imaginary of a rural exodus from supposedly "deserted" toward more "developed" areas, the story is more complex, as I explained previously: emigration flows from West Africa to North Africa and Southern Europe mainly originated in urban and coastal areas of relatively prosperous countries such as Ghana, Nigeria, Senegal, and Côte d'Ivoire (see also Molinero Gerbeau and Leonel 2018). On top of these existing mobility patterns toward the cities, mines, and cash-crop producing regions of West Africa, future emigrants also prefer to spend time in big cities in order to accumulate the money and the contacts necessary for the realization of their journey—a possibility that also opened up as a result of the free movement of persons between member countries of the Economic Communities of West African States (ECOWAS), which contributes to porous borders and historical "South-South migration" (see also Flahaux and De Haas 2016).

West Africans who ended up in Southern Italy almost invariably concentrated in the area between Naples and Caserta, specifically in Castel Volturno and Villa Literno, where the first Burkinabè migrant workers had laid the foundations of a more stable African presence in the area.[20] But in contrast to the West African plantations, where they had been able to acquire some form of autonomy and recognition from customary authorities (at least until the regime change imposed by Henri Konan Bédié in 1995), African migrant workers in Southern Italy were being confined almost exclusively to the nonresidential, informal space of the ghetto. As Benoit Hazard (2010) recalls, the ghetto thus initially represented a kind of a-topical place: a site that offered a shared space of transit along established migration circuits as well as a platform from where to collectively organize one's livelihood. For the Burkinabè and other West African migrants in Italy, the central form of livelihood at the time was the day jobs they could find around big southern cities, accessed on what were locally called *piazze*, or *ronde* (in Villa Literno, one such site had the nickname *piazza degli schiavi*: slave market). One term they used for such occasional labor was *kalifoo* (or *califo*). Ghanaian migrants, who picked up the term in Libya, likely adapted the French word *carrefour*, which means intersection or crossroads, a possible pickup point for jobs (Lucht 2012, 30).[21] In Italy, the term immediately acquired a connotation of invisible work and illegal labor—including the transport of drugs, and sex work.[22] In addition to such occasional day labor, some African migrants started expanding their trajectories from the urban zones toward surrounding rural areas. This happened especially between May and January, when the farming season in Southern Italy spreads out from the suburbs of Naples with the seedlings of potatoes and tomatoes and the strawberry harvest, followed by the tomato, olive, and vegetable harvest in neighboring Puglia and Basilicata, and the mandarin and orange harvest in Calabria.

In her ethnography of Villa Literno, which for almost four years constituted the major African ghetto in Italy, Olivia Schmidt di Friedberg highlights the fundamental dilemma that drove the initial government intervention in this arena: while local agricultural firms—increasingly in the grip of neoliberal market dominance—needed the flexible labor of precarious migrant workers, the local presence of thousands of "illegal migrants" constituted a thorn in the eye of local communities, NGOs, and populist movements, which did not cease to emphasize in the local media and public arena the insalubrious, unhygienic conditions of the ghetto, which was, it needs to be said, rather the consequence than the cause of the lack of social and spatial integration of this African workforce. As the police chief of Villa Literno, whom Schmidt di Friedberg interviewed, put it, the boundary between Africans and locals was as demarcated as it was intractable; for the locals, the ghetto was the place of only Black people (*i neri*). So while the social and spatial organization of the ghetto reflected the interwoven patterns of African lifeworlds in mobility, including the many commercial activities and religious practices associated with informal African urbanity,[23] the public administration kept approaching the place as a complex emergency rather than a permanent feature of the way capitalist food production actively rooted itself in the local context. For the entire period that Villa Literno operated as a main labor reservoir in the Caserta area, the place kept being deprived of water and electricity. No toilets or sewage systems were being installed, and the makeshift shelters inside the ghetto kept being overcrowded with bunk beds so close together that it was difficult to pass between them. In an area largely abandoned by state intervention, the only relationship between the ghetto and the white

Italian population was that of market exchange—except for a few Italian antiracist associations who hurried to the African migrants' support after the killing of
South African activist Jerry Masslo (see chapter 1).

In parallel to the antiracist protests that erupted in reaction to Masslo's death,
the circulation of African workers in Southern Italy adopted a more ethnicized
and fragmented character. Migrant workers who already had settled in a specific
area started calling on their family members who had migrated to other regions
or were employed elsewhere in Italy. These circulations tended in fact to reinforce their more permanent resident settlement (Molinero Gerbeau and Leonel
2018, 67). But whereas in West Africa this phenomenon had led to the growth of
informal *cités* and *enclos* (enclosures) where migrant workers gradually gained
some form of autonomy and self-government, the lack of political rights of these
same workers in Europe would further consolidate their impermanent political subjectivity. Instead of feeling united as Black marginalized workers, most
workers in fact preferred to remain invisible and organize their livelihoods in
the confines of their ethnicized social networks. Labor discipline predominantly
took the form of small packs of laborers centered on a boss (*caponero*), who
would subsequently ensure the connection and accommodation of his workers
from Campania (Caserta, Villa Literno) to Puglia (Foggia, Stornara, Cerignola),
Basilicata (Venosa, Palazzo San Gervasio), and Calabria (Goia Tauro, Rosarno).
Though these seasonal migration trajectories remained stable for thirty years, a
certain social hierarchy could be noted after some time: the older, first-generation
migrants benefited from knowing the places of employment as well as the practice of planting and harvesting, and sometimes established direct contact with
the white, Italian labor intermediaries who recruited them on the account of
agricultural firms.

For a long time, this kind of circular, seasonal migration left no almost permanent traces in the landscape. Beyond the immediate Naples area, the only
remains after the harvesting season were the cardboard and abandoned clothes
left behind in the workers' temporary shelters or in one of the abandoned *caso-
lari* (farmhouses) that dot the Southern Italian fields. Since 2009, and especially
after the more repressive border and migration management regime in Europe
after the outbreak of the Libyan war, some more stable communities started
to emerge. Examples include Ghana House close to Cerignola, and the Grand
Ghetto close to San Severo, in Puglia. While Hazard and other anthropologists
who attended these places at the time described them as relatively homogeneous
spaces that conglomerated around a West African and Muslim identity (Blion
1996; Schmidt di Friedberg 1996; Hazard 2010), they also admit that national
and ethnic cleavages remained an important factor of social and cultural division in these sites, and would become even more so as a result of the deepening

segmentation and segregation process that followed the increasing securitization of European borders in the aftermath of the NATO operation in Libya in 2011–2014. After explaining these important geopolitical changes in the next chapter, I want to highlight some of the deeper infrastructural consequences in terms of boundaries and connections in the Southern landscape of rural Basilicata.

TERRITORIALIZING LABOR

As I said previously, I consider migrant agricultural labor not merely as the end-product of a process of commodification, in the classic Marxian sense. I am interested instead in the processes of sociospatial differentiation and stratification that end up producing what can be regarded as the fundamental boundary that upholds the predicament of formal industrial development, which is the distinction between the formal, "free" wage laborer and the racialized and informal "unfree" worker. Following Orlando Patterson's argument that in order to understand unfreedom, one must analyze the complex, tense, and at times contradictory interaction that underpins its social production and reproduction, I will describe this interaction as a dynamic process of proletarization and deproletarization—in the sense that agricultural workers are both "too free" to be able to negotiate their place and "not free enough" to negotiate the terms of their adverse incorporation in the globalized value chains (Brass 2014, 571). Though they are constrained to offer their labor power at the will of agricultural entrepreneurs, I regard their lack of choice as an effect of the technologies of boundary making.

In the case I am describing, the terminology of "bordering infrastructures" becomes important in understanding the dynamics of this differentiation and stratification process. As the physical networks that facilitate flows—in this case of labor migration—these infrastructures do not just embody territorial differentiations, but they actively create those differences, and, indeed, the technologies of separating, disciplining, and coercing migrant labor increasingly act as filters that separate "the desirable from the undesirable, the genuine from the bogus, the deserving from the undeserving" (Gargiulo 2021, 15). One focal point in this context will be the gang masters (*caporali*) or labor brokers whose function it is to simultaneously make migrating workers fit for flexible employment, while outsourcing the cost of the protection, care, and social reproduction of labor-power directly onto the networks of racialized and sexualized workers. Another important bordering infrastructure involves the instrument of territorial residence, which, especially in a context of progressive securitization of migration flows, increasingly keeps migrant workers tied to the land and to their employer as unfree workers. After a short description of the current border regime that characterizes Mediterranean border and migration management, I will turn to the specific infrastructures that have been put in place to coerce and discipline migrant labor in the context of Mediterranean agri-food supply chains.

Respingimento

In Italian, the term *respingimento* signifies both expulsion and refusal, a physical distancing of the undesired. It is widely accepted now that the organized chaos of Tunisia's and Libya's subsequent regime collapses around 2011 profoundly shook not only the foundations of the European migration regime but also the entire structure of geopolitical relations between Europe and Africa. That year, the fall of the Ben Ali regime in Tunisia and the Gadhafi regime in Libya unleashed a massive population movement on the southern shore of the Mediterranean. The record numbers of people who sought to reach the EU by boat, combined with an increasingly repressive migration regime, led to unprecedented numbers of deaths at sea (Heller and Pezzani 2016).[1]

During the NATO intervention that sought to contain the geopolitical consequences of these Mediterranean currents, the Italian government initially launched a humanitarian operation called Mare Nostrum, which officially aimed at saving migrant lives. The operation took off after what is still considered one of the worst maritime incidents of the post–World War II era: the October 2013 capsizing of a ship off the island of Lampedusa, in which 386 Eritrean, Somali, and Ghanaian migrants died. Yet the operation did not prevent bordering technologies from thickening around these moving bodies (Garelli and Tazzioli 2016). While the multiple surveillance mechanisms (including satellite imagery, military vessels, and aircraft) that NATO deployed close to the Libyan coast came to operate as a "halfway bridge to Europe," it motivated human smugglers to operate with ever more precarious and unseaworthy means, thus counting on European humanitarian assistance to rescue migrants swiftly. With the subsequent transformation of the Mare Nostrum operation to Triton in 2014, Heller and Pezzani (2016) also observed a critical blurring of humanitarian and security logics in systems of monitoring mobile populations: if Mare Nostrum signaled a pretense of European state sovereignty across borders, Triton inaugurated the tactical ebbing of migrant assistance at sea. However, this withdrawal was only temporary. Instead, it was replaced by an increasingly overt privatization of surveillance over moving bodies, as well as the deliberate subcontracting of sovereign control to nonaccountable agencies. This development will be the main subject of this section.

It is important to note the effects this progressive criminalization of migration had on the lived experiences of African migrants along the Sahel-Saharan routes and in Libya during this period. With the curtailing of migrants' rights to travel legally and claim a legal residence and employment contract, their living space became gradually violated and invaded by criminal elements like human traffickers, militias, and moonlighting state officials. Several observers point at the "clandestinization" and criminalization of African ghettos along migration routes and in the Libyan capital, Tripoli. Julien Brachet summarizes this shift succinctly: Whereas in the past "migration through the Sahara was irregular but not clandestine [and] there was an unofficial social control of migrant transport, by transporters themselves, by their relatives who knew what they were doing, and by state officials, which blurred the boundaries between the legal and the illegal, and firmly rooted passenger transport within the licit economic sphere," today human trafficking practices are manufactured by the very migration policies that were drafted to control them: "The degree of illegality and secrecy of the transport provided depends directly on the harshness of migration policies and on the ways in which they are implemented"—effectively creating a category of "people smugglers" that is forced to operate in secrecy. Such is the performative dimension of the "fight against criminal networks of smugglers," he concludes (Brachet 2018, 30–31; Tinti and Reitano 2017).

The consequence of this criminalization was that, on Libyan territory, the migrants' living space became invisible and marginalized. Ghettos increasingly acquired the function of clandestine stopover places for what francophone migrants refer to as *le tuyau*, the pipeline of illegalized human traffic across the EU-African space (Kohl 2015). As Gadhafi's containment policies unfolded, African migrants were forced to change their social practice as their lives became more and more confined to the ghettos. Marthe Achtnich reveals how migrants from Africa progressively became caught up in a clandestine economy where a heterogeneous set of actors profited from their mobility aspirations. In a kind of mirror of the institutionalized spaces of containment on the European continent, where incoming migrants were locked away in formal camp infrastructures that had the deliberate objective to usurp time for the purpose of migration control (Andersson 2014), the Libyan informalized space of migration transformed migrants' time into a source for capital accumulation and their bodies into commodities for purposes of extracting value. The migrants' community networks, which became increasingly localized in the ghetto as well as the detention centers along their trajectories, gradually became incorporated in these economies of mobility as they provided the localized social reproduction of the "frail, often temporary, measures through which migrants negotiate lives in transit and reproduce the conditions for their own mobilities" (Achtnich 2021, 11). As a result, migrants' "time capital" (Andersson 2014, 806) never became an intrinsic given but continued to be produced through social relations of care, labor, and endurance that also formed the backbone of the social reproduction of migrants' community networks once they arrived in Europe, as I will explain further in the next section.

On the other shore of the Mediterranean, the NATO intervention in Libya provided the context of the so-called North Africa Emergency (in Italian "Emergenza Nord Africa": ENA). Adopted in 2011, right after the Libyan regime collapse, the ENA introduced a series of exceptional measures targeted at migrants escaping violence in North Africa.[2] In the footsteps of earlier reforms, these measures did not materialize in a centralized asylum regime on the Italian peninsula, however. They rather spurred a "diffuse" system of migrant reception involving a small core of cooperatives and civil society organizations working in the domain of refugee protection—thus explicitly making nonstate agencies, such as charity groups and cooperatives, the main respondents to provide for migrant accommodation and social and legal assistance.[3] Within the framework of the Dublin regulations in Europe, migrant mobility remained nevertheless extremely restricted: while asylum seekers and refugees in Italy were allowed residence only in their first country of arrival, they could travel for limited periods provided they carried an affidavit from the prefecture council's office of their legal home (Fontanari 2017; Pinelli 2017).

In terms of migration reception in Italy, ENA had two immediate effects. First, it intensified pressure on existing accommodation: with few places available,[4] nonstate organizations responsible for accommodating and servicing incoming migrants were already working against the tide of diminishing government support. As their requests to increase the number of available places did not always elicit an adequate infrastructural response, some associations decided to move ahead by erecting an alternative circuit of private accommodations across the peninsula, called *accoglienza diffusa*. Particularly in rural areas, where reception capacities were typically low, public and private organizations started to systematically repurpose abandoned infrastructures, like hotels, farmhouses, and public buildings, to host migrants traveling through the central Mediterranean route.

Second, Italy experienced the transit of increasing numbers of migrants who had no intention of applying for asylum in the country, or whose request for asylum was subsequently rejected in the territorial commission. The presence of so-called *transitanti* (transiting migrants) resulted in the growth of informal migrant occupations up and down the peninsula. Throughout 2013–2015, a network of squats, shelters, and other temporary settlements appeared across different Italian cities. Parallel to the Mare Nostrum operation, the Lampedusa tragedy had also motivated a movement of solidarity throughout Europe, which helped these informal occupations to grow both physically and politically in importance. Though predominantly managed by "autonomous movements" (predominantly anarchist groups and radical labor unions), these settlements partly amalgamated with the already existing forms of self-organized settlements and ghettos that had existed on the Italian peninsula since the mid-1980s (see chapter 2). In 2016, the medical charity Médecins sans Frontières estimated the number of asylum applicants and refugees living in "informal" habitats at around ten thousand (MSF 2016). Strikingly, though, MSF did not include in its study what it called the "informal labor camps": sites like Borgo Mezzanone and Rignano Garganico (Puglia), San Ferdinando (Calabria), and Boreano (Basilicata), where thousands of migrants continued to flock each year to harvest grapes, oranges, and tomatoes for Italian enterprises and the big distribution networks, but which increasingly took on the function of informal migrant relief sites during this period. In its next report published in 2018, MSF noticed not only a growth, but also a growing geographic and ethnic fragmentation of such informal settlements, apart from the already noticeable absence of local social and health services, water, food, and electricity (MSF 2018).

Based on this evidence, it is clear now that Europe's and NATO's reaction to North African regime collapses led to a progressive criminalization and securitization of migration across the EU-African space. While the humanitarian relief operation of Mare Nostrum indeed saved thousands of lives, the systematic reorganization of asylum at a European level resulted in a repressive border politics that significantly reconfigured the authority over migrating bodies. During 2012–2014, Schengen Agreement signatories reiterated the principle of the European common policy adopted in Dublin in 2001, which stipulated that so-called first countries of arrival take responsibility over the migrants' asylum claims. With the refugee crisis in the Mediterranean unfolding, this framework automatically resulted in border states like Italy, Greece, and Spain taking on the bulk of charges in this regard. Despite the many protests on the part of Mediterranean countries in this context, in 2013 the Dublin III negotiations not only reconfirmed this principle of first arrival, but the European framework also instituted a novel set of technologies that were set on securitizing and digitizing border controls. Officially, Dublin III was meant to counter the phenomenon of "asylum shopping": the tendency of an admittedly small minority of migrants to try their asylum demands in different member states. From a diplomatic viewpoint, however, it was clear that, without a real possibility of filing their asylum requests at the European embassies in their country of origin, migrants who were seeking asylum in Europe had no choice but to engage in a perilous journey across the desert and the sea. Concretely, Dublin III introduced a series of measures that created an increasingly hostile environment for incoming migrants across Europe.

One of the more systematic changes since Dublin III has been the EURODAC system: a digital database where fingerprints of arriving migrants are stored, scrutinized, and shared. From EURODAC emerged a series of logistical reorganizations that made the Mediterranean route not only more dangerous and repressive but also opened the gates to the progressive racialization of migration control. Upon their arrival on European soil, incoming migrants were now forcefully obliged to leave their fingerprints so they could be identified for future bureaucratic and security purposes (Amnesty International 2016). In broader, ontological terms, therefore, one could say that EURODAC introduced a form of digital "epimerization": the rendering of skin as digitized data becomes "the exercise of power cast by the disembodied gaze of certain surveillance technologies ... that can be employed to do the work of alienating the subject by producing a truth about the racial body and one's identity (or identities) despite the subject's claims" (Browne 2015, 109). As Glouftsios and Casaglia argue (2022, np), EURODAC thus became part of a wider data infrastructure that "stigmatizes" postcolonial "others" with codes to control their mobilities: in order to prevent and contain the potentially rebellious ramifications of transnational mobility,[5] they write, the data base became a system to brand "non-European, racialized bodies ... with codes ... that give them meaning and identity, and that attach them to specific, racialized categories."

In reaction to protests and subversions, the border regime became even more repressive. This became apparent when, under pressure of European member states, Italy abandoned its humanitarian operation in 2014 in favor of a more aggressive border security intervention under the name Triton. It is no surprise that border violence increased particularly after this change of course: suddenly, Italian migration and border officials started to forcefully extract fingerprint data from incoming migrants. During the same period, the reaffirmation of Dublin regulation also led to the emergence of a new category of migrants: the *dublinati*, or migrants who were sent back to their first country of arrival after filing an unsuccessful asylum claim in third countries and being identified through the EURODAC database. During 2015–2016, the number of *dublinati* significantly rose on the Italian peninsula because of the pressure of neighboring states to fingerprint incoming migrants on the Italian border. The immediate result of this shift was a diminishing of so-called extraordinary reception centers across the country. In addition, the Renzi government also openly blocked ENA refugees from acquiring their temporary residency permits in Italy during this period: in 2016–2018, the denial rate for the renewal of humanitarian refugee permits rose from 60 to 80 percent.[6]

After the signing of yet another cooperation agreement with Libya in 2017,[7] the refoulement of African migrants started to take on an even more systematic character, as the Italian sociojudicial association ASGI wrote on its website at the time: "Italy and the European Union . . . delegate border control to the Libyan authorities, effectively preventing departures, making the escape of migrants from Libya even more dangerous thanks also to the equipment that is inevitably used by the Libyan authorities to attack NGO ships during the rescue operations, and making the living conditions of migrants even more dramatic" (ASGI 2017).

It was in fact more than ironic that Italian governors defended the bolstering of multilateral cooperation with Libya's transitional government in light of the "extreme pressures" they were supposedly experiencing from "illegal migration"— and despite the rising evidence that Libyan warlords had been directing human trafficking operations directly for some time now.[8] In this ensuing diplomatic fight over migrant bodies, neighboring states like France and Austria also started to systematically send back "Italian" asylum applicants across their borders— sometimes using outright illegal means[9]—a reason why the term *respingimento* progressively signified both legal and illegal forms of migrant refoulement.

Another shocking consequence of the systematic refoulement of migrants from European soil was the Libyan "slave markets." As I noted above, the later days of Gadhafi's regime were associated with the proliferation of discriminatory acts toward the Black African population in the country—expressed through systematic arbitrary detentions, armed criminality, and involuntary returns.[10] As Libyan militias overthrew Gadhafi, and the fight between warring factions made life increasingly insecure on the streets of Tripoli, a dramatic series of events would bring to the surface the even more systematic exploitation of Black Africans in Libya's expanding prison complex. In 2017, news erupted about "slave auctions" in Tripoli. In a video fragment distributed by CNN, several men appeared onscreen as they were being sold as plantation laborers: "Big strong boys for farmwork," an invisible voice shouted. Even if African slavery has a longer history in Libya, the news generated a stream of indignation. The UN secretary general, António Guterres, denounced crimes against humanity in the international press. Mali and Burkina Faso withdrew their ambassadors from Tripoli. And Rwanda offered to host thirty thousand stranded refugees. Throughout 2017 and 2018, evidence continued to emerge about the systematic abuse and exploitation of African refugees in Libya, where they were forced to work as sex laborers, domestic servants, and in the agricultural industry.

Subsequent visits of the United Nations High Commission for Human Rights to the Libyan Directorate for Combatting Illegal Migration (DCIM)—the body of Libya's government of transition overseeing the detention centers of refugees who had been intercepted at sea—revealed what the UN body called a methodical organization of African slave labor in the country's expanded prison complex (UNIMSIL, UNHROHC 2018). While denouncing the squalid conditions of detention camps—often located in abandoned warehouses, apartment blocks, farmhouses, garages, or former prison sites referred to as *campos*, the UN documented the torture and ill-treatment of African prisoners, including acts of sexual violence that DCIM members perpetrated with impunity. At any given time, the UN reported, between four thousand and seven thousand detainees were held in DCIM centers in western Libya. These numbers even multiplied in late 2017 to nearly twenty thousand people, following the arrests of thousands of migrants and refugees in the aftermath of fighting between armed groups in October 2017, as well as the increased support that the Government of National Unity received following its agreement with Italy in the same year.

While it is difficult to sustain the accusation of "slavery" in a context of war and state collapse, the subsequent changes in the Libyan regulation and coercion of migration during this period indeed show a proliferation of slavery-like practices of detention and forced labor.[11] Building on Orlando Patterson's definition, the argument that African migrants were enslaved in fact gains strength in the face of their systematic abjection and abuse in the context of Libya's war economy. As Patterson argues, slavery should never be reduced to the mere imposition of force and the right over life and death for unfree humans: it also involves a form of *social death*. More concretely, it produces an instance of bare life, in which the person is violently stripped of genealogy, cultural memory, social distinction, name, and native language—that is, of all the elements of Aristotle's *bios* (Ziarek 2008). In hindsight, that is exactly what has been taking place in the detention centers of the Libyan prison complex: at al-Kararim, Janzour, Tajoura, Gharyan, Tarik al-Matar, and Tarik al-Sikka, prisoners were not only subjected to forced labor, but also, and more significantly, they were denied their very humanity. In a rogue version of concentration camps, the DCIM outsourced the control over the detainment, coercion, and depositing of migrant bodies to private militias and gang members who increasingly considered inmates as their private property. The United Nations Support Mission in Libya reported male migrants and refugees to be routinely taken out of captivity for forced manual labor, including construction and farmwork, as well as military tasks. One of these tasks included the removal of bodies of detainees who had died in custody.

In this context of proliferating abuse, it is important to signal the role of the women. Their systematic sexual exploitation in the prisons, where they were treated as the cooks, cleaners, and sex slaves of gang and militia members, was increasingly coupled to their subaltern employment in the domestic service and sex industry. Women frequently reported being transferred out of detention by smugglers and traffickers to carry out domestic work without remuneration. This simultaneous treatment of woman on equal footing when it came to forced labor, but at the same time as nannies and servants who needed to subject their identity and personhood to the sexual domination of the male bosses, in fact constitutes yet another confirmation of Angela Davis's argument that we need to appraise women's roles in the context of slavery and its aftermaths foremost and essentially "as workers" (Davis 1983, 10–12): "As slaves, compulsory labor over-shadowed every other aspect of women's existence," she writes, while as mothers and companions, "they were simply instruments guaranteeing the growth of the slave labor force. They were 'breeders'—animals, whose monetary value could be precisely calculated in terms of their ability to multiply their numbers." (For a discussion in the Italian context see Rigo 2022.) In Libya's war complex, it is exactly this denial of personhood that forms the backbone of Black Africans' social deaths.[12] In the face of the rising abuses and denial of humanity that Afri-can migrants were subjected to in this moment, but also considering the system-atic predation of the Mediterranean plantation economy on the reproduction of migrant labor for which women continued to be in large part held respon-sible, it becomes outdated, indeed insulting, to still talk about the Mediterranean as an open frontier, a zone of experimental bordering practices and strategies of refoulement. Rather, we should consider these practices as a new mode of government within which the control over life and death becomes operational (see also Klute and von Trotha 2004; Humphrey 2004). What we are seeing here is neither a "collapse" of authority, nor merely a "criminalization" of economic markets, or a "violation" of human dignity, but a reconfiguration of sovereign authority that decides over the life and death of vulnerable migrants. Impor-tant in this context is less the question of *who* owns the right to decide over this exception, than *which* connections between legal provisions, political institu-tions, and physical infrastructures have generated, and continue to generate, the platform from where this sovereign power is actively exercised. As I said previ-ously, the widespread concern with criminality as a cause of premature migrant death in fact prevents us from asking the more pressing question of whether it is still sufficient to consider the sovereign right to make life, take life, or let die as a mere matter of sovereign exception, or whether we must instead confront the bio-economic issue of how one's precarious life and premature death are conditioned by one's position in capitalism (Tyner 2019, x). In the next section, I will try to answer that question by describing and analyzing how the changing migration and border regime in the Mediterranean has effectively changed the policing of migrant labor through such reconfiguring connections and modes of government.

Securitizing Labor

The reorganization of the European border also left its noticeable mark on the Southern Italian tomato plantation economy. During the 1980s and '90s, as I wrote before, the retail revolution had already contributed to a growing concentration of capital in a small oligopoly of tomato processing firms. The Italian tomato business thus appeared to represent a textbook case of a neoliberal market economy, of high capital concentration combined with a spatial differentiation between producing firms and transforming industries. The crucial factor that underpinned these divisions in the Italian agrarian economy was the availability of precarious migrant labor. From then mid-1980s, agricultural firms had started to fill their persistent labor shortages with migrant workers from the Maghreb and Eastern Europe. Following their predecessors, public administrators and entrepreneurs continued to justify these inequalities as a necessary pathway in the grand teleology of modern, capitalist progress.

"To resolve this situation," one mayor told me, "we will need years, if not decades. . . . I often compare this situation to our own, as Italian emigrants in Switzerland, for example. . . . After years and years, we integrated there gradually [*man mano*]." Time and time again, this reasoning occurred centrally in the public narrative of why migrant workers were suffering the plight they were. While making abstraction of the concrete infrastructures that prevented migrants from obtaining access to fundamental human and labor rights, this discourse did not surprise me at all, as it exemplified the cultural habitus of Southern Italians since the country's independence from the Bourbon ancien régime: the need to subject one's expectations and desires to the hegemonic territorial order in fact reflected the layered manner in which the social relations of production articulated in this agrarian frontier. In practice, though, this meant that African migrant laborers, just like the Italian *braccianti* (day laborers) and industrial workers before them, had to bear the cost of their social reproduction.

In the context of humanitarian security that characterized the Mediterranean border crisis, I nonetheless noticed a significant discursive and material shift toward the criminalization of labor migration flows. Dines and Rigo (2015) identify two important factors that have contributed to this shift. First, the almost exclusive focus on the Mezzogiorno in public media outlets and in government interventions led to a consolidation of the imagery of an underdeveloped and criminal South. Rather than highlighting the material conditions that led to migrant precarity, legislative efforts concentrated on the criminal aspects of labor intermediation, the illegal monopolies of gang masters and their informal hierarchies located in Italy's labor slums. The humanitarian management of migration tended to overshadow the centrality of labor relations in Italy's agrarian economy, while producing what the authors call a "refugeeization" of labor (2015, 4). By this they not only mean a numeric shift toward refugees and asylum seekers in the composition of the agricultural workforce. But they also highlight the radically conflicting grounds upon which the stratification of labor was constructed in the context of neoliberal market reforms. They write that the increasing differentiation of migration flows in the context of Triton and the Italian-Libyan treaty contributed to the growth of a precarious labor force composed of refugees and asylum seekers inclined to accept ever more detrimental labor conditions. Among the 1,356 migrant workers the humanitarian NGO Caritas assisted in the ghettos of Puglia and Basilicata between 2014 and 2017 in their Presidium project, for example, 64.3 percent resulted in having some form of refugee status. For the diocese of Acerenza in Basilicata, these numbers are even higher: 71.1 percent (Perrotta and Raeymaekers 2022). This is emblematic of a situation in which refugees and asylum seekers have increasingly taken on the jobs of precarious seasonal laborers, not just in Italy, but in Europe more generally. According to a 2015 European Parliament inquiry, noneconomic migrants already constituted between two-thirds and three-quarters of all third-country nationals entering the labor markets of member states. In countries like Germany, Italy, and France, the inversion of the relationship between permits for protection and for work reasons is now a consolidated trend, as Rigo and Caprioglio (2021) write. Despite temporal and geographic fluctuations, different forms of humanitarian protection now permanently cover at least a quarter of the total number of residency permits issued annually in the European Union. These statistics confirm that the binary between "legal" and "illegal" entry is unable to account for the multiplicity of legal statuses of migrants, nor for the way current legislation on international protection and asylum circumscribes the actual living conditions of migrant workers on the European labor market. Rather, they seem to reconfirm the statement I made earlier that the boundary between regular labor and irregular work is in itself the result, the outcome, of a deliberate strategy that undermines the emancipation of workers' rights in favor of a migration policy that frames these rights in terms of humanitarian security.

Sanitizing the Labor Force

The tendency to reframe migrant labor in humanitarian terms became apparent in the post-2019 efforts of European states to contain the so-called food crisis that erupted because of the COVID outbreak. As I wrote in the introduction, the pandemic patently brought to the fore the internal contradictions of the global food regime: while trying to formalize the "essential" labor need for the survival of agri-food enterprises, very few questioned the massive exploitation of human and of natural resources this survival was, and is, based upon (Bello 2020). In March 2020, the Italian government (a technical government of national unity under the guidance of Giuseppe Conte) voted a legal provision, a sanatory law (*sanatoria*), which had the dual objective of formalizing "irregular" employment in a number of circumscribed professions deemed essential for the national economy and well-being, while granting applicants a formal employment status for six months. At the expiration date of this sanitation effort, in August 2020, the Ministry of the Interior received approximately 207,000 applications: 85 percent came from domestic caregivers, and the remaining 15 percent (around 30,000 applications) from the primary sector.

Besides being significantly lower than the estimate of six hundred thousand "irregular" workers that the minister of agriculture had announced to be the main objective of this measure in Parliament,[13] the limited impact of this sanatory law can be related to two immediate causes and one structural cause. First, the law did not take note of the net transformation that has taken place in the last few years in the so-called seasonal workforce: a growing segment of migrant agricultural laborers is now made up of refugees and asylum seekers who try to build a way of subsistence as agricultural workers in the absence of state support: today, 40 percent of foreign agricultural workers have a humanitarian permit or refugee status (Rigo and Caprioglio 2021). As many pro-migrant associations wrote at the time, these workers thought twice before betraying the real reason for their refuge in Italy and transforming their status, *post factum*, from political refugees to economic migrants. The second factor relates to the persistent feudalism incorporated in contemporary capitalist relations. Migrant workers who wanted to signal and overcome their informal status were asked to declare their status through their employer. Based on this, it is fair to say that the sanatory law of 2020 remains perfectly in line with the established tradition of emergency measures the Italian state has inaugurated to tackle the problem of irregular migrant work in the country, and which systematically bolstered migrants' subaltern labor position and political subjectivity. Quite like the Renzi and Salvini governments that actively produced the "irregularity" of asylum seekers in terms of territorial residency permits, the 2020 *sanatoria* did not eliminate the causes that continued to contribute to the formation of new irregularities. On the contrary, the state's efforts to eradicate informal work remain entirely framed in terms of migrants' irregular territorial status, which shows again that the purpose has never been to encourage entrepreneurs to get workers out of informality but only to skim the excesses of a power relationship that had now become structural. It is this curious blending of humanitarian and security instruments to channel migrant labor that I will now analyze in a local context.

Territorializing Labor Power

In 2014, the regional administration of Basilicata made a more concerted effort to "securitize" its agricultural migrant labor force. Mirroring the national narrative around border security that had taken shape in this period, the administration's intervention was founded on a strong discourse of criminality and illegality. In an interview with me in July 2016, the regional administrator for migration used the term "*caporalato* online" to describe what he found to be the main source of labor exploitation in Basilicata: "The *caporalato* system is a paramilitary type of organization. . . . During the harvesting season, one phone call is enough to mobilize thousands of workers at the time," he told me in his office.[14] The administrator appeared mostly concerned by what he regarded as a small group of Burkinabè intermediaries who, in his view, concentrated their violent grip on agricultural labor in a couple of ghettos situated in the tomato district. He had become convinced that eliminating the ghetto as a key migrant infrastructure would be the right strategy to also eliminate gang-mastering "altogether," he told me in October of the same year. "If we succeed in eliminating the *tangente* of the *caporale*, we have solved the problem."[15] With this term *tangente* (cut, kickback) he wanted to highlight the mafialike structure of the Burkinabè gang masters, who in his view based their power on a system of blackmail (*ricatto*) and violent coercion. The ghetto had to be eradicated because of this central function in the system of criminal enslavement, he found. In addition, ethnic and family affiliations to these *caporale* figures made it even more difficult for workers to escape from such tormenting exploitation (*sfruttamento*), he concluded ("finché loro abitano lì non c'è' possibilità di rompere questo sistema di reclutamento").

As it turned out, this official narrative closely followed the national discourse of labor exploitation and migration policy at the time. On the one hand, Basilicata's approach toward labor migration contained a clear reference to the Italian experience of organized crime and its "business of protection": like the mafia, African *capineri* were seen to keep their clients in their grip through an astute system of blackmail and extortion. On the other hand, the vision appeared to be that this criminal system operated according to a strict cultural code and ethnic divisions that also explained the violent competition between labor gangs. If only one could eradicate the ghetto as a key infrastructure in this web, the administrator concluded, one could relocate workers in more decent housing conditions where they would be free from extortion but still live according to their "cultural habits." Once more, executive government representatives deployed in rural development boiled down the problem of labor exploitation not to the organization of production but rather to a discrepancy between conflicting cultural economies, traditions, and ethnic affiliations.

In 2014, Basilicata's regional administration decided to intervene in the domain of seasonal labor accommodation. After three years of absence, the administrator for migration assigned the management of a new seasonal labor camp to the Italian Red Cross (the term used at the time was *centro di accoglienza per lavoratori stagionali*). The center was located on the outskirts of one of the rural towns. Its decrepit buildings were to function as a warehouse, where workers could be divided into compartments. In the main square, shower and toilet containers were to be installed for a total of three hundred workers. In neighboring Borgo San Pietro, that same year, the mayor inaugurated what he describes as an "experimental project."[16] Officially declaring the migrant ghetto located in his municipality as unfit (*inagibile*), he not only foresaw its imminent eviction, but also engaged in a fourfold strategy to drive away migrant workers from these "insalubrious" sites.

To keep the migrants out of the ghettos and in the seasonal camps, different public administrations in the municipalities of Basilicata's tomato district used four kinds of pressures. The first concerned taxation. In a joint operation with the *questura* (police headquarters), the regional administration put pressure on the farmers to seal their abandoned warehouses, or else face the payment of a house tax (called IMU).[17] The second method concerned public hygiene. During the harvesting season, the public health agency ASP[18] started going around to verify the hygienic conditions of the abandoned farmhouses in the different municipalities. The result was that landowners gradually started to close and fence off the buildings they had hitherto rented out to African workers out of fear of being incriminated. Several landowners I interviewed confessed that these government actions provided the main reason why they had started closing off the entry to their buildings or tearing them down completely. A third instrument to evict the migrant ghettos was that of physical repression. Considering labor migration increasingly as a problem of public order, this repression also seemed justified, considering the persisting migrant "crisis." In her interview with me, the councilor for social affairs of one municipality put it in forthright manner: "If we continue to provide services [to the ghetto], we haven't solved the problem. Listen, we are dealing here with people who are a hundred years behind compared to us . . . concentrated in a place without rules. . . . And so, we must impose the rules, there where there is no public force [*forza pubblica*]. If you ask me, the best we can do is to improve the conditions of the [seasonal labor] camp and work with the security forces."[19] Humanitarian and labor union workers equally evoked cultural backwardness as a prime reason why their intervention appeared to be received "with a certain diffidence" by African workers.[20] "At some point, I start to doubt whether they don't want to be in this mess," one humanitarian volunteer told me.[21] Following a similar line of thought, the regional administrator for migration changed his depiction of the ghetto as the "*bancomat* [cash machine] of the farmers" to a zone of lawlessness: "We are dealing with a lawless zone [*zona franca*] that needs to be eradicated," he told me in August 2016. Interestingly, the executive invoked the term *bonificare* (sanitize, reclaim), which is exactly the terminology the Fascist government used during the 1930s in its attempt to demographically colonize the southern marshes and pastoral lands (see chapter 2).

Whether willingly or unconsciously, therefore, the regional administration for migration had just reinforced the idea of an uncivilized countryside that needed to be conquered and pacified through a specific set of spatial reorganizations. The most important of these, for the time being, was to force seasonal workers to move from the unhealthy and criminality-infested rural settlements to a strictly controlled infrastructure of seasonal labor camps. As the new anti-*caporale* legislation envisioned, these labor camps were to "logistically" accommodate seasonal workers—a term that clearly indicated the shift of perspective toward labor securitization.[22] Driven by this same purpose, the mayor of Borgo San Pietro ultimately decided to send in the security forces to tear down what remained of the ghetto in his municipality. When I interviewed the regional administrator about this intervention, he reiterated his point of view about the insalubrious illegality that characterized this site. He proudly showed me a picture of the site before and after the intervention, telling me that "we've gone there with our bulldozers, making sure to close off all buildings and to tear down all shacks. Even if there remain one or two *caporali* present in the area, there are a lot less of them now."[23]

A final instrument the regional administration uses to coerce agricultural labor is what I call bureaucratic power. Building on Irus Braverman (2011), I envision bureaucratization to involve the erection of an infrastructural assemblage intent on controlling population movements. This process includes the assignment of personal security status that makes migrant movements amenable to control. And it comprises a conscious manipulation of the instrument of state territoriality to make this control possible. As she writes, the territorialization of state power does not exclusively pass through the physical design of mobility control, land, and population enclosures: it also involves population registries, identity cards, permit systems, and other crucial bureaucratic techniques to control population movements (Braverman 2011, 283). This bureaucratic power assumes the form of an infrastructure assemblage, or a mode of ordering heterogeneous entities. Such assemblages are both productive, in the sense that government arrangements typically create agency, and they are desired, in the sense that they voluntarily associate elements that were hitherto disconnected (Müller 2015; Nail 2017).

The Task Force for Migration constituted an interesting case of such an emerging governance assemblage. Established in 2014—the same year Mare Nostrum changed into Triton—it brought together CGIL, Caritas, the Red Cross, and the regional councilor for migration in consultation with local town councils.[24] With the official purpose of eradicating the *caporalato* hierarchy, it concentrated its efforts on the systematic erection and management of seasonal reception centers, the formalization of labor contracts, and the betterment of living conditions for migrant workers through concerted action between town administrations, labor unions, and charity organizations. More widely, the objective of the task force was to reestablish what Ferguson and Gupta call state verticality. The purpose of state verticality, they write, is to convey an understanding of state administration as a "concrete, overarching, spatially encompassing reality" (2002, 981). Verticality serves the precise purpose of reifying the notion of state government as a single entity with spatial properties. It serves to reiterate what they describe as the property of vertical encompassment: the idea of a state that is simultaneously superior to, and encompassing of, other institutions and centers of power. Together, the operation of these metaphors materializes in what they call the spatialization of the state: the reproduction of spatial orders and scalar hierarchies through concrete bureaucratic interventions. Through this planned containment of labor power as well as the eradication of alternative grounds, state regulators were exactly trying to reach this aim in a context in which state rules remained highly fluid and contested by the multiple participants in the agricultural economy.

Next to coordinating the seasonal labor camps, from 2014 onward, the main purpose of the task force became to identify, register, and watch over seasonal farmworkers to make sure their movement followed a predictable and manageable pattern. Humanitarian organizations in turn developed a sophisticated surveillance system to work toward this end. Whenever seasonal laborers turned to the NGO for assistance, its local operators filed their personal data. In a next step, they made sure to send these data onward to the local police station for a security check. After receiving clearance, the NGO operator then called the reception of the seasonal labor camp, where Red Cross operators prepared an identification that allowed the workers in question to reside in the camp—but only if they agreed to the internal regulations of the camp. These regulations included the respect for opening and closing times (after midnight the gate closed), as well as some rules of behavior (alcoholic beverages, for example, were not allowed in the camp). Finally, official inhabitants of the Red Cross camp were allowed a renewal of their territorial residency papers, or *permesso di soggiorno*: when agreeing to be watched over by this mix of state and nonstate organizations, labor migrants obtained the right to an official residence for another two or five years—depending on their migration status.

The most important purpose of this ensemble of bureaucratic techniques, therefore, was to uphold the territorial power of the nation-state over other, competing powers and registers of regulation. More widely, they were put in place to uphold what Ferguson and Gupta (2002, 982) call the technology of encompassment: the promotion of a taken-for-granted scalar imagery of a state that contains and directs its localities, regions, and communities. Through its networked association of different institutions in a hierarchical framework, the task force directly tried to incorporate the different communal administrations of the tomato district into a single hierarchy that also reformulated political powers in a new topology of executive population control. As the regional administrator made clear to me several times, the new system of bureaucratic control had the main aim of standardizing a response that had been hitherto divided between different communal administrations. And it was quite clear that not everyone had the same opinion on what would be the best strategy of intervention.

While the Task Force for Migration formed a good example of territorializing state power in the domain of labor mediation and coercion, its operation did not stop the controversy over who was to decide the fate of mobile land workers. On the contrary. Many criticized the Red Cross for managing the seasonal labor camp in a "militaristic" manner. When I visited the camp in the early summer of 2017, the manager told me that the Red Cross's lack of transparency over actual numbers of the camp's temporary inhabitants concerned a matter of privacy.[25] This answer did not satisfy the local associations that were socially and legally assisting labor migrants. The issue of Red Cross management remained controversial throughout my fieldwork in the area. Not long after the camp's establishment, it became clear that only a minority of labor migrants chose to permanently stay there (during my visit in the middle of the harvesting season I counted fifty). Some ended up there at the end of the season with the hope of getting their papers renewed. So rather than a logistical solution envisioned by the law, the Red Cross offered only a partial service of temporarily filling the gaps of a divided state administration repurposed toward controlling population movements.

Time and time again, the Red Cross and state regulators invoked the need for security to prevent transparent oversight of the camp's management. Regional authorities in turn emphasized the destructive attitude of "black and indigenous actors of the *caporalato* industry" who resisted the Red Cross reception infrastructure.[26] Off the record, several NGO workers told me that the issue of the *permesso di soggiorno* continued to trigger serious frustrations with migrant workers, some of whom effectively turned their anger on camp infrastructures.[27] Rather than the usual terminology of culture and social capital, administrators started to invoke "public security" as the main motive why things kept turning out the way they did. When I discussed the issue of the *permesso di soggiorno* with the demographic registry office (*anagrafe*), the executive used strict security terminology to explain why he fiercely disagreed about handing out residency papers to temporary workers. Though he had to act in compliance with the task force, he said, he found it problematic to deliver such identity papers in a very brief period and without a proper security check: "If a bomb explodes somewhere, I will be held responsible," he said, clearly referring to the terrorist threat that was regularly evoked in the media in relation to so-called uncontrolled migration across the Mediterranean. He told me the government needed to be wary of infiltrators (*infiltrati*) who may use such gaps in security to obtain legal status.[28]

To contrast this increasing surveillance of their lives, migrant workers kept invoking their right to territorial residence as a key condition to becoming visible to the state. Since the administrative reform under the Renzi government in 2014 (the "Piano Casa"), and in clear continuity with the "invisible border" of Italian residence laws since the 1930s (see chapter 2), people with no fixed address could not obtain residency papers unless they actively registered with an official institution, such as a migrant reception center or a communal administration. At the same time, though, official residence rights formed a prerequisite for obtaining a formal employment contract, with pension and unemployment contributions. Needless to say, this measure posed enormous difficulties for ghetto dwellers, squatters, and nonresidents, as they could not formalize their presence on Italian territory and thus remained excluded from their rights as refugees, asylum seekers, and migrants more generally. In my interviews with legal counselors, they all insisted on this anomaly in the current Italian legislation. The director of the association Avvocati di Strada (Street lawyers), which legally assists the homeless, already denounced this paradoxical situation in 2014: "Without residence," he said, "you cannot vote, you do not obtain health care, you cannot receive a pension nor benefit from local welfare, you cannot obtain formal employment, you are not entitled to legal assistance.... [In short,] taking away the residence permit from people who occupy a building literally means placing those people outside of society, making them invisible, erasing in one single shot the possibility to confront their difficulties. . . . It is remarkable that a plan, which should help families to confront the current crisis, precisely bears these consequences," he concluded about the Piano Casa legislation in 2014 (Godio 2014).

The conflict over residency papers highlights once more the visible contrast between the official logistics of temporary migrant housing and the informal accommodation of migrant workers who remained concentrated in the ghetto. Temporary labor camps figured as a segregated space of population containment. But it was equally clear that they failed in the task of logistically solving the problem of uncontrolled migration. Every year, NGO operators placed the same temporary infrastructures inside the decrepit buildings that were repurposed for this aim, and every year the controversy re-erupted over the scarce services and lack of personal liberties. The lack of solid responses did in fact thicken the political debate around rural migration as humanitarian organizations and local activists accused the regional authorities of mismanagement. After the destruction of Borgo San Pietro's ghetto, one humanitarian operator told me, "It cannot be that he [the head of the Task Force on Migration] closes the ghetto in June, and then expects the laborers to spontaneously come to the reception center when it is opened in mid-August. In the meantime, it is clear they have all already dispersed."[29] Volunteers (many of whom were unemployed Basilicata youth) continued complaining about the unjustified division of labor between the task force and civil society organizations: while the Red Cross continued to hide the center's numbers, different charity organizations continued to work toward a more systematic accommodation of migrant workers with the help of social councilors in the different municipalities. But with the fierce resistance of the demographic registry (*anagrafe*) in the different municipalities, this proved to be a tedious task indeed.

The main effect of the securitization policy in the Alto Bradano area in 2014–2020 was a growing criminalization of labor in and around the infrastructure of the white gang master industry. With only a minority of seasonal workers living in the town centers, the actual result of the task force policy was that labor became mainly concentrated in the ghettos of San Giuseppe and San Donato, respectively situated on the territories of Borgo San Nicola and Borgo San Rocco. Already closely in the grip of the white *caporale*, these ghettos benefited from the eviction of other, smaller ghettos, which subsequently forced other, more autonomous groups of workers to accept the two ghettos' primacy. In this context, one could argue, the ghetto of San Giuseppe reinforced the informal inclusion of the African labor force in the industrialized agricultural economy dominated by the white *caporali*, while the official camp structures prevented the same workforce from formally integrating in local society. Whether intended or not, the region's pushback policy resulted in a system of communicating vessels, whereby the violent segregation of African workers went hand in hand with their social exclusion. This labor geography was a clear outcome of the systematic securitization of migration that emanated from state policies of mobility control in the context of Mediterranean humanitarian security politics.

Humanitarian Surveillance

The previous section meant to highlight that there is indeed more to state spatialization than the policing of territorial borders alone, but these politics also involve a more active implementation of bordering infrastructures through "borderwork." In a recent contribution on the EU-African borderlands, Vammen and colleagues theorize borderwork as a concept that allows us to track the specific systemic practices not just of states but also of other "organizational actors" who are engaged in the "complex, laborious" process of translating bordering technologies into concrete arrangements that affect the shape and scope of political power across multiple geographic scales. This necessarily requires a more engaged analysis, not just of the multiple events and places, but also of the multiple actors that take part in the everyday (re)production of borders—that is, how citizens and migrants, state and nonstate actors, construct, navigate, and facilitate border control under constrained circumstances at various levels of intervention (Vammen, Cold-Ravnkilde, and Lucht 2022).

When moving away from the performance of Europe's border regime in the Mediterranean it is indeed worthwhile to look at the "less dramatic, multiple, mundane domains of bureaucratic practice by which states reproduce spatial orders and scalar hierarchies," as Ferguson and Gupta (2002, 984) argue in their essay on the ethnography of neoliberal governmentality. Taking the example of the Task Force on Migration, I have tried to show how the spatialization of contemporary borderwork involved the configuration of a networked topology of heterogeneous associations aimed at controlling population mobility in the territory of Basilicata. It is clear though that this government assemblage did not produce the intended effect of reinforcing the state's vertical encompassment of municipal administrations and civil society organizations. What it did produce was a permanent controversy over who controlled the means of protecting this mobile labor force. Bureaucratic power proved to be only a limited instrument to convey the state's territorial sovereignty, while state repression turned out to reproduce the informal labor hierarchies it officially claimed to contest. In that sense, it is important to highlight the limits of state governmentality in a context where the terms of regulating mobility are contested and institutionally diffused. Rather than uncritically accepting the spatial optic of an all-seeing state that acts as a unitary depository of power, Tania Li (2005, 383) reminds us, we should carefully deconstruct and analyze the presumably "messy, contradictory and conjunctural effects" of failed state schemes. Whenever policies fail, she reminds us, we should ask ourselves what power conjunctures and configurations they reveal that are not covered in high-modernist or neoliberal reformist agendas. To explain in depth what this failure of state power did produce in the domain of agricultural labor, I now turn to a specific instance, or event, I came across during my fieldwork in 2016.

In many respects, 2016 was a peculiar year for the tomato harvest in Basilicata. Heavy September rains prevented the few available machines to enter the fields. As usual, tomatoes in Basilicata were harvested quite late in comparison to neighboring Foggia (Puglia) because of higher altitudes and, thus, a slower ripening. The industrial processing plants in Salerno had established their usual price fork at the beginning of the season to determine the conditions of production, so farmers were trying as best they could to anticipate their output. In contrast to Emilia-Romagna, in Basilicata farmers use their own planting machines, their own harvesting equipment, and their own groups of laborers for the harvest. "When the planting season starts in May, one or two workers are enough to do the job," one farmer confessed to me. "But when in September it all comes together, it becomes a slaughterhouse [*un macello*]. . . . Especially when it rains, things are even worse, because you need to find your workers immediately [to harvest the crops]."

In this dramatic context, the slow response of regional authorities in setting up the seasonal labor camps raised even sharper critiques than usual: where would the laborers needed to pick tomatoes be found on such short notice? While some migrant workers had been flocking together again in the different ghettos since early June, the decision of Borgo San Pietro's mayor to evict the ghetto situated in his municipality resulted in an unprecedented concentration of workers in San Giuseppe, in the vicinity of Borgo San Nicola. This concentration of workers further strengthened the grip of the local *caporale* organization on the migrant workforce. Assured of a steady flow of manpower, the gang masters made sure that all labor in the fields would pass under their firm control. An audio clip that was circulating in the public media at the time overheard one of the *caporali* talking about contracts to farmers and migrant workers, passing papers around and citing his key assets. Two names continuously were on people's lips: a certain K. and a Mr. M.P. The latter was cited as the owner of a house in front of San Giuseppe that gained notoriety as a central node in the *caporale*'s business of protection. "One day M.P. even came around while we were doing our usual round in the ghetto to offer assistance," one humanitarian worker told me: "He asked us what we were and were not doing around here."[30]

Humanitarian agents noted a certain level of complicity between these labor intermediaries and the local administration, in the sense that M.P. and his aides could continue their illegal activities undisturbed, even though the crime of illegal labor intermediation had passed from an administrative fine to a penal offense in 2016 (see chapter 2). Ironically, the administration also recognized this as a problem. According to one councilor I interviewed, "the owner [of the land on which the ghetto is situated] clearly agrees with this situation. . . . Some say people are even paying rent. . . .. But I ask myself: what are the police doing? Remember, it's not the first time we see this happening. . . . But why don't they organize a roundup, why don't they go there and shut the place down?" Meanwhile, the humanitarian organization that was providing its social and legal assistance to migrant workers in the area kept encouraging ghetto occupants to move to the official labor camp in Borgo San Nicola.

One major problem in getting workers to move to this official camp infrastructure was the distance between the camp and the workplace. If not picked up by the drivers working for the *caporali*, day laborers had to cycle or walk for hours to reach the fields, often to discover that their place had already been taken by someone else. In their annual report, the medical urgency group MEDU furthermore denounced the poor hygienic conditions in the temporary labor camp:

> The standards and the location of the reception facility do not seem to fully respond to the actual needs of foreign workers. From the visit carried out on 12 September [2016] by the MEDU team, a series of critical issues emerged in relation to the facilities available to the guests of the center . . . : some essential services are missing, including the distribution of sheets, pillows, and blankets for the cots; there is no infirmary or health worker who can deal with emergency situations. The staff is made up of volunteers and operators of the Italian Red Cross, but cultural mediators and social workers with specific knowledge on immigration and labor rights are absent. (MEDU 2017, 7; my translation)

As usual, the Red Cross volunteers blocked information about the management of this public site. Whenever associations or NGOs asked to obtain what were essentially public data—for example the number of registered occupants, or available cookers—they met the silence of the Red Cross and the task force. At the end of September, the regional government in Potenza finally communicated the number of 280 workers who had presumably visited the center—clearly a mirage of the total number who annually came down to Basilicata to harvest. In November 2016, the Red Cross decided to close the camp. Several inhabitants protested in front of the gates against this situation, saying that their promised residency papers had been refused by the town administration. Once again, humanitarian agents and the public media denounced this situation as a spiteful abuse of power. In a widely circulated report in November 2016, the popular news outlet *Striscia la Notizia* (Break the news) provided testimony to the anger of African workers in Borgo San Pietro after their forced eviction from the labor camp. Demanding an explanation, one humanitarian agent received the response from the task force's president that the regional government had to check first whether they weren't dealing with "infiltrators."[31]

In this climate of mutual suspicion, I tried to form a firmer idea of how the humanitarian agents who claimed to protect the rights of exploited migrants connected their narratives and practices to the wider security environment that the new *caporalato* and asylum legislation had meant to establish. How did humanitarian values become so intermingled with the politics of border securitization in the context of contemporary agri-food supply chains? A critique I had often heard was that humanitarian emergency assistance in this context consolidated the exclusion of migrant workers from local society, since organizations concentrated their efforts in the ghettos and not in town or in the fields. Reaching the offices of one NGO, I assisted a conversation between two humanitarian agents and a Burkinabè worker who, so it appeared, had obtained his driving license through the organization's assistance. One agent suspected that the worker was acting as a *caporale*. "You have to be good [*devi fare il bravo*]," one of them said, while the other agent kept asking questions about the worker's whereabouts: "Who do you work for? . . . Is the van you drive actually yours?" The Burkinabè worker looked visibly nervous as he was driven literally into the corner of the room. "I still have a doubt about the use of this license," concluded one of the agents. Smiling at me, he faced the worker again: "If you're not [convincing us], I will take away your permit." Subsequently, the two agents went on to tell the man that he should get his friends in the ghetto to go to the official labor camps, which, they admitted, hosted not more than eighty people at the time. Given we were in mid-August, this number could not be considered a success. The Burkinabè worker answered, "If you ask me, they should close those places." He continued to say what everyone knew already: that the labor camps were too far away from the fields and that workers were not willing to move there because it made them even more dependent on the *caporali* for their transport (no means of transport were provided by the Red Cross or the regional authorities at the time); and he observed that in the labor camp there were not enough stoves to enable people to cook. He continued, "We need to make a lot of noise [*tanto casino*] to obtain what we need there." The agent answered, "Noooo, you don't need to make a fuss at all. . . . You just need to convince your friends to join you there."

Just how deeply enmeshed the humanitarian intervention in Basilicata was in the securitization of migration I learned a few days later, when I joined the NGO team on one of their tours (*giri*) of the ghettos, as they would call them. In the late afternoon, we left for the ghetto of San Giuseppe in their van, accompanied by a young woman who wanted to do volunteer work with the NGO. During the trip, she told me she still felt a bit disoriented and unprepared. All the people in the van, except the NGO president, were young volunteers from neighboring towns. While driving through the fields, the president of the organization confirmed that this year, tomatoes were maturing more slowly than other years because of an illness that attacked the plant at the root and let it burn as soon as the sunlight became stronger. According to the president, this explained why very few workers had arrived on site. When we pulled up to the ghetto, I noticed several men building shacks; I counted five shower cabins, a restaurant, and several barracks fabricated out of wooden poles and metal sheeting. I also noticed an older man I had met several times before in the ghetto of Borgo San Pietro, where he used to run a shop. But when I made attempts to greet him, he waved me away, answering me in French: "Forget about it, [that place] is gone now."

Turning back to the NGO staff, I noticed that the president had gathered a group of ghetto dwellers around her. She was insistently waving her hands as she repeated the narrative she had already presented to me back in the office: that it is better for them to leave now, that the ghetto would be cleared soon—look at what happened in Borgo San Pietro, she said, referring to the recent eviction and destruction of the ghetto there. They should pack their bags, she said, and go to the reception center in Borgo San Nicola and register there. I moved away, toward a young ghetto occupant who visibly was not convinced by the president's discourse: "You are police," he said in Italian to me and another NGO agent who had just joined us. "What do you mean?" the agent responded. "Can you not read?" He pointed to his name tag with the name of the humanitarian project. The young man repeated his judgment, visibly unconvinced. Amusingly, he went back to work on constructing his barrack. This encounter clearly confirmed the impression I had been having for a while: instead of offering humanitarian support, the main purpose of the NGO intervention had become the channeling of population movements toward the official labor camps and away from the informal space of the ghetto.

Just as were leaving the ghetto, another van entered. Two women stepped out. "Nigerians," said one agent, whisperingly. Though the agents knew that a brothel was operative in the ghetto, they would avoid talking about prostitution in the women's presence. "Prostitution is very common here," the president told me later in the car, "because it is normal for them." She said another colleague of hers who worked in the same sector saw girls of African descent sell their bodies at the age of twelve or thirteen years. The same colleague told her that, in a project she ran to help girls break free from the prostitution rings, she observed that victims of human trafficking would stay on board of the project for two or three months, but then most of them ended up on the street again, "because they realize that with such [sex] work you earn much more with much less effort."

Besides the obvious gender stereotyping that was going on in the NGOs and which associated female presence in the ghetto exclusively with sex work rather than the wider economy of intimacy that characterizes life there,[32] the situation I witnessed at the local NGO offices confirmed to me what Heller and Pezzani (2016) call the humanitarian security dynamics that unfolded in the Mediterranean in the aftermath of the Libyan crisis. In line with the wider shift toward a securitization of migration, humanitarian agencies assumed a role that became increasingly associated with population control, state repression, and bureaucratic power (see also Ticktin 2017). They did so by imposing bureaucratic procedures that aimed to insert the migrants' movements into a system of state oversight operated by the Task Force on Migration. And they justified this treatment by insisting on the migrants' inferiority as hapless victims and vulnerable noncitizens. Humanitarian agencies and state bureaucrats continued to represent migrant workers as bodies that needed to be saved: being both needing and less (or "not yet") civilized Others, the migrants needed to be channeled and directed through a modern and efficient bureaucratic infrastructure that would ensure their inclusion in the state's territorial system of rules and laws, and in Italian society. At the same time, they persistently viewed migrants' rescue as a function of bureaucratic power that was defined predominantly in technical terms. As Irus Braverman highlights in another context, of the Palestinian-Israeli border, the technologies that are being depicted as a "more human" and "more civilized" way to manage human flows in fact thus become part of a progressive effort to normalize the violence that the process of adverse incorporation inherently generates. What is important to remember here is that the formal, bureaucratic infrastructures of state administration cannot sustain themselves as exclusive technologies of control. Rather, the threat of violence is always implicit, particularly in the way formal, material infrastructures literally push the boundaries of control toward an outside space that is located off limits, beyond the protective realm of official state infrastructures (Braverman 2011, 267). This double mechanism—of bureaucratic power and often implicit (and at times explicit) physical violence against those subjects the state identified as the objective of humanitarian rescue—led to what I would call a progressive securitization of labor in Basilicata's agrarian economy. I see this securitization conglomerating around three key elements: bureaucratization, militarization, and labor coercion. Let me briefly turn to these elements before analyzing the impact these left on Basilicata's agrarian landscape.

At first sight, the mechanism of state control that the Task Force on Migration instituted could be seen as a classic case of state territorialization: in his elaboration on Michel Foucault, James Scott explains state territorialization as the attempt on the part of state administrations to control the movement of people who, for various reasons, escape the oppression of state-making projects like slavery, conscription, taxes, *corvée* labor, epidemics, and warfare (Scott 2009, ix). A recurrent term in this context is that of floating populations (*populations flottantes*), which designates those mobile forms of life that state government has difficulty capturing and controlling because of their ability to evade taxation and bordering policies (see chapter 2). One could also read the attempts of the Italian state to make rural migrant laborers visible to the state as a desire to incorporate previously uncontrolled populations and economic activity into its sovereign realm. Yet while historically the mobilization of state power in Southern Italy's agrarian economy could be observed to reflect this logic of capitalist enclosures as a dispossession of the peasantry's means of production, the instruments of neoliberal governmentality have clearly ceased to share this ambition to spatially fix floating populations and their assumed wealth in the confines of the colonial plantation economy. Instead, the territorialization of labor occurs nowadays through a combination of bureaucratic mechanisms that define the boundaries of migrants' legitimate presence on the territory, and an expanding infrastructure of surveillance that crosses the boundaries of the state's traditional domain of action. This makes it all the more important to investigate the active borderwork that goes into bounding such mobile labor as a complex, laborious process that involves not just state agents but a whole range of agencies and sources of authority. Where humanitarian agencies visibly work toward securing state visibility—to use James Scott's paradigm—state officials remain noticeably complicit with illegal gang masters and their grip on the local economy even as they continue to condemn them formally.

Rather than seeing this blurred authority as a "failure" of government schemes, however, I suggest we read its apparently messy effects as signs of a changing spatial optic (see also T. M. Li 2005). This active policing of labor market boundaries reproduced what Nicola Phillips (2013) calls the "adverse incorporation" of informal activity into the realm of industrial production: the way unrecorded labor is actively subcontracted, outsourced, and informalized into different allied arrangements with industrial development, while at the same time it is formally excluded, made invisible, and precarious.[33] Two associated dynamics have precipitated this adverse incorporation of migrant workers into the formal capitalist domain.

On the one hand, the growing concentration of migrant workers in the rural, nonresidential area of the ghetto basically precludes them from possessing any palpable political rights: despite their active, cyclical employment in agriculture, they cannot claim formal protection from the state as long as they do not formalize their territorial residence through the *permesso di soggiorno*—a procedure that needs to also involve their employer, on whose benevolence their territorial status consequently depends. On the other hand, workers who do claim visibility from the state—to be recognized as territorial residents, to claim access to social services and so on—are forced to accept the system of humanitarian surveillance, which channels their movement through an increasingly militarized and centralized logistical infrastructure and thus takes hold of their mobile subjectivity in a quite intransigent manner. As they are unable to renew their paperwork outside the space of this humanitarian surveillance, it is fair to say that this preclusion *ex ante* of the migrants' territorial belonging in the technology of the *permesso di soggiorno* forms indeed a legalized blackmail that serves not to stop the arrival of so-called illegal migrants, but to coerce their labor and exercise power over them. In what indeed started to look much like a war on migration through infrastructural means in the European Mediterranean (Garelli and Tazzioli 2016), itinerant workers remained increasingly trapped in a deadly triangle between their unstable means of survival, their need to secure a livelihood, and their "exceptional" humanitarian status—all of which resulted in their increasing impermanence as laborers in the agrarian frontier. Finally, this form of labor securitization also highly depends on the persistence of informal forms of discipline and coercion that continue to be implemented by the *caporalato* "industry," as regional authorities kept calling the work of labor intermediaries who actively maintain the connections between workers, entrepreneurs, and public authority. In the absence of alternative trajectories of formalization, the migrants' existential need for obtaining formal employment and territorial residence still makes them explicitly dependent on the services of the *caporali*, who enthusiastically fill this gap generated by the state's bureaucratic territoriality.

On a wider scale, I emphasized previously that a central problem regarding the exploitation of agricultural workers regards the cost of social reproduction, more specifically of the way in which the intersection between a repressive legal climate and the deliberate outsourcing of labor market organization to illegal intermediaries generates a situation whereby the workers and their wider social networks bear the cost of reproducing their own labor force. In the next section, I will provide further detail to this observation before drawing some preliminary conclusions from this chapter.

The Cost of Social Reproduction

A more systematic analysis of the factors of agricultural production and reproduction in Basilicata's tomato district indeed reveals that the main problem concerning the social reproduction of Basilicata's agricultural economy does not concern so much the concentration of *caporalato* criminality in the migrant ghettos, but rather the lack of social integration of an increasingly diversified workforce. While looking up official employment data,[34] I find further confirmation of this hypothesis: according to the *centri per l'impiego* (CPI)—the labor bureaus that basically serve as formal intermediaries with the agricultural firms—the fifteen hundred to two thousand migrant laborers employed officially in Basilicata each year for the tomato harvest predominantly (around 70–75 percent of the laborers) report one to two contractual employments for a period of four months. This is an important indication of labor market integration: if workers moved constantly between employers, this percentage would be much lower. Instead, the CPI reveal that workers often return to the same workplace. In the municipality of Palazzo San Gervasio, also evident during these years is an exponential growth in the working days of extra- and neo-EU laborers (in the case of non-EU workers, the growth is 64 percent). This shows a growing stabilization of employment relationships.

The main disturbing factor concerns the contrast between actual versus official employment. Only a very small percentage of migrant workers exceed a contract period of sixty days. Migrant employment in agriculture remains characterized by a high level of precarity: 54 percent declare a contract of a maximum of thirty days, so below the minimum established to be entitled to unemployment income. And only 25 percent of workers declare to have a permanent employment throughout the year. These numbers reflect again the lack of market integration of the migrant workforce at a micro scale: in case of an employment longer than a month, workers obtain the right to unemployment benefits and to a pension contribution; in the absence of such a contract, they even face difficulties in renewing their residency papers. So rather than highlighting the need of having a secure place to stay, these data confirm a systematic exploitation of migrant agricultural workers based on the persistence of economic informality: being employed formally for a limited time, workers find themselves in a permanent gray zone where their rights are neither claimed nor implemented.

A second factor of importance I find is the discrepancy between the official and the actual place of stay of seasonal workers. One must note the difference in Italian law between the official residence (*residenza*), or the principal seat that makes people legible to the state, and the domicile (*domicilio*), which can be temporary. Workers usually feel quite free to accurately declare their domicile, as this is not tied to any official relation to the state apart from their temporary employment. Of all the workers officially registered at the CPI during the harvesting season in 2015–2016, a vast majority declare to have their domicile in the main *comuni* of the tomato district. A striking element that emerges from these declarations is that a large majority of seasonal workers do not live in the urban center of the *comuni*: a total of 78 percent declare to live in the rural periphery. Interestingly, most of them indicate their temporary domicile as either "ghetto" or *campagna* (countryside). A further 7 percent declare to live in the two temporary migrant reception centers, which—as I explained before—mainly serve to get migrant paperwork renewed but do not serve as the main habitat in the area.

A final factor I discovered concerns the contrast between the place of stay and the place of employment of seasonal workers. While a vast majority of employment contracts concern agricultural enterprises located in Lavello (over three hundred, in comparison to around one hundred for the other municipalities), most seasonal workers declare to live in other *comuni* (around five hundred in Palazzo and Venosa, compared to just under two hundred in Lavello). In crude terms, this means that Palazzo and Venosa take on the social reproduction cost of the labor invested in firms in Lavello. This appears in contrast to the interpretation of labor unions and humanitarian organizations that ascribe the informality of labor to the seasonality of the workforce in the region: contrary to all-year workers, they claim, seasonal laborers prefer to stay in the ghetto, where they can cut corners and remain invisible to the state. What emerges instead is a structural market dis-integration of these workers by agricultural entrepreneurs, who prefer to subcontract their labor reproduction costs to the informal space of the ghetto, while reaping the benefits of migrant precarity through the imposition of so-called gray labor—that is, the temporary employment of workers who remain secluded from social and political rights.

The (anonymized) mayors' testimonies, triangulated with the data from the CPI and the Italian pension fund INPS, confirm quite clearly the already observed adverse incorporation of workers in the Vulture–Alto Bradano region. On a micro scale, these data contrast quite sharply with the dominant perception among trade unionists, entrepreneurs, and regional authorities that seasonal workers are generally reluctant to seek their protection because of the workers' lack of "social capital." Data from my study show the contrary: workers seek contracts; and they are embedded in rural society—even if mostly informally. But they remain officially underrepresented and marginalized compared to their Italian counterparts (remembering that Italian employees in agriculture represent 30 percent of the official workforce but obtain 70 of the remuneration: Osservatorio Placido Rizzotto 2014).

Based on these findings, one can firmly conclude that because of their lack of official market integration, seasonal workers employed in Basilicata's tomato economy are persistently caught between the hammer and the anvil of their fragile political status and a necessity to earn a living. On the one hand, the numbers, and testimonies I shared here, clearly show how the *caporale* figure remains a kingpin in a system of violent labor intermediation that starts with the deliberate withdrawal of state protection and ends with an active abandonment by humanitarian and administrative institutions. In this situation of active withdrawal, *caporalato* has practically supplanted the state-sanctioned mediation between labor and capital that existed up until the early 1990s. While the CPIs have become mere registration offices of migrants' official employment contracts, the *caporale* fulfils the role of coercing and disciplining the labor force through an explicit violence that is implicitly backed by the state.

The role of humanitarian organizations, on the other hand, mainly has become that of policing human mobility. They are there to make sure that migrants flow toward the official accommodation where agents of the Red Cross supervise and discipline their presence on the territory. Interestingly, recent labor legislation in Italy has further consolidated this humanitarian role in security, notably by framing of labor accommodation as a logistical necessity: article 9, paragraph 1 of the anti-*caporale* legislation (voted in November 2016) says that in order to improve the working conditions of agricultural laborers, measures will be adopted for their "logistic accommodation and worker support," including "experimental methods" of labor placement that will be territorially implemented (see also chapter 1). Rather than laborers being considered political subjects with aspirations, grievances, and rights, therefore, the deliberate withdrawal of the state in the domain of agricultural labor market organization has transformed those laborers into mere working bodies that have to be simultaneously channeled, secured, serviced, and accommodated outside the "normal" networks of civil society, and inside the ghettos, camps and abandoned sites that continue to be located on the margins of this expanding capitalist agro-economy.

The Territory of Migrant Labor

The way migrant labor is incorporated in Basilicata's firms visibly shows how formal development policies—in this case of the Task Force on Migration—reproduce the informal as a constitutive outside space that continues to produce economic value but remains deliberately unaccounted for in official state planning. If taken from a teleological, modernizing perspective, the formalization of agricultural labor can in no way be called a success, as informality continues to be the dominant paradigm in agriculture. However, the way this formalization process unfolded also demonstrates the deep market fundamentalism that characterizes state intervention in contemporary rural development.

A key element for understanding how extractivism persists as a form of labor exploitation is the way it is socially and culturally reproduced through operations of unsettlement. On the one hand, the instrument of state territoriality can be observed to act as an intersectional boundary that imposes a strict hierarchy of "regular" and "irregular" statuses (notably of the resident, nonresident, refugee, asylum seeker, illegal migrant worker) as well as a combination of social criteria (specifically of race and gender) that divide and weaken the migrant workforce politically. This boundary produces what Mezzadra and Neilson (2013) call a "differential inclusion" of the workforce: through the intersecting technologies of bureaucratic power and humanitarian management, workers are actively integrated into the national labor market as divided, fragmented subjects. Following Nicola Phillips (2013) and Francisco Blanco Brotons (2021), I prefer the term "adverse" incorporation because it highlights the deeper transformation of geographic scales in the process of labor securitization I have tried to make explicit in this chapter.

In the aftermath of the Mediterranean migration "emergency" of 2011–2014, the increasing visibility of migrants' structural, while precarious, contribution to economic wealth motivated a joint regional response in Basilicata to address what its stakeholders saw as the root causes of the migrants' socioeconomic vulnerability. Instituted in 2014, the Task Force on Migration officially centered its activity on the double axis of humanitarian emergency and border security. To reach its public aim of containing the impact of illegal labor mediation in the domain of agricultural production, the task force elaborated a plan to formalize the migrants' labor and housing facilities. Through the instruments of temporary labor camps and territorial residency papers (the *permessi di soggiorno*), the task force (composed of the regional administration, humanitarian organizations, and representatives of the main labor union FLAI-CGIL) agreed on their joint objective of channeling laborers logistically in their "temporary" labor condition by actively destroying their mobile settlements in cooperation with local sanitary services, the national *procura* (prosecutor), and police forces. While these attempts remained partially a failure—in the sense that many workers kept turning up in the ghettos regardless of these systematic repressions—it is important to note the compromise that the task force worked out at a local level: without upsetting agricultural firms, it succeeded in bypassing the authority of resistant *comuni* and civil society organizations that continued to oppose these plans. At the same time, the task force consolidated the economy of *caporale* labor mediation as a constitutive "outside" sphere to formal agrarian development in the sense that it did not abolish the gang masters' central function in the agrarian economy, but rather displaced the concern over its impact to the imagined space of illegality, insalubrity, and uncivility of the migrant ghetto.

One could argue that securitization of the migrant workforce in Basilicata ended up generating a discrepancy between those who profit and those who invest in the reproduction of the labor force that is needed to produce and harvest the fruits of the land. Since Basilicata, and Italy more widely, continued to benefit from the growth of a migrant workforce to fill the gaps of massive proletarization of workers in agriculture, the labor used in agri-food production remained highly precarious and disposable. Next to the already mentioned difficulties in obtaining the necessary land and water resources, farmers in the region complained that it was indeed harder and harder to keep their head above water, between the various mafia infiltrations in the supply chains and the illegal intermediaries who control and coerce the seasonal labor force. The only remaining resource at hand to confront these many critical factors, they kept repeating, was to cut the cost of labor. In that sense, the deep reliance of local farmers on the services of organized crime constituted a public secret among agriculturalists and the local administration. Both silently acknowledged that nothing structural could be done to avoid illegal labor mediation in this case. "The problem," the councilor of agriculture of Borgo San Pietro said in a public meeting I attended on August 25, 2016, "is that many times, agricultural employers do not even know their workers." So, the only thing that unites them is the phone number of the gang master. Other administrators disagreed: "In my opinion, many workers already know the farmers they work for . . . at least this is my hypothesis. . . . But from there to go on and tell that this one is a *caporale*, just because he goes out more often to the piazza or speaks better Italian, I don't agree. . . . I honestly don't see all this slavery, I don't see all these things, and I don't think I want to see them, just for a matter of personal conscience."[35]

Next to the outright racism that characterized state intervention in this domain, what continued to align policies was a predominant, Cartesian template of modern progress and individual emancipation that had underpinned rural development in Basilicata since the late 1800s. Public authorities overtly neglected the evidently unequal ways in which local agricultural enterprises in the South kept being integrated in neoliberal market structures. Instead, their discourse involved a historical retrodiction of some sorts, a speaking back to history through what its narrators interpreted as a sequence of modern progress. I recall the municipal councilor's reference to African workers as lagging "a hundred years" in modern development, a gap that could only be filled with the imposition of public force (*forza pubblica*).[36] Next to assigning exclusive responsibility to those who are deemed lacking the qualifications of modernity (a strategy that can be defined as "blaming the victims": Howard and Forin 2019), what prevailed in this discourse was the perception of modern progress in the form of building blocks, of "social capital" and its associated medicine of market integration. But such a template was never meant to reflect the complex changes that society is or was going through. Rather, it serves to bolster the dominant idea of what constitutes an appropriate distribution of power in the spheres of "nature," the market, the state, and civil society as presumably "separate" realms of social interaction—a separation that lies at the foundation of rural capitalism in the Mediterranean. At the end of the day, the adverse condition of the agricultural workforce along a line of "not yet" civilized, "not yet" emancipated emigrants and indigenous communities who continued to form the backbone of Southern Italy's agricultural economy seemed to contribute to a rather more important unequal redistribution of the cost of social reproduction in what most Italians erroneously continued to interpret as an ongoing migration emergency. That rural workers had to be placed into the waiting room of history, so to speak, was felt as an acceptable price in order to maintain the historical balance of forces that keeps Mediterranean rural capitalism in place as a dominant mode of production.

IMPERMANENT TERRITORIES

The previous chapter sought to analyze the regional government of Basilicata's frenetic attempts to tie migrant labor to the land while at the same time excluding workers from rural society. This chapter takes a complementary look into migrant ghettos as emerging rural infrastructures. As I have tried to make clear, such infrastructures are an essential component of the agrarian economy of cash crop production in the Italian South but are also deliberately excluded from the formal social, political, and economic sphere. Thus, while migrant ghettos continue to be regarded in contemporary development planning as "shameful" places that need sanitation and redeeming, they are also important relational spaces grounded in the necessity to organize lives in mobility.

To explain the dynamic tension between the inclusion and exclusion of migrant laborers from rural society, I return to the two key terms I introduced in the introduction: "bordering infrastructures" and "natural racialization." The terminology of bordering infrastructures helps me to explain the important sociomaterial dimension of migrants' included exclusion in contemporary agricultural supply chains. Again, infrastructures are physical networks that facilitate and direct flows. In Larkin's words (2013, 329), they are material in that they are "matter that enable the movement of other matter," but they are also defined by their social relations, as infrastructures necessarily emerge through social arrangements and processes. What this terminology brings to the fore is not so much the structural foundations of what, in Marxist terms, are defined as the social relations of production and reproduction (foundations I have discussed at length in the previous chapter). Rather, it seeks to highlight the material-discursive "cuts" that actively co-constitute the agrarian frontier as an assemblage of intra-acting physical and social forces (see Barad 2003; Squire 2014). Indirectly, this approach also corresponds to Nick Blomley's observation that the production of territory requires conscious "cuts" in the processual networks through which social spaces are produced. Like Neil Smith, Blomley does not see "space" as something that is situated outside our social and political life, but is actively folded into and produced through forms of interaction and relationality: "Space, then, is always in the process of becoming, as relations unfold. It is not a container, but rather is contained in networks. It is not a coherent system of discriminations and categorizations but is itself expressive of multiplicity and flow" (Blomley 2010, 205). Read in this way, territorial spaces and their technologies of rule are only one form of geography, a form that is actively engaged in a consequential production and parsing of space. While this form is clearly a powerful one—as I have tried to show through the example of the *permesso di soggiorno* and the boundary between "informal" ghettos and "formal" labor camps—it should be clear that these territorial cuts do not efface prior patterns of use. On the contrary, their attempt to channel and control flows and relationality always opens up new tensions and negotiations.

The terminology of natural racialization allows me to describe the specific manners in which territorial infrastructures are effectively "naturalizing" a racialized humanity into a stratigraphic order of "not yet," "not quite," and "nonbelonging" subjects, with all the violent struggles and negotiations that this dynamic entails. As I will try to show, the "Black spaces" that emerge in this context thus need to be understood as a direct result and a desired outcome of the politics of separation carried forward by today's bordering infrastructures. As places that are both materially and discursively singled out as standing somehow "outside" the perimeters of civility, migrant ghettos tend to reproduce migrant workers as "bodies-out-of-place" in a political ecology that is quite significantly charted along racial lines (see also Pallister-Wilkins 2022). In my view, the politics of natural racialization reflects a kind of slow, incremental violence that gradually permeates the lives of marginalized workers through dynamic spaces, of bodies, ecosystems, and natural resources (Nixon 2011; see also Amira 2021). But whereas such slow violence can be seen as a debilitating mechanism that actively deforms the spatial characteristics that make a place livable, it is also actively remolded and contested through practices of what I would call *ruinification*—or the poetic repurposing of ruined sources of life. Returning to the abandoned sites where migrant workers reconnect, sustain, and reproduce their alternative ways of life, I ask myself what kinds of life can emerge and thrive in the ruins of capitalism. Aligning myself with the idea that in "a global state of precarity, we don't have choices other than looking for life in this ruin" (Bear at al. 2015, 6), I tend to take this invitation quite literally while looking for the ways of life that are actively rooted and routed in the abandoned nodes of the Mediterranean agrarian frontier. Here I discover that abandonment needs to be indeed interpreted in an active sense, as a life on the edges, where the contours of what constitutes the human and the nonhuman are given new form.

In the first section of this chapter, I will describe the politics surrounding labor migration flows in the Alto Bradano area from the mid-1990s until today, to then dedicate a more ethnographic reflection toward the racial dynamics of exclusion that have underpinned, and continue to underpin, these policies and containment efforts. The starting point of my analysis is what Alessandra Corrado and others call the globalization of the Italian countryside. As I explained above, the redrawing of agricultural supply chains, combined with a shift in geopolitical forces, contributed in the 1980s to the intensification of migration flows across the Mediterranean, in particular to a sharp increase of West African migrations to the Southern Italian peninsula. In correspondence with the emergence of a new, corporate, food regime, these emigrants ended up lending their labor to Italy's agri-food producing firms. While the increasingly restrictive border regimes that were progressively conceived at the European level did in no way stop these migration flows, they did nonetheless foster a selective mechanism of enforcement and adverse incorporation of the migrant workforce in the national labor market. In a recent analysis, Caruso and Corrado (2022, 25–132) observe two complementary trends I have also noted in Basilicata: on the one hand, they write, the increasingly diversified production of agri-food farms has contributed to a growing stabilization of migrant agricultural labor contracts in the area as agricultural production now takes place all year round. On the other hand, the authors note a rapid shift in the ethnic composition and stratification of the agricultural labor force from a predominantly EU "communitarian" (Romanian, Polish, and Bulgarian) makeup toward an African (Maghreb, West African) preponderance. Yet while this African presence can be noticed progressively in the agro-towns and villages, both in terms of the demographic composition of the agricultural labor force and the social fabric of rural society more broadly, migrant workers with African backgrounds continue to suffer a fundamental exclusion and separation from Italian society that cannot be cast simply in legal terms. In this chapter, therefore, I want to highlight the racializing dynamics that underpin this persistent separation from an infrastructural point of view.

A Separate(d) Place

In late August of 2016 I meet with Antonio Cialdone, the mayor of the small town of Borgo San Rocco.[1] He asks me to go down with him to one of the abandoned farmhouses in his *comune* where a group of day workers has asked for his help. When I arrive, Antonio briefly introduces me to Mamadou. Mamadou says he is from Burkina Faso. He comes to harvest tomatoes every year in Basilicata with the same group of workers. We set off together in the late evening with my car. After a fifteen-minute drive, Mamadou tells us to take a right turn and wait in front of a metal barrier. The night is dark, and it is starting to get cold. Mamadou makes a phone call. After a few minutes, three dim lights slowly descend from the hilltop in our direction. The lights come closer, and a couple of faces appear in front of the car. One man opens the gate for us. Carefully, I continue my drive up the mud track. We reach a small patch where people are silently gathered around a fire. There are around fifty men: some of them are quite young, like Mamadou (who told me he is twenty-seven); others are older. Around the patch I notice a small farmhouse and a warehouse that appears to serve as a mosque. Before entering the building, men hang their coats on the wall. After that they kneel and start contemplating their night prayers. All of this appears like a slow daily ritual. After exiting the building, some men move closer to us. We shortly exchange greetings.

Then the mayor starts talking. He says he has heard that the ASP (*aziende pubblica di servizi alla persona*: the local health service) has visited the farmhouse to verify hygienic conditions. He asks the men if this is correct. They confirm and add that the *carabinieri* have come as well, and that they have given a deadline for them to leave. All this information is translated into Italian by Mamadou. The mayor tells them he knows about the situation. He adds that, luckily, the ASP is working under his responsibility, and he can guarantee that no one is going to be chased from the premises for now. The men explode in joy. The mayor says he is happy. But he adds that he has only limited powers. If at some point the regional authorities decide to evict them from the farmhouse, there is nothing he can do about it. The men nod in agreement. Some of them have already left to go on with their activities. After a short chat, Mamadou accompanies us again to the gate, and we set off on the road back to town.

Later in his office, Antonio tells me that he does not at all agree with the regional policy to force people to the reception centers. He says the head of the Task Force on Migration has personally asked him to find the landlords of abandoned farmhouses and force them to send the squatters away. "I find this totally absurd," he shouts, adding that "I will not tear down any farmhouse. Because the consequence will be that they [the migrant workers] will end up on the street [*in mezzo alla strada*]. Assuming they do go to [the reception center]," he adds, "this will open the gates to criminality. Because over there, they have nothing on their hands." Instead, the mayor says, "we need to place these men in the condition to work." In his view, this would mean organizing a decent transport service to and from the workplace. And it would mean enforcing a decent workday, "instead of spending fourteen hours a day picking tomatoes. . . . For us to say that we are a civilized country," he concludes, "we need to organize a fund to renovate the abandoned farmhouses of the agrarian reform project and accommodate these workers decently."[2]

During his interview with me, the mayor shares a plan he has proposed with some local associations to offer houses for rent to migrant workers, instead of forcing them to stay at the temporary reception centers. Five young workers from Burkina Faso have already decided to permanently reside in the town. In any case, he adds, his town is practically empty, as most of the inhabitants have emigrated abroad. Of the remaining residents, few young people are willing to stay in Borgo San Rocco. The mayor tells me his two daughters live in the North of Italy, "and I know for sure that they will never turn back." The problem is that the emigrants do not want to give their homes away to migrant workers. Part of the reason has to do with prejudice: Italians who have emigrated fear that these foreign men will ruin their family houses. But in Borgo San Rocco, the situation seems slightly different, the mayor tells me: lots of migrants are already living in town. The town's councilor for social affairs has joined us, and he adds that of the sixteen hundred residents in town, seven hundred are immigrants. Most of them are from Romania. "They are all hard workers," he confirms, "and they don't cause any problems." "But obviously," the mayor adds, "you imagine it to be difficult for a population already suffering from unemployment and the absence of state support to accept that there may be people in their municipality who may take subsidies, who may have a higher living standard than they do. . . . Therefore, I find it crucial to avoid having them [the migrant workers] roam around aimlessly [*vadano a zonzo*]." He adds, "The most important problem here is work."

The situation in Borgo San Rocco is indeed revealing of the rapidly changing social demography of rural Basilicata, and rural Italy more generally, over the past ten years (see Caruso and Corrado 2022). In practice, Basilicata's foreign workforce has changed its composition from a presumably floating, migrant population toward a population of immigrant residents, predominantly of Eastern European, and nowadays also African, origin. *Comuni* like Palazzo San Gervasio, Venosa, Montemilone, and Lavello—which form the core of the tomato district—are undergoing a steady demographic reconfiguration that is in great part determined by capital's needs. On the one hand, farming enterprises benefit from a persistent dispossession of the labor force to advance their economic growth. As I wrote in the previous chapter, the active exclusion of migrant workers from the formal economic sphere generates a wrong impression of "seasonality" of a workforce that in practice has become a stable factor in rural South Italy. On the other hand, the permanent sense of emergency that tends to characterize migration and border management in Italy, and Europe more generally since the Libya crisis, has generated an artificial gap in agricultural labor power, in the sense that mobile, laboring bodies are now predominantly viewed through a lens of humanitarian intervention and border security. These developments form only the tail of a much longer process of adverse incorporation that began in the early 1990s.

When the first migrant workers started to arrive in Basilicata in the mid-1990s to work as harvesters around Irsina (on the border with Puglia), their presence went largely unnoticed. This changed when in the early 2000s some local volunteers decided to occupy a vacant building in the periphery of one of the *comuni* to host workers who, once again called by local employers, had decided to move toward Palazzo San Gervasio but were unable to find a flat or house to rent.[3] Between 1999 and 2008, the municipality acted as the formal sponsor of this site, which nevertheless remained under the autonomous direction of the migrant workers who returned there every year to pick tomatoes and olives between August and November. Gradually, however, official pressures started rising. Defining the camp as the "*bancomat* [cash machine] of the farmers," the regional administrator for migration, Pietro Simonetti, publicly associated the site with illegal activities of drug trafficking and gang mastering. In 2009, a conflict erupted in the camp between two groups of workers after some *capineri* had started to monopolize the water supplies there, which caused some resentment among the workers. Though peace returned quickly to the informal camp, some migrant workers decided nonetheless to move away and set up their temporary premises in some abandoned warehouses across the border, in neighboring Puglia.

For the workers who decided to remain at the camp, their fate turned out to be more problematic. During a substantial police intervention, national security forces and *carabinieri* arrested all the people present. But they released them quickly again when they noticed the majority had resident papers. Seeing in this action another sign of deeply rooted institutional racism against migrant workers in the area since the troubles at Villa Literno (see chapter 1), a local antiracist collective under the lead of the Osservatorio Migranti Basilicata decided to file a complaint at the tribunal of Melfi (according to the *Gazzetta del Mezzogiorno* of September 3, 2010). Despite the protest of several associations and the center-left Democratic Party representatives (which at the time still represented the political majority in Basilicata), the regional administration decided to enforce the closure of the communal labor camp during the next four years. This had the immediate effect of dispersing the few remaining foreign laborers to the surrounding countryside. Just like in Rosarno and Villa Literno before, administrators felt increasingly reluctant to provide any form of official accommodation to migrant workers, as their presence was increasingly narrated as a security risk.

In the autumn of 2010, a group of African workers decided to remain on the camp premises despite its official closure after the end of the harvesting season. After that, dynamics accelerated quickly. Fearing "another Rosarno" (*Gazetta del Mezzogiorno*, August 4, 2010) regional authorities planned to open a temporary labor camp in the vicinity of Borgo San Nicola the next year. While some Burkinabè workers moved toward a former *riforma* settlement in the municipality of Borgo San Pietro, a smaller, Sudanese group occupied an abandoned farmhouse toward the border with Puglia. In both locations, the presence of Black African workers generated growing resistance from local communities, resulting in the forced eviction and destruction of these precarious habitats. In Borgo San Pietro, a restaurant owner helped workers move back to the evicted camp in the vicinity of Borgo San Nicola with his van, and, when they returned to Borgo San Pietro, he threatened them at gunpoint. Dispersed by fear, the workers then decided to occupy a hamlet in the vicinity. As the controversy came under increasing media attention, newspapers and other national media denounced living conditions at the site as inhumane and unhygienic. A fire that destroyed part of the settlement gave final justification to the mayor of Borgo San Pietro to evict the site in 2016.

Despite this active politics of migrant dispersal, however, it is interesting to note that the immigrant population of rural Basilicata did not cease to grow during this same period. In 2017, for example, the demographic registry (*anagrafe*) of Palazzo and Venosa reported, respectively, 400 immigrants among a population of 4,600, and 450 among a total of 12,000 (8.6 percent and 3.75 percent respectively). The same year, Lavello reported 1,100 foreign residents in a population of 13,700 (representing 8 percent). In absolute numbers, these percentages are among the highest in the country (in the North, for instance, Milan counts 14.4 percent immigrant residents, Brescia 10 percent, and Bergamo 8 percent). Though it has largely gone unnoticed, this changing demography of Italy's Southern rurality has produced a significant impact on the functioning of public services and the agrarian economy more generally. During my interview with the mayor of Borgo San Rocco, he made it no secret that his town's public infrastructures—public hospitals and schools in particular—subsisted thanks to the steady immigration of the past years. Without the immigrants, urban infrastructures like schools and hospitals would simply face decay and abandonment because of the lack of state support and citizens to service them. In addition to contributing to local consumption, sending their children to school, using the hospital and the post office—and thus keeping state personnel employed in these services—immigrants also contributed enormously to the local economy through their employment in local firms.

The mayor of another municipality presented his argument in the following way: "By now our classes are made up of twenty to thirty percent of children of foreign origin," he told me. "The problems of segregation we were facing in the early years have more or less vanished now," he added, while praising the multiethnic association with whom the municipality actively planned and implemented the newcomers' social and cultural integration.[4] Significantly, the mayor used the term "immigrants" (*immigrati*) instead of "migrants" (*migranti*). While admitting that during the harvesting season, some workers continued to occupy abandoned buildings here and there, he preferred to envision a longer-term integration through a policy of social housing and formal employment, he said. In contrast to neighboring *comuni*, which live off crops that require low labor input, like wheat and olives, his agro-town had become a major site of industrialized greenhouse production, predominantly of fruit and vegetables, for export to the rest of Europe. This meant farmers needed workers not just occasionally, but the whole year through. Yet, the mayor added, the issue of *caporalato* should not be disregarded. In his municipality, he had made plans to unite the efforts of security and judicial forces to combat illegal hiring in town. Contrasting the dominant perspective of the Task Force on Migration and its insistence on the ghetto as a center of criminality, the mayor added that the organization of illegal hiring in the area was more refined and advanced than we usually assume, as gang masters nowadays work through close relationships of family and kin. Rather than limiting their services to a ghetto, some *caporali* had already established a strong base in the rural towns. That is why the social integration of workers should become a priority for the *comuni*, he concluded. In one of the former *riforma* hamlets, his administration already planned to renovate thirty homes. The mayor also proposed to invest in agricultural innovation by introducing new technical training and equipment. "With these interventions I hope to contribute to a major social integration," he concluded.

Detailed analysis of the factors of agricultural production and reproduction in Basilicata's tomato district indeed point at the lack of social integration of agricultural workers—in the sense that their persistent segmentation and stratification reproduces their adverse incorporation into the rural economy of which they form a central component. In the next section, I will detail the consequences of this adverse incorporation on the reproduction of rural lifeworlds in Basilicata more broadly.

Fragments

As I was trying to map the trajectory of West African labor migration in the Alto Bradano, I met Youssouf Dialo and Karim Boukary, two Bissa Burkinabè workers who had taken up residence in one of the district's municipalities around 2010 (see chapter 1). Karim had a somewhat convoluted migration trajectory, he told me. As a former member of a police force, he had fought in the war between Burkina Faso and Mali in 1985. In the 1990s, he was one of the early rural capitalists who succeeded in setting up his own small plantation in his hometown: a horticultural field he ran in coordination with a local NGO. As I wrote before, the development of Burkina Faso's "peripheral" savanna areas depended to a great extent on two factors: the investment of return migrants engaged in agricultural labor in neighboring Ghana and Ivory Coast, and the development assistance of international organizations implicated in the World Bank's small-cropper program. The development programs and investments were modest, however, and they failed to provide a stable source of subsistence. So, male workers in particular continued to move around cyclically in the search of income. Karim's son worked in Libya, where he engaged in different jobs in construction and the petroleum business. Youssouf instead had grown up in Côte d'Ivoire, "on the plantation," as he said. In the early 2000s, he left and took a boat to Europe, on a perilous journey across the Mediterranean, leaving his wife and daughter behind. Once more, these personal histories showed the highly gendered and racialized patterns through which the Black Mediterranean plantation was unfolding in the context of the migration "crisis" that occupied so much of contemporary European public debate. I first met Youssouf and Karim in the warehouse of a farmer who had earlier helped Youssouf in acquiring his official residency. Youssouf, Karim, my farmer friend and I started our conversation around a regional road map on which I asked them to indicate their trajectories.

"Youssouf, you told me you arrived in [the municipality] in 2009?" I asked. "So where did you live before that?" While looking at the map we laid out on the table, he indicated a point in the middle of the fields: "First in Borgo San Pietro, and then in Borgo San Nicola." I asked him to be more precise. "In 2008, there was another ghetto, not the one we know now, but another one, toward Borgo San Rocco." Youssouf asked my friend the farmer to indicate the road between the different *comuni* on the map. Then he continued: "When you pass in front of [village *x*], you cross a bridge, and then you redirect toward Borgo San Rocco." "So where did you come from to reach this place?" I continued. "Youssouf laughed: "From the camp." In understood he meant the temporary labor migrant reception center that the town administration had given in concession to some local associations at the time. Confirming my interpretation, the farmer completed his sentence: "These guys here received a complaint for the illegal occupation of government premises back in 2009."

Youssouf continued:

> Yes, first we lived there, in the camp. After the tomato harvest, we all went away, toward the ghetto. Then in 2009, we returned, but we found

the gates were closed. We stayed there for a while, but it was difficult to find any employer. So we decided to go to Borgo San Pietro, not the site I indicated here on the map, but to a proper village, where the church is [he indicates the name of the ghetto, in the municipality of Borgo San Pietro]. But we did not stay more than a day over there, because the owner of the restaurant over there, he came to tell us that "no, you don't have a right to be here, because this is the road to my restaurant. If you are here nobody wants to go to my restaurant. . . . I pay my taxes," and so on. "It's not that I don't want you here. I'm not the problem, the problem is the customers." Then he placed all of us and all our stuff in the van, it seems to me ten, eleven people, like that, and he brought us back to the camp. We entered there anyhow, even if the site had not opened *officielle*. We simply had nowhere else to go. Then I went to town, and I asked one NGO worker, and she told us the center would open in August, so we decided to stay. But the time had come to close once again, toward the end of October, beginning of November, like that. And this guy, I can't remember his name, came to tell us the date has arrived we all have to go, but we did not go away.

"Why?" I asked.

"Because we had nowhere else to go. . . . Then at some point all the *carabinieri* of Basilicata came to evacuate us, and we decided to go to the *casa abbandonata*, right to the north of Borgo San Nicola."

After this first meeting, I decided to spend more time with Youssouf and Karim to systematically map the traces of migrant trajectories in the tomato district. Through this participatory research, I hoped to uncover the traces of rural settlement and displacement in the buildings and infrastructures that we visited together, to find out the specific ways territories were taking shape in and through mobility. We decided to take my car and visit all the places Youssouf and Karim had indicated on the map.

As we were making our way over the many potholed roads, Youssouf suddenly told me to stop near a dilapidated building: "Here we are in Puglia," he said. Karim pointed to a few plastic bags that could be seen dangling from the broken ceiling of the building: "That is a clear sign. When strangers move into this house, they will place some plastic bags on the roof to prevent the rain entering the building." He laughed. "That's what I call a trace." Clearly aware of my desire to find proper clues and indications, Youssouf continued, "In this place, you must know there lived only Sudanese migrants. There were also Malians here, but they had their own ghetto."

Youssouf tells me how agricultural work always follows a clear ethnic segmentation: "The Sudanese, they do not plant or weed, because they do not know this practice back at home, coming from the desert and all that. . . . So, they only come for the harvesting season. Instead, the Ghanaians, Burkinabè, and Malians, they arrive already early on, to do the planting, hoeing, and weeding of the fields. That is why they have their own ghettos here." And he adds a clarification: "The Burkinabè are not all from the same place. While some are from Béguedo, others came from Boussouma, and [still others] from Garango": these are different localities, with different connections. "Just talking to each other like that, we may discover to be acquainted in some way," Karim says, "but are actually different people, and we have different connections here."

I asked them if this situation resembled their trajectories in Ghana and Côte d'Ivoire: "You know, as a geographer, I always thought you needed to pay your allegiance to a local representative, a chief of some sorts, who acts on the right of the firstcomer."

Youssouf nodded. "Yes, I understand. I used to live for twenty years in Ivory Coast, and there it effectively works like that. But here the situation is different. In the ghetto there is no chief. The oldest member of the community only has the title of elder. But this is a mere decoration, as he is old and so it will be the younger one who will take him to work." Karim completed: "Yes, in fact the real problem of the ghetto is the problem of relations [le problème du ghetto c'est le problème des relations]. When I arrived here, for example, in the territory of the Sudanese, I did not know anyone. I must go with these Sudanese. So, if I want to work it becomes complicated, that is to say, if I do not associate with then, I cannot work. . . . So, it is the logic to know and to make myself known." Youssouf added, "When we arrived here in 2008, [the territory of Alto Bradano] was controlled by the Sudanese, and partly by the Arabs [les arabes]. We were highly welcomed by the agriculturalists because, you know, the Arabs work less well, and so they needed the workforce [main d'oeuvre]. That is when we decided to settle here. . . . In short, that is the situation, because Borgo San Pietro is, in fact, not their [the Sudanese] territory."

What became gradually clear though my journey with these African workers was that racialization happens at different layers, and it gets kneaded into territory through ghetto encounters. As our journey continued, we passed another abandoned building on the side of the road. Its entrance was blocked by big concrete bricks. Karim tells me, "This is where the Ghanaians used to live." After a brief stop, we continue to ride a mud track, which connects the provincial road to a local road. Several abandoned houses dot the fields: like the former Ghanaian ghetto, they all make up part of the former riforma settlement, the administrative center of which used to lie a few kilometers ahead. Karim and Youssouf appear to be increasingly at ease, even as we find entrances impeded and we cross into judicially impounded terrains. At another stop, as I continue to look for clues, they both sift through the remains of what appears to be a not-so-long-ago human presence. "Last year we stayed here with a group of Burkinabè," Youssouf tells me, adding that the owner of the building does not mind them occupying the warehouse and former pig stalls, if they do not touch the private house standing next to it. As I observe the tuna and tomato cans that are piled up in the vicinity of the building, Karim carries away a television set from the warehouse, which, as it appears, must have done service as a "connection" house, or *macquis*, as the Burkinabè prefer to call it.[5] A drawing on the wall depicts a nude woman penetrated by a giant penis. Just underneath, a female necklace and shoe, as well as some counterfeit CD covers, lay scattered across the floor.

At another abandoned settlement a few kilometers ahead, we need to crawl through a hole in the entrance. The building has been impounded since an official eviction in 2016. Using our phones to light the darkness, we observe several rooms packed with mattresses, clothes, and furniture. In the glare of our flashlights, slowly the contours appear of a living place that has been abruptly abandoned. The rooms smell of charcoal, of sweat and fermented waste. But while images of violent destruction disturb my imagination, Karim and Youssouf do not appear fazed. Instead, they continue digging through the dirt, inspecting a vest, a table, and some tools, which they will carry with them to the car. After a while we leave the dark building and set off to Santa Maria, the abandoned warehouse in the vicinity of Borgo San Nicola. While busy on his phone with a local employer, Karim shows me to the entrance of the building he occupied in the winter of 2009. Youssouf tells me, as in conclusion, "The problem here was, well, we did not want to go to the ghetto. But the *proprietari di casa* [*sic*: house owners] did not want to rent us their homes. . . . We offered several times to rent, but they said that we could not pay the house. . . . To us this came as a surprise, since the Romanians, Albanians . . . them, yes, they obtained a house, but not us." Karim adds, "They did not want us; they did not want Blacks." Asking what the alternative was, he concludes, laughing, "We had no choice, did we? We had to live in the abandoned houses. It was that or nothing."

Naturalizing "Black Spaces"

In hindsight, the trajectories of Karim and Youssouf appeared to me as firsthand evidence of the way rural labor infrastructures have effectively maintained, and continue to maintain, a boundary between the white spaces of what are presumed to be the centers of Italian rurality and the Black spaces of migrant lifeworlds on the margins. As I wrote in the introduction, this infrastructural lens helps me explain the process through which the commodified value of migrant labor is actively integrated into the formal mechanisms of economic development from the edges of a naturalized and racialized "outside space." Yet while Blackness is frequently invoked as a figure of nonbelonging and permanent exclusion in this context (see also Merrill 2018), I see in this exclusion a more dynamic process of natural racialization. As noted, the term "natural racialization" refers to the specific manners in which the experience of racism effectively *naturalizes* a group into belonging to the nation and to national citizenry through "inclusionary forms of exclusion" (Carbado 2005, 638); but also, and importantly, it signifies how the question of who is categorized as a legitimate territorial presence in the modern nation-state is partially an effect, a product of a spatial politics of racial differentiation and of managing difference through spatial dispersal (Hawthorne 2021a, 5).

Again, my work with MIC|C provided a fertile background against which I could examine these transient intersections. My collaboration with MIC|C had the intent of challenging and questioning the intricate ways in which ruined infrastructures became part and parcel of the adverse incorporation of migrant labor in today's agri-food supply chains. MIC|C's intervention sought to capture life at the margins as it had existed. It sought to highlight and denounce the persistent impermanency that was both functional to capital and to the way it could simultaneously exhort and expel forms of life at its disposal. One could say that MIC|C highlighted the articulation of the boundary between the displaced and the settled, the discarded and the preserved, as it detailed the impermanence of life as it had existed: like the ashes of a fire, or the remnants of a camp that had moved on, the maps and objects displayed on the website and displayed in the few artistic events to which MIC|C was invited revealed how this stratified boundary was actively mapped into the landscape and, layer upon layer upon layer, strata upon strata, generated an increasingly fragmented and fractal space that organized functionalities into productive modes and provided the gravitational space around which capitalist operations were both organized and reproduced.

Three elements emerge as particularly striking in this context. One regards the stratification of humanity on the boundary between "informal" and "official" places of refuge. As I wrote in the previous chapter, a central instrument (or political technology) that is used to distinguish between different strata of humanity in this context is clearly that of the territorial residence. Though refugees and asylum seekers have a right to a territorial residence, they need an official address to be able to renew their papers. Next to the popular consensus that the continued exclusion of migrant workers generates in Italian public opinion (a consensus that is notably sustained through the permanent sense of emergency attached to their presence), this differentiated status of migrant workers also works to the benefit of agro-capitalists who subsequently exploit the difference between "not yet" (in the case of asylum seekers), "not quite" (in the case of refugees), and dehumanized subjects who cannot claim full rights of residence. The dynamic map on MIC|C's website effectively shows how, over eight years (2009–2017), the fluctuation of official temporary labor camps has been accompanied by an equally important ramification of migrant workers' ghettos that continue to fulfill a central role in the commodification of migrant labor.

To some extent, one could argue that the situation described by Karim and Youssouf resembles what Loïc Wacquant and colleagues (2014) call the territorial stigmatization of postcolonial citizens in the context of neoliberal urbanization. Wacquant argues that the permanent seclusion of migrant lifeworlds in the urban peripheries of Europe effectively attaches a blemish of place on their already existing stigmata associated with poverty, ethnic origin, and postcolonial immigrant status.[6] The territorialization of identity thus acquires a more topological dimension in an era in which both territorial borders and processes of urbanization should be interpreted as morphological assemblages that are in many ways multilocalized and multiscalar. As I explained in the introductory chapter, this multiscalarity should indeed inspire us toward a more processual analysis of capitalist supply chains and the role of migrant labor therein.[7] Seen from such perspective, the trajectories of West African workers in Southern Italy's rural economy appear indicative of a more persistent, though apparently impermanent, process of urbanization of the countryside that goes paired with this reconfiguration of migrant identity in the margins. The deliberate politics of exclusion that defined their nonbelonging to white rural society effectively seemed to reproduce not so much a fixed border but rather a compartmentalized system of spatial exclusion that lodged their spatial dispersion into every relation they maintained and undertook. A key aspect of this dynamic, I argue, concerns the rather overt instrumentalization of race as a central determinant of this logic of separation.

The terminology of the Black Mediterranean helps to explain the color line that continues to racially separate humanity in this context. Again, this scholarship starts from the premise that Black subjection is not a matter of mere exceptionalism or the result of current policies based on racial prejudice, but forms an essential component of the way capitalism has unfolded in this part of the globe since its earliest stages. While contemporary migrant trajectories usually are associated with a state of liminality and rites of passage,[8] it is both shocking and meaningful to see how for men like Youssouf and Karim, this state of liminality never appeared to resolve itself. On the contrary, their in-between state of nonbelonging had become part and parcel of a permanent state of being that characterizes life in the global agrarian frontier. While they were among the few African migrants who managed to obtain a house in the towns—mostly thanks to the relentless efforts of local antiracist associations—their fellow citizens continued to live a life at the margins and in the makeshift homes they continue to construct year after year in the rural *case abbandonate* and the ruins of the previous agricultural reform. The improvised homes of my friends included, for instance, a shack in one of the deserted farms' backyards, an abandoned barn, and a haphazardly refurbished room in an isolated part of town. Significant also was the fact that none of the friends I made during my long period of fieldwork among West African workers invited me to their home, even though we spent considerable time together in the ghetto. One friend explicitly told me that the owner did not accept any visitors on his premises. Whenever we agreed to meet, I had to call him in advance so he could come down the dirt track to meet me at the side of the road. An interesting conversation about the concept of home developed one time when I was hanging out with some West African migrants: as one of them said, the places they inhabited in Italy could not be called a proper home (*chez soi*), because here one remained in any case excluded from the wider social relations that form the foundation of stable prospects.

In reconsidering the active politics of spatial dispersal and social differentiation that underpin contemporary bordering policies from this perspective, it is indeed significant how the Mediterranean has come to represent a space of continuous suspension for these West African men, whose labor power is systematically absorbed by the societies that continue to refuse their presence as a matter of permanent exception and nonbelonging. Read in this way, one could say, the African ghetto has not only assumed the function of an "outside" space that is selectively incorporated into capitalist processes of valorization; but also, and increasingly, it is considered as a "naturalized" space of which the life forms are both materially and discursively constructed as uncivilized and threatening. This natural racialization, it should be said, is functional both to supply chain capitalism and to the power of the nation-state, because it actively reproduces the formal, sovereign borders of the former as the gravitational space around which operations of capital can be fulfilled and replenished. This double functionality of the ghetto as an "outside" and a "natural" space that reconfigures human lives in distinct ways to feed capital reconfirms my earlier statement that racial capitalism is not primarily about skin color identity but is a chromatic structure of power inherent in the capitalist mode of production and accumulation (Lombardi-Diop and Romeo 2014; Melamed 2015; Miapyen and Bozkurt 2022).

The theory of racial capitalism in the Black Mediterranean clarifies the central place of race in profit maximization and capital accumulation, but it also puts to the foreground how capitalist dispossession is never a completed process but relies on the constant valorization and revalorization of forms of life located on its edges (Edwards 2021; Miapyen and Bozkurt 2022). I once again recall the public administrator's reference to African workers as lagging "a hundred years" in modern development, a gap that, according to this public official, could only be filled with the imposition of public force (see chapter 3). This logic of redeeming the countryside through acts of territorial state expansion had known its culminating expression in the politics of agricultural reform, or *bonifica*, and the—admittedly unsuccessful—attempts of the modern Italian nation-state to colonize and render efficient its operations of rural capital accumulation in the South and in the colonies (see chapter 2). Yet while *bonifica* historically referred to the rationalization of peasant agriculture through infrastructures of modern development, the term now indicated a rather different intent toward eradicating the foundations of alternative forms of life on which capital feeds itself. In this sense, the state's destructive interventions toward migrant ghettos since 2014 can be read once again from the double, and corresponding, dynamics of the spatialization of nature and the naturalization of space I highlighted in the opening paragraphs of this book. Contrary to dominant public opinion, however, the main objective of these seizures and evictions was not to eradicate the migrant workers' informal settlements per se, but rather to render their living space unlivable, hazardous, and inaccessible so as to mold their labor power to the needs of rural capital. During consecutive ghetto evictions in Basilicata, security forces made sure that the roofs of evicted buildings were destroyed, and the access to abandoned buildings was blocked with bricks and wires. In one case, I could observe how public authorities had deliberately blocked the access to a water pump that was also used by local farmers. But they never prohibited workers from returning to the same site to reconstruct their makeshift camps.[9]

What emerges because of these state interventions, therefore, is not a neat dividing line between the "civilized" society of rural towns and agro-capitalist operations and the "uncivilized" hinterland of outcast migrants, but indeed a complex compartmentalized system of spatial exclusion that lodges the separation between the "Black space" of the ghetto and the white space of Italian rural lifeworlds geographically at every scale. In this bordered landscape, furthermore, one notices the expansion of such racializing dynamics beyond the frequently discussed domain of Mediterranean bordering infrastructures. As mentioned earlier, both Villa Literno's eviction at the end of the 1990s and the subsequent evictions of migrant ghettos in Basilicata directly contributed to a growing ethnicization of the workforce, in the sense that different ghettos now host different ethnic communities. This is also the reason why I place "Black space" in quotation marks, because from an ethnographic perspective, ghettos are not at all a unified space but rather should be considered as an interconnected archipelago of ethnicized labor enclaves. In contrast to the—admittedly naïve—belief that their inhabitants' condition of rural outcasts automatically generates the foundation for a common cause and protests, the operations of racial capitalism reach so deeply that even workers from the same ethnic background frequently end up competing for the same jobs and in the same domain (a dynamic that is frequently referred to as the "war among the poor"). Rather than romanticizing the ghetto as a social space where power hierarchies are dissolved and camaraderie prevails, I am pushed by my observations to say the contrary.

In this context, I keep reminding myself of a conversation that developed one time when I was hanging out with some West African migrants in the *macquis* of Borgo San Nicola in August 2018. While I was talking to some acquaintances, one of my friends, visibly drunk, asked me for money to buy him a drink. At some point, a local *caponero* stopped by with his car. I did not know the two men were acquainted. The *caponero* approached me. As we had known each other for some time, we started chatting about the goings-on in town and in the neighborhood. I mentioned to him the World Cup match we watched some days earlier in the ghetto (that year, France won against Croatia). The *caponero* responded, while pointing at the satellite disk on the roof of the *macquis*: "You see, all this is the work of K." [the Sudanese *caporale* who controlled the local zone]. Then he turned to my drunk friend, asking him if he had finally decided to work. My friend shrugged, standing aloof for a moment, and then answered, "My fate is in the hands of God." Looking back severely, the *caponero* responded, "Your fate may be in the hands of God, but K. does not live in heaven, you know [*K. n'habite pas au ciel, tu sais*]." After saying goodbye to me, he took off again in his car.

This encounter—like many others I took part in or witnessed in the same period—made me acutely aware of the strict hierarchies that characterized the multiple, overlapping territories of agricultural extraction in the Italian context (see also Perrotta 2014). Even as they lived their lives in the "periphery of the periphery" as it were, my Burkinabè friends repeatedly complained how their lives were constrained by the presence of their fellow citizens who resided in the city and on whose social networks their lives and livelihoods depended. Some confided to me that this constant surveillance within their own social networks was exactly the reason they did not want to leave the countryside and set up a residence in town, even though they desperately needed the official residency papers there to legitimate their presence on Italian territory. The general sense I gathered in the ghetto, therefore, was that of a fractal space, which offered room for solidarity and conviviality—particularly during the "off months" outside the harvesting season—but also remained rife with tensions and unresolved conflicts. Whereas social hierarchies remained loose in these "off" periods, and small groups of workers attended the Burkinabè *macquis* in relative autonomy from each other, the hierarchy of the *caporali* firmly held the ghetto in its grip during the summer, providing its "services" but also superimposing the presence of other workers in the increasingly overcrowded rooms. During such peak periods, all worker teams had to pay allegiance to the same hierarchy, without exception, as it was the protection of the *caporalato* hierarchy that ensured each and every one access to regular employment contracts and jobs. This is also the main reason why I decided to distance myself from the theory of resistant autonomy that some Italian antiracist organizations associated with the ghetto in this context, but which in my view does not take sufficiently into account the Black struggles that characterize the ghetto as a racially naturalized space (see the next chapter). The archipelago of ghetto settlements that took root in the Alto Bradano area between 2009 and 2017 instead looked to me more like a capillary system of loosely related islands, the relations between which tightened and loosened according to the agricultural seasons. If I were to choose an imagery, I would compare this temporal movement more to a lung, or a compression chamber, which ventilates flows of labor across the plains with the rhythm of seasonal demands.

Instead of seeking a class conflict where there is, in fact, very little, a more fruitful way to conceive of the ghetto is that of a shared space of life in mobility. Through my work with MIC|C, I became aware that Black migrant ghettos are also incredibly layered places where memories of belonging and nonbelonging overlap, and where social boundaries are constantly redrawn, renarrated and re-envisioned. With the often deliberately invisible and marginalized connectivity of these sites with rural society, migrant workers also conceive of them as poetic places in the sense that they contain the traces of these narrated memories and narrations of belonging. I continue to recall the many insightful moments we shared while I was traveling through Basilicata's agrarian archipelago with Karim, Youssouf, and other African workers. Sifting through the remnants of these sites, what comes to mind is in fact not so much their cyclical valorization and devaluation toward capital's needs but their active articulation as sites of collective memory and identification. The notion of "ruins" indeed feels inadequate in this context if one considers the ruptured multiplicity of these sites in the face of capital's operations. As Gastón Gordillo (2014) notes, this multiplicity forces us to rethink not just what is destroyed but what is created by apparent processes of ruination. Contesting the abstract space that capitalist operations generate when they "hit the ground" in specific places (Mezzadra and Neilson 2019, 2), Gordillo writes, we need to move beyond this abstract homogenization that does not resonate with the sensuous texture of actual places and objects.

Through the research I did with MIC|C, and later in my ethnography of migrant labor in Basilicata, I indeed seek to reach beyond the first impressions of waste and debris one encounters in the abandoned sites that are cyclically repurposed by mobile workers. Instead, we found that these sites were full of absent presences that actively narrated the life that had animated them, and would animate them, throughout these cyclical processes of abandonment and revitalization. I draw back to the observations of Vicky Squire and of Karen Barad I quoted earlier. Considering ghettos as rural infrastructures not only reveals the wide variety of agents, platforms, and architectures through which migrant labor is actively connected and disconnected from global value chains. But this perspective also highlights the material-discursive cuts that actively co-constitute the agrarian frontier as an assemblage of intra-acting physical and social forces. Though one of the principal objectives of the politics of ruination that characterized rural interventions during my field research was in fact to erase migrant ghettos as abandoned spaces and a reflection of a shameful past, people like Karim, Abou, and Youssouf continued to actively reuse and repurpose these sites as part of their own trajectories. However fragile they are, these attempts require us to consider capitalist ruination primarily also as a "lived process" (Mah 2010, 399) that opens potential trajectories toward an alternative future, as it is indeed in these sites that migrants reconnect and imagine possible pathways. Many were the instances we found intimate objects and personal belongings, and many were the indications of such reconnections: whether in the form of someone's short, written statements and drawings, or poetic narrations, migrants who passed through these sites often left personal traces with the direct aspiration of being read by others. In the abandoned ghetto of Irisina (Potenza Province), where Moroccan workers lived during the early 1990s, one Arabic graffiti was left on the wall: "Morocco is not going well. And those who live in Potenza are living in dismay." In the ghetto of Mulini Matinelle, one poem read, "The person who lives in exile is ruined." One of the Arabic poems on the wall of Grotta Paradiso (a cave where migrant workers found refuge after their expulsion from the formal camp infrastructure in Palazzo San Gervasio) read, "The cavern of madness." Another one said, "Bye bye darkness."

In our subsequent collaborations and performances in MIC|C, we tried to reinscribe the meaning of these objects and poems into a performative space, by actively connecting them to the lifeworks of migrant workers who had experienced existence in the ghetto. One performance I mentioned in the introduction involved the construction of a makeshift shelter on the central square of Matera (Basilicata) during a cultural festival. Another series of events involved a more active cooperation with a theater company from Bologna called Cantieri Meticci. In these different performances, our main purpose was to give a new meaning to the objects and memories we had gathered during our research in Basilicata by connecting them directly to the personal experiences of African refugees who were also members of the company. On one such occasion, I was surprised to hear how the jerry cans that workers use in the fields are the same as those migrants use on their trajectories through the Sahel and Sahara Deserts: the cloth in which they wrap these bottles serves to keep the water cool under extremely high temperatures. By placing the narrations and memories of these objects in performative juxtaposition, we presented new interpretations of the connections and disconnections that make life livable and unlivable in the widening space of the EU-African borderscape. As Hicks and Mallet write about their similar project of the archaeology of Europe's undocumented in the Calais "Jungle," these performances indeed have the power to show the larger history of the movements of people, goods, and ideas, rather than seeing them as separate, and therefore different, processes. This interconnectivity provided a powerful counterpoint to the logic of separation that continued to underpin border and migration policies in the Mediterranean, and in Basilicata in particular, during this period of mass displacement and dispossession.

As we were re-elaborating the meaning of these objects and poems together, I was reminded once more of Karen Barad's neologism "intra-action" (see introduction). With this term, she tries to indicate the inseparability of the discursive and material elements that lead to particular (re-)configurations of the world. In her reading, "the human" is conceived as a product of the world in its "open-ended becoming" rather than as a pre-given category, so people as well as things are actively made as more or less "human" through the active "cuts" that they experience in their coming together. Read in this way, the traces we found and elaborated together on the MIC|C website should in fact be seen as a sign of the material-discursive cuts and interconnections between migrant trajectories and their intra-action with the physical environment; I find this intra-action as important to consider as the—admittedly only partially successful—attempts to reconfigure their lifeworlds as an abstract space made amenable to capital's needs. Building on MIC|C's work (but see also De Silvey and Edensor 2012) I would like to think that infrastructures are also sites where the human and the more-than-human are embroiled in a mutually constitutive relationship, as authors like Karen Barad, Vicky Squire, and others have been trying to tell us. The convergences in today's rural infrastructures—which, I repeat, bring together state and nonstate actors, human and more-than-human elements in specific times and locales—sustain a racializing hierarchy that singles out mobile bodies as "not yet" (in the case of asylum seekers), "not quite" (in the case of refugees), and "nonhumans" (in the case of "illegal migrants" cast into the "natural sphere" of the ghetto). But they also involve another kind of layerdness that is as graspable as it is unaccounted for in current scholarship on borders and migration. In my view, more attention should indeed be given to this layerdness and the ways it is, is not, and can(not) be made visible as an alternative reading to the supposedly abstract spaces that constrain our lives to the needs of global capital.

During our interventions with MIC|C, we tried to make this layerdness part of the discussion about the historicity of cycles of capitalist expansion and contraction that had characterized, and continue to characterize, rural development in the Black Mediterranean. Whereas the strata of objects, belongings, memories, and narrations we displayed during our short interventions indeed show us the displacement of marginalized subjects in this fluctuating frontier, they also demonstrate how such places constitute an attempt toward new forms of rootedness through webs of dependencies and relationships. They show us how abandonment and impermanence can become themselves an active form of government. In that sense, I again link up with contemporary archaeologists Hicks and Mallet whom I quoted earlier that there is more to discover and share in the intersection of geography and archaeological inquiry into the ruined lives of modernity; indeed, that intersection can "open a window to spatial and temporal processes" of contemporary migration that highlights not only the material entanglements between people and their environment in the context of hypermobility but also gives these connections new meaning by placing them into a new performative context.

Restless Lands

During my last year of field research in northern Basilicata, the situation there would become increasingly grim. As the regional government's politics of ruination met with rising opposition, not just from the migrant workers but also, and increasingly, from local agriculturists who saw its effects in their own pockets, frustrations came regularly to the fore—including in open protests and manifestations of anger. On one such occasion, a group of workers—clearly instigated by the *caporale*—refused to work if the municipality did not allow them to use the site of the ghetto for their makeshift accommodation (as in other neighboring *comuni*, the Borgo San Nicola was considering the closure of the site, which in this case was on the premises of this gang master's close ally). The strategy of concentrating migrant labor in one central site benefited only a few entrepreneurs who were working in close complicity with the white gang master hierarchy and infrastructure. In the process, however, it had clearly increased the bargaining power of the gang masters in their relationship with the state. This upset not a few workers and entrepreneurs who were unwilling to bend their activities to the will of this small clique of "friends of friends" of the local *caporale* syndicate. While I continued my fieldwork in 2017 and 2018, however, I was struck by yet another factor that I had hitherto ignored, and which involved the "relational and ongoing nature of the state-society contract" that is expressed in concrete infrastructure planning and use. As Charlotte Lemanski noted (2020, 9), we should be aware that the active negotiation of infrastructure use also involves a consideration of citizens' and noncitizens' relation with the state.

I was reminded of this relationship on two occasions. The first involved a drive through the town of Borgo San Nicola one evening in the winter of 2019. At some point and without warning, the streetlights suddenly turned off, leaving us in pitch dark. Perceiving my annoyance, my friend who was sitting next to me responded that this was a quite frequent phenomenon, as electric facilities are badly maintained. The problem of power cuts not only affected the ordinary citizenry, obviously, but also restaurants, bars, and small enterprises in town, as we would hear later in our conversation with one of the restaurant owners in town. The second occasion involved a ride with my friend Franco through the fields in the autumn of 2018. While we were navigating rudimentary streets and dirt tracks, he jokingly told me that "you northerners have decided to leave us all the potholes"—explicitly recalling the Meridione's historical marginalization. At some point, Franco indicated a system of ruined irrigation canals: "all abandoned," he said. When I asked him the reason, he said that some years back a band of thieves systematically stole the copper wires that comprised the electricity grid of the irrigation system (farmers need electricity to pump the water of their wells—some of which lay at a 150-meter depth—into the fields). Later, checking the local newspapers, I noted that such theft has become quite common in the area: in 2013, one man was arrested in Genzano for copper theft amounting to 10,000 euros. In 2014, three men were arrested in Irsina for stealing copper wires from a telecom business. And in 2019, a man and a woman were caught in Ferrandina (Matera) for stealing wires from the state-owned electric company ENEL (*Gazzetta del Mezzogiorno*, March 14, 2014; *TG24*, March 20, 2019). That same year, the *carabinieri* of Potenza arrested a gang responsible for stealing 100,000 euros worth of copper wire from state companies as well as private firms. The police intervention brought to light a total of sixteen thefts, committed in the period between November 2017 and December 2018, in which about twelve thousand meters of copper cables were stolen, with a market value of around 100,000 euros and damages of over a million euros.

Looking more closely, I relate this deteriorating electricity infrastructure back to the state of the roads. One winter, I find my route to the South blocked because a bridge on the Bologna-Taranto highway has collapsed. When I explain the reason for my delay to my friend Franco, he comments—partly joking, partly serious—that "we have become a second Palestine" now: isolated from the civilized world but included adversely through the extraction of its resources.[10] In Basilicata that winter, I find my way on secondary routes regularly impeded by deep fissures in the concrete paving. Furthermore, streams often overflow the roadway and force vehicles to ford deep channels of water. The only sign of remediation I find during these journeys are the signposts put up by local municipalities closing roads or warning of such impasses. But these warnings appear rather a vain exercise, it is as if to say: drive here at your own risk. I experience this risk quite abruptly during a snowstorm in January as the road tarmac is quickly covered in a white carpet. While I keep my hands gripped on the steering wheel I see trucks sliding off into the ditches; my wife prays to all her ancestors to keep us alive. There is no sign of a snowplow or salt machine until we reach the vicinity of Bari, a hundred kilometers from the border with Basilicata.

During all these misadventures, the more quotidian question I keep asking myself is how ordinary life goes on in such a context of rapid and overarching ruination. Though some people tend to romanticize rurality in the dark winter months, when life presumably takes on a calmer dimension in the rural villages and snow covers the Apennines, the constant movements of my acquaintances in the African and Italian communities give a different impression. While older folks tend to remain in place, young African workers who have been able to save some capital take advantage of the low work opportunities during winter to travel back home until the start of the next agricultural season in March. I am struck by one comment Franco makes when a local gang that is waging its violent extortion of indebted farmers in the community decides to burn the car of one citizen on the small square in front of his door (organized crime has been increasing its grip on agricultural activities for years). Sadly, he says, "Only the worst people stay behind here now." Partly also for that reason, young Italians from the community are eager to travel and seek opportunities elsewhere. While some of my friends were taking up occasional jobs in the North, others went on with their studies or helped their families in the household and on the farm—but very few remained permanently in place.

After getting acquainted with a group of male Italian youths from one of the local *comuni*, I notice a seasonal pattern to their wanderings: while most young people stay in Basilicata in the summer to work on the farm (frequently also in conjunction with migrant laborers) and take some holidays, they tend to travel rather intensely in autumn and winter. Such cyclical migration primarily finds its origin in the historical and spiraling youth unemployment in the region: reaching as high as 60 percent in some parts of the country, such unemployment predominantly affects the South of Italy. Indeed, what strikes me most in my conversations with young people is the sense of desolation and rootlessness they identify with their lifeworlds. A term that continues to arise in our conversations is *abbandono*—abandonment. On one occasion, a young man who had been working abroad for many years as a waiter shares with me his perplexity about the investment he just made in a local restaurant. Despite the long working hours (we meet at midnight to share a drink) and the personal investment he has made to set up this business, he says he is ready to drop everything and move abroad once more if an opportunity emerges. Another young man, in his thirties, initially tells me of the advantages of living in a remote rural town: as a musician, he can concentrate on his music and survive with low-paying jobs because of the low cost of living. After some months, however, he shares with me his decision to migrate as well, preferably to a big city where he can find multiple opportunities to work and earn a living. In late 2020 I meet him in a town in the North of Italy where he has decided to move for good.

I am particularly struck by the trajectories of two former students, one of whom had returned to Basilicata after finishing his degree, to work on the farm with his father. Despite earlier ambitions, he tells me one evening, he is looking for an administrative job at the municipality, adding that there are few other stable jobs for people like him, who have a degree and do not want to work on the farm all their lives. This appears to me a common path of young returnees around here: while they may nurture ambitions to start a new business, to set up networks and initiatives during their time away, many of them end up emigrating again after encountering frustrations at home. These frustrations may take many forms, but they usually include a combination of bureaucratic hurdles and lack of economic and investment opportunities, as well as family and other obligations that take away their personal liberty. More generally, young people complain about the local mentality. In fact, a mantra among the youth I encounter is that "it is the mentality here"—a mind-set they find rusty, backward, and antithetical to any notion of personal development. One young man sums up his perplexity with me while we are preparing an art installation at the Matera 2019 cultural festival. Looking at the introductory text on the folder we prepared for the festival—which mentions the margins as a center of change—he says, "Ah, so you want to be in the margins. . . . Listen, don't think that your Black friends are the only ones who are occupying that space." While we are loading stones on the truck to drive to Matera, he adds, with an ironic tone, "Here we are all n——— [*negri*]. I mean, I also dirty my hands in the land all day."

Overall, I find in the testimonies of these young men a strong re-evocation of the marginalized rurality that continues to push forward capitalist accumulation in the Italian South since its independence from the Bourbon kingdom in the mid-1800s. The desolation, abandonment, and rootlessness of a population that has been living through the experience of emigration for generations cannot but leave its permanent traces in the mentality and lifeworlds of these youngsters as they try to make sense of opportunities and carve out a possibility to create a personal trajectory. The anthropologist Vito Teti (2004, 2017) uses the term *erranza* (literally, wandering, roaming, but also a feeling of being lost) to make sense of the way people reinvent their rural lives between constant abandonment and returns. While Teti focuses on Calabria, I likewise see Basilicata's youth captured in such a state of hypermobility, between their desires to invest their lives at home and the need to earn a living somewhere else that is usually far away from the place where they grew up and root their childhood memories. The sphere of personal development of these youth, I find, is often situated between these concrete opportunities and an imagined space where a possible future can thrive.

At the same time, I cannot but connect this *erranza* to the mobile lives of African workers, whom I have spent years with in this agrarian frontier. For them as well as for the Italians who are "left behind" in this rural environment, the term *abbandono* characterizes quite well their collective search for autonomy and a collective identity because it simultaneously describes the active process through which their lives are ruined and disinvested while they remain forced to subject their plans and ambitions to the material conditions of a social order from which they are increasingly excluded. The feeling I gather from these African and Italian youth is indeed that of a floating condition: simultaneously drifting and trying to stay afloat. They relate a feeling of disconnectedness, of bodies that keep being torn between different spaces, without having the possibility to root their existence in a stable place. More and more, this situation seems to me to come to a crisis point, however, a point where the proceeding rural globalization generates tension, not just between emigrants and immigrants, formal policies and informal lifeworlds, but also between dynamics of urbanization and agrarian change, modern progress and state abandonment, violent exclusion and adverse inclusion.

The Infrastructures of Impermanence

In the rapid globalization of rural lifeworlds across the Mediterranean, a social differentiation process is taking root that I have tried to highlight here. While the town folk regard ghetto dwellers as somewhat backward and "not yet" part of the modernizing, progressive logic of neoliberal self-liberation, the social space of the ghetto reveals a strong division on which the relations of production continue to be based. As the frontier of supply-driven agricultural production proceeds, it not just radically upsets existing social and cultural normative systems, but also introduces new elements of rupture, division, and detachment. That is why I insist on not limiting the analysis of rural urbanization to questions about the built architecture, state development plans, and material infrastructures that seem to underpin this process. One must widen the scope toward the social networks that facilitate the flow of goods, people, and ideas and allow for their exchange over space.

I found it instructive to view the ghetto in a wider set of connections between rural capital, labor, and public authority on the one hand, and the social connections it is apparently capable of maintaining with agrarian society more widely on the other hand. Spending more time in the ghetto served as a catalyst of this itinerary. It was here that I discovered the intimate relations between some of the local Italian youngsters and migrant African workers. It was here that testimonies about the *caporalato* hierarchy and its violent grip on society could be debated and contested. And it was here that I discovered the deep social divisions that governed relations between workers, local entrepreneurs, and the public administration. Without exaggerating its political potential for structural change, the ghetto offered a social platform where some of the closed chains and networks that people from different backgrounds experienced in their everyday lives could be discussed and temporarily broken. Although the relations between the ghetto and rural society remained indeed deliberately marginalized, they did form a starting point to question the apparent failures of state administration and public authority in a local context. Situating myself deliberately in these margins helped me to open the black box of this infrastructural power, to reveal the multiplicity of institutions that have been involved in mediating rural labor and the way they have been implicated in a wider reconfiguration of power in the space between labor, capital, and identity.

CITIZEN RECOGNITION

This chapter concerns the citizenship rights of Black African workers in Southern Italy in the context of the deep geopolitical, social, ecological, and economic
transformation the Mediterranean region has been going through in the period
2014–2020. The high reliance of agricultural firms (both seasonal and nonsea-
sonal) on migrant laborers has generated a demographic shift across the rural
spaces of the Mezzogiorno and the Sahel. In Southern Italy in particular, the
social cost of globalized agri-food production appears to have fallen increasingly
on the shoulders of geographically and culturally segregated rural communities,
which include migrants in the ghettos, as well as immigrants and Italians in the
towns and rural hamlets. At the same time, this shift appears to be generating a
deeper fissure in the country's perception of its postcolonial national identity:
What does it mean to be an Italian, a migrant, or an immigrant in this current
era of geopolitical and economic crisis? What does it mean to be a citizen or a
noncitizen when relations between national belonging, political sovereignty, and
state territoriality are so rapidly reconfiguring in the Mediterranean? This chapter addresses those questions from the perspective of what, in previous chapters,
I have come to call the racial naturalization of African lifeworlds in the Black
Mediterranean.

In line with the Black Mediterranean scholarship on which this book builds,
I address the politics of belonging that unfold in this racialized space from a
perspective of racial capitalism; that is, I emphasize how the connection between
race and nation is actively forged into a moral boundary that places categories of people into an unequal relation of power with regard to contemporary

operations of capitalism. This line of argument is based on the presupposition that any attempt to theorize capitalism without cornering the lived experiences of those who are defined as not-quite (or not yet) human, not-quite (or not yet) modern and civilized, necessarily reenacts the racializing violence that makes capitalism thrive as a modernizing project. I continue to refer to the myriad ways in which Italy's colonialism in North Africa and the Horn of Africa, as well as its own internal colonization of the Mezzogiorno, has actively established a potent repertoire of racist practices, imagery, and modes of sociospatial organization that significantly shapes the lived experiences of Black African communities in Italy to this day (for a discussion see Giuliani and Lombardi-Diop 2013; Proglio 2016; Merrill 2018; Frisina and Hawthorne 2018; Pesarini and Tintori 2020; Hawthorne 2019a and b, among others). I also detail how this boundary actively separates and segregates individuals in the realm of contemporary capitalist supply chains, more specifically through the stratified organization of labor in the space of "national" development. In the context of Italy's cash crop economy, I hope to highlight how such stratification has become part and parcel of a racist teleology of "integration," which opens up new connections, but also new divisions, among Black subjects who are differentially positioned in relation to Italy's "racializing juridical assemblages" (Weheliye 2014, 79). One becomes part of a "nation" through her or his insertion into racial hierarchies that have a determining effect on the differentiation of contemporary citizenship. I clarify this process through an analysis of the political struggle over the redeeming of informal Black migrant workers' infrastructures, or ghettos, in the context of Italy's anti-gang-mastering legislation and policy. This analysis is predominantly based on an intermittent series of research stays in Casa Sankara, an initially informal and later formalized site of migrant reception close to San Severo, in Puglia. While my experience at Casa Sankara brought me back to Cedric Robinson's invitation to look beyond the law as a source of sovereignty, I in fact consider the wide range of actors and positionalities implicated in drawing the boundary between deserving citizens and undeserving outlaws, a dynamic that I will hope to show remains closely linked to what are considered productive and unproductive subjects.

This chapter focuses on the planning and coming into being of a migration reception center in the Southern Italian province of Foggia, where I engaged in two-year participatory research. It also focuses on the forced eviction of one of the most significant migrant settlements in the area during 2015–2019, the Grand Ghetto of San Severo.

The chapter will temporarily move away from Basilicata as a main area of interest, to return to it later with these new insights in mind. Both regions are intimately linked, notably in the way public institutions tend to address the issue of migrant labor in agriculture. Especially in the post-ENA (North Africa

Emergency) years, public authorities have progressively concentrated their efforts on the formalization of migrant labor. In Puglia and Basilicata, these efforts involved, among other things, the erection of regional platforms for labor recruitment (the *liste di prenotazione*), as well as the institution of labor camps, which ideally should have constituted an alternative accommodation to the informal ghettos that continue to form a central node in the agrarian political economy of both Northern and Southern Italy.

Complementing the materialist and sociological analysis of the last two chapters, I will highlight the cultural logic of such state interventions and explain the reasons for their apparent failure. I once again follow Tania Li (2005) in her invitation to never stop short of investigating the compromise that modernist government schemes end up reaching in practice, rather than uncritically accepting that regulations simply "roll out" in space. As she writes, the grandiose state-driven projects of rural and urban planning to "improve the human condition" (as James Scott [1998] writes) remain, in their many caesuras, utopian attempts to remake the world according to criteria of rationality and aesthetics, with spaces neatly divided and populations listed and classified. Less visible, however, are the "countless, often competing, local tactics of education, persuasion, inducement, management, incitement, motivation, encouragement" that take shape in domains like public health and rural development (Li 2005, 386). It is these tactics that the current chapter will now turn to.

My conceptual objective is once more to counter the metaphor of an all-seeing, all-encompassing territorial state that is both willing and perfectly capable of upholding a neat boundary between the formal and the informal spheres of politics and the economy, and rather ask how the state reconstitutes itself in the margins, on the boundary between these spheres. The intense processes of social and spatial differentiation through which state interventions are concretely "worked out" in the domain of rural development can provide useful information about the territorial nation-state as an always unstable project that remains divided between its ambition of the will to rule over populations that work and extract the land, and the practical implementation of these ambitions in a specific place. Focusing on these social and spatial differentiations, I hope to highlight and analyze the tense relation between tentative government policies and the frames of recognition on which they remain unsteadily founded. I argue for a dynamic understanding of labor as an inherently political process, the making of which the workers themselves—next to entrepreneurs, and state administrations—partake and participate in. Turning to the category of citizenship as an inherent part of this process, I highlight how labor formalization has been deeply affected by the current Mediterranean border "crisis" and its insistence on emergency rule and surveillance.

Capo Free–Ghetto Off

The ambition to formalize the lives of thousands of migrant workers and their "lawless" urbanization of the "Grand Ghetto"—as the regional administration in Puglia continued to define the migrant labor settlement on the border of Rignano and San Severo, in the province of Foggia—should be situated in the unstable frontier that has characterized state interventions in the domain of agricultural labor markets and rural development planning. This chapter builds on what Charlotte Lemanski (2020) calls forms of citizenship and noncitizenship in action in the domain of contested infrastructure projects. With reference to postapartheid South Africa, she writes, citizens have become increasingly apt in adapting and consuming existing infrastructures in ways that may be deemed illegal and uncivil by the state, but which may instead by seen as legitimate given the visible state abandonment and neglect. The Italian politics of eviction and forced resettlement that has characterized rural development planning this past decade potentially offers an interesting, complementary way to understand the racializing juridical assemblages that underpin such contested infrastructural uses, especially because, as in postcolonial South Africa, those assemblages force us to adopt a dynamic understanding of the relationship between citizenship and infrastructure that goes beyond a narrow urban or state focus.

Some of the contestations around the eviction of the Grand Ghetto in fact resonate quite well with Lemanski's conceptualization. In her discussion of contested infrastructure projects, Lemanski builds on James Holston's (2008) terminology of insurgent citizenship and Faranak Miraftab's (2009) notion of insurgent planning. Both concepts aim at highlighting the forms of (inter)action that actively challenge the state's allocation of public resources in the infrastructural domain, while also emphasizing the important relational character of their concrete planning and utilization (Lemanski 2020, 9). Infrastructures, these authors argue, also function as a dynamic embodiment of citizenship and citizen-noncitizen relations. In this chapter I want to return to the fundamentally racial dimension of this question by highlighting how infrastructures of migrant labor have also become part of a process of racial normalization, whereby the productive labor that is necessary to keep the agricultural economy up and going is actively separated from the bodies that generate it. While certainly not confined to Black bodies, racialized normalization is both driven and underpinned by a strong cultural fetish of the Black body, which, if left untamed, risks, in the popular imagination, liberating the forces of uncontrolled energy that challenge the foundations of civilization, and of citizenship, in the nation-state order.

The convoluted way the eviction of Puglia's Grand Ghetto took shape constitutes, in my view, an exemplary case of the active negotiation over the terms of citizenship that goes beyond a discussion of the architecture and urban or territorial planning involved in contemporary infrastructure projects. Critical urbanists like Holston evoke the rebellious character of non-formally planned infrastructures such as urban slums, squats, and migrant occupations, because they supposedly "subvert the proclaimed equalities and universals of national citizenship" (Holston 2008, 53). In the context of Israel-Palestine, Oren Yiftachel (2009) writes how the politics of spatial segregation that characterizes ethnocratic statehood may indeed become an active way to place populations that are not deemed worthy of civilized government between the "lightness" of legality, safety, and full membership, and the "darkness" of eviction, destruction, and death. At the same time, such "gray spaces" may offer a platform for the emergence of alternative political subjectivities, he writes. The "creeping apartheid" that characterizes such spatial politics also causes a change in the political articulation of targeted communities. Yiftachel specifically mentions practices of deliberate permanence (in Arab: *sumood*, or hanging on), memory-building, and autonomous politics.

In the Italian context, the literature on the spatial politics of migrant ghettos unfortunately continues to be divided between opposed interpretations. One interpretation associates the ghetto with the phenomenon of *caporalato*: the form of illegal labor mediation labeled as being responsible for the notoriously detrimental circumstances to which migrants employed as agri-food commodity labor are increasingly subjected. As I wrote in chapter 1, the *caporalato*-ghetto nexus figures prominently in a narrative frame called "neo-abolitionism"—the struggle against extreme labor exploitation that is perceived as affecting the individual in a way that is comparable to slavery, and as such forms an embarrassment for public authorities deemed unwilling to protect (or incapable of protecting) workers captured in systematic exploitation (Howard and Forin 2019). Other scholars insist instead on the sociality of the ghetto as a place that provides a sense of community in a context of widespread institutionalized racism. As Perrotta and Sacchetto (2014, 87) write, "One of the most important pillars of the system of illegal hiring is the construction of a sense of 'community' that binds the [African gang master, also called *caponero*, or Black boss] with 'his' workers. It is a 'community' made up by bonds of kinship, friendship, respect, and trust. The workers closer to the black boss . . . do not question his role and profits, or the organization of his home and daily life. Farmworkers are bound to him by ties that go beyond mere economic considerations." In these narratives, ghettos appear as central nodes in a system of weak social ties: a kind of marginal urbanity that offers a practical response to the spatial and social marginalization of people of African descent in an era of extractive capitalism and proliferating borders.

While I generally agree with these observations, I see a need to also capture more precisely the racial politics through which the migrant labor ghetto, as a space of emergent rural urbanity, is actively incorporated in global capitalist supply chains. In this chapter, I will insist on the central role of migrant labor infrastructures in the active renegotiation of citizenship in Italy's postcolonial context—particularly how the negotiation over migrant infrastructures also reflects a struggle over membership in a society that continues to spatially exclude a considerable section of its productive population in marginal and segregated sites. I will also describe the ghetto's infrastructural reconfiguration in this context. Particularly, I want to show how the boundary between formality and informality, legality and illegality, of public and private realms of citizen-state interaction forms an integral part of the racialization of contemporary global workers and the ways in which the experience of racism effectively naturalizes these into the nation-state space through "inclusionary forms of exclusion" (Carbado 2005, 638).

The eviction of the Grand Ghetto took place in the context of a wider regional intervention called "Capo Free–Ghetto Off." In the early 2000s, various charity organizations started engaging in a series of humanitarian interventions that aimed at bettering migrants' living conditions on the site. One of these was called *Io ci sto* (I am here; later renamed to *ghetto vivibile*: livable ghetto), directed by a Swiss priest. Another project involved the Christian charity Caritas. Through its diocese involvement the charity provided water and sanitation, as well as sociolegal assistance. On April 2, 2014, the regional councilor for social affairs Guglielmo Minervini approved the project *Piano di azione sperimentale per un'accoglienza dignitosa e il lavoro regolare dei migrant in agricoltura* (experimental action plan for a respectable reception and regular labor of migrants in agriculture)—also know as "Capo Free–Ghetto Off" (literally meaning: erasing *caporalato* equals erasing the ghetto), which was to combine these different actions in one government plan. The original plan envisioned the replacement of the Grand Ghetto by five alternative sites, where migrant workers would be hosted. And it comprised a series of measures to formalize their working conditions. In addition to some legal measures, Minervini introduced a quality brand, called Equipuglia, which would grant economic incentives to those firms who did not use illegal labor (*lavoro nero*): "Our invitation thus regards all consumers inside and outside Puglia who choose products which do not exploit illegal labor, and which do not contribute to maintaining a situation like that of Rignano," the governor concluded at the time.[1]

One central measure proposed by the Capo Free–Ghetto Off plan involved the establishment of digitalized employment lists (*liste di prenotazione*). Through these, the regional government incentivized employers to recruit their agricultural workers on a state-sanctioned platform, which served as the unique infrastructure to register the formally employed. An electronic database that connected the different employment centers in the region (the *centri per l'impiego*, or CPI; see chapter 1) would ensure that this recruitment could take place in a rapid and transparent manner. The overall idea behind the *liste di prenotazione* (which later reappeared in Basilicata and Piemonte as well) was that if employers were given incentives to recruit their workers through formal state channels, illegal mediation would become less attractive, because workers could now be found online and not through the networks of the *caporali*, and unregistered employers could more easily be traced and sanctioned. Off the record, the government stakeholders acknowledged that digitalization could only become effective when combined with an additional geographic technology called the terrain-work balance (*indice di congruità*), which associates the surface dimensions of agricultural properties with the labor time needed to plant, grow, and harvest specific crops like tomatoes. This balance could be easily calculated whenever employers were filing their subsidy requests with the regional planning agency (Piano Regolatore Agricolo). To receive European subsidies for their crops, entrepreneurs are obliged to report their utilized agricultural surface (UAS, or *superficie agricola utilizzata*) for that year. This number could easily be made congruent with the amount of labor time needed to plant, weed, and harvest the crops for which the firm was asking subsidies. Based on a net estimate of required labor time that the European Directorate for Agriculture and Rural Development recalculated each year, state agencies, it was thought, could maintain a systematic overview of agricultural capital and labor while intervening through ad hoc inspections—including the use of unmanned drones to check on the actual goings-on in the fields—to keep employers in line with state regulations.[2]

Despite all these good intentions, the *indice di congruità* was never implemented, for reasons I was not able to clarify completely. The consequences of this absence, however, were clearer, and included the growth of what Rigo and Caprioglio (2021) call gray labor: the underreporting of actual labor time in order to skim off or preclude the payment of social welfare contributions like unemployment and pension benefits. Through its insistence on the supposedly insalubrious space of the ghetto as a center of illegal recruitment, the project of formalizing migrant labor in Puglia thus clearly obeyed a territorial logic that is typical of state interventions in the domain of rural development: by associating informality with an "outside" space that thrives on illegality and disrespect for state laws, state institutions are motivated to capture and incorporate these informal activities and populations in order to (re)establish law and order (Roy and AlSayyad 2004; Roy and Crane 2015; T. M. Li 2005). While the attitude toward agricultural firms followed a strategy of carrots and sticks ("ethical" firms would get rewarded with monetary incentives, "unethical" practices would be punished through police interventions), the planned eviction of the Grand Ghetto took a more convoluted course, with partially unforeseen effects. It is this process I will turn to in the next section.

Casa Sankara

The first time I met Hervé Faye was in the summer of 2015. We greeted each other at the station with Marco, who had himself spent several years in Northern Africa and decided to accompany me on this first research trip to Southern Italy. After a short introduction, Hervé invited us to Casa Sankara, the concession he and his uncle Mbaye Ndiaye were occupying on the road between San Severo and Foggia. The premises resembled what I experienced as a West African *foyer*: a central square and a few container buildings, around which children played, while women were busy cooking the meal we would consume later around the fire.

Two years earlier, in 2013, Casa Sankara had been granted a government concession to operate as a diffuse migrant reception center (*accoglienza diffusa*). In cooperation with a local cooperative and charity organization, the families who now occupied this site worked together as *cooperanti*, similarly to the many subcontracted sites that were servicing refugees and asylum seekers across the country at the time (see chapter 3). In practice, this meant Hervé and his fellow *cooperanti* became the cooperative's employees. Living permanently on this site, they serviced a total of ninety people at the time, taking care of their accommodation and nutrition, as well as their often-complex relations to public institutions, for a period of eight months. In Casa Sankara, asylum seekers from Pakistan and Bangladesh lived side by side with fellow migrants from Africa who had traveled across the Mediterranean. Being migrants themselves, Hervé told me, they took care of "those people who live the conditions of marginalization on their own skin."[3] In agreement with the director of the charity organization, they named the site Casa Sankara, after the revolutionary Burkinabè president Thomas Sankara, who was assassinated in 1983. And with the regional administration they jumpstarted the Capo Free–Ghetto Off project, which had the ambition to replace the informal migrant settlement of San Severo with more dignified accommodations. As the regional administrator in charge of the project told me, the ambition was to make Casa Sankara into an autonomous, self-sufficient place.[4]

But after two years, the project collapsed. The families that had sustained the regional project found themselves broke, without a formal contract and without official residency papers, illegally occupying this former regional concession. The situation felt absurd in an environment that not long ago had greeted Casa Sankara as a potential alternative to migrant marginality and as a model of hoped-for social integration. While the war of words went on around the initiative on social media and in the press, I felt there was something more going on than a simple standoff between a cooperative and its workers.

To some extent, Casa Sankara could be seen as emblematic of a much wider conflict that the Mediterranean border crisis was generating at an intersubjective level. On the one hand, its contested occupation took place in the context of the tightening grip over migration in the aftermath of the North African Emergency (see chapter 3). As I wrote earlier, the inauguration of Triton as a border control operation in 2014 caused a shift from a humanitarian paradigm to one of security. Whereas the repression of humanitarian aid in the central Mediterranean visibly contributed to active migrant dispersal and dispossession at the time, it also risked throwing a growing migrant population into a prolonged state of liminality owing to the latter's constant illegalization and refoulement across national borders. Omar, an inhabitant of Casa Sankara, told me not long after my arrival,

> I'm really tired of Italy, tired of this whole system. . . . At one point, I was forced to leave Libya, where I worked for several years: every month I earned my salary working on construction sites; there, I did not have to pay for water, electricity, or petrol, it was all for free. Then they put me up in two reception centers for two years, in Benevento and Caserta [Campania]. The only thing I did was eat pasta with tomato, pasta with tomato, . . . The shopkeepers did not want to sell us anything with the vouchers from the center. They were just racist. . . . From one day to the next I was thrown out of the reception center. The managers told us that the contract had ended, so we had to leave. From Caserta, I decided to go to Brussels for some time. When I returned to Italy, I ended up working in the ghetto.

In conclusion, Omar shrugged: "Look at what they've accomplished, the leaders of Europe: *La nouvelle Libie* [New Libya]. . . . They've chased us Africans away from the continent. . . . Now they lament that too many migrants are arriving at their doorsteps. But who has created this problem, this chaos in the first place? It is them!"[5]

While Hervé and Mbaye insisted repeatedly that their shared condition of being migrants generated a fragile sense of community around this common fate, in practice, they told me, "we were confronted with a mentality of exploiters."[6]

The Racial Contract

To understand the implications of the conflict Casa Sankara generated on a wider scale, it is useful to take a small step backward. First, I need to explore the background of the two men who became the protagonists not just of Casa Sankara but also of the eviction of the Grand Ghetto. Hervé and Mbaye told me at length how they had first moved into Casa Sankara in 2013 after a fire destroyed a large part of the ghetto of San Severo. Like many others, they had ended up there after a series of misadventures. Having lost their official permit to stay in Italy after a short study in Milan, they ended up as clandestine, ambulant traders in Naples, where they were arrested and released. Without papers and without work, they decided to go to the ghetto as a metaphorical last chance to put their life back on track. But the harsh living conditions and the violent monopoly of the *caporali* there were insupportable to these two Senegalese men who were used to quite a different life from that of the ghetto (both belonged to a family of griots, or pre-servers of the oral tradition, of the Lebu people). Their open rift and fight with a *caponero* in the Grand Ghetto was followed by the destructive fire that devastated part of its premises—a cataclysm that changed their life for good. Roaming around aimlessly in San Severo, they bumped into a local cooperative, L'Albero del Pane (the Bread Tree), which was offering meals as part of their charity. The men started talking to the cooperative's local president, who decided to hire them as *cooperanti* (humanitarian agents) in his migrant reception initiative.

A second note needs to be made about the organization of the *accoglienza diffusa* in the ENA context. As I said in a previous chapter, the Mediterranean emergency inspired the Italian governments of Mario Monti and Matteo Renzi to assign structural funds to cooperatives, volunteer groups, and aid associations, as well as private entrepreneurs, to host and service the growing population of asylum seekers and refugees that was reaching Italian shores. The access to these funds occurred through public bidding processes that were not always completely transparent. This opacity reached such an extent that it motivated a judicial investigation, called Mafia Capitale. Among other accusations, the prosecutor highlighted the tight complicity between social cooperatives, public institutions, and criminal figures in the management of public funds intended for migrant reception in the Italian capital.[7] Though the alleged links to organized crime later disappeared from the accusations, the Roman investigation showed the tainted way public funds for migrant reception were managed across the country. During the emergency, episodes of violence-tinged corruption erupted repeatedly in the national press. Several migrants complained about the conditions of host centers located in abandoned and dilapidated buildings. And some even testified to episodes of violent repression. Critics talked about a "business of migration" feeding off those who needed protection the most. In my interview with a close aide of the governor of Puglia, he personally denounced what he called a "parallel system" of corruption that characterized migrant reception in the region. He accused several associations in his region of working "at the expense of the immigrant and making them into their own business."[8] It was in this context of detrimental service delivery and violent corruption that the conflict over Casa Sankara eventually burst into the open.

Hervé and his fellow workers accused the president of the local cooperative of exploiting Casa Sankara and its inhabitants for his personal benefit. The nub of the disagreement was the refusal of the president to sign a formal employment contract with the *cooperanti*. Hervé and the other migrant members of the cooperative protested that they desperately needed such a contract to renew their residency papers so that they could gain access to social benefits and regain their legal residence. According to Italian immigrant decrees, formal employment is the only alternative to obtain legal residence in the country in the absence of the prerequisites for political or humanitarian asylum. Without such a contract, migrants not only risk deportation, but they also practically lose their chance of obtaining a legal accommodation in the form of a rented flat. And their legal right to social benefits such as unemployment and pension contributions become nonexistent; in effect, they cease to be considered a legal person.

The standoff between Casa Sankara's employees and the cooperative's president partly reflected what Andrea Muehlebach (2011, 2012) identifies as the culture of volunteerism (*cultura del volontariato*) that has taken root in Italy's post-Fordist order: the highly moralized forms of citizenship that emerge concomitant with the proceeding privatization of social services. In Italy, such compassionate labor is heavily mediated by the state, she writes, as its institutions actively try to mitigate the consequences of their own withdrawal by hoarding a narrative of citizen responsibility, solidarity, and sacrifice. The pioneers of this narrative are situated on both ends of the political spectrum, with "white" and "red" cooperatives competing in this new affective market economy. The case of Casa Sankara shows that compassionate labor operates not only as a mitigating force against marginality and exclusion, but also as a vehicle for the production and maintenance of a new exclusionary order founded on racial categories and racist exclusions. Yet while the unwaged labor regime that supports charity work relies on good feelings like trust, reciprocity, and magnanimity—all of which are considered "essential to the social contract" in a "disarticulated" society, Muehlebach writes (see also Caltabiano 2002, 19–21)[9]—I find it useful to emphasize the fundamentally racist underpinnings of the culture of volunteerism that characterized working conditions in Casa Sankara. With their noncitizen workers, the outcome of this process of social reconfiguration turned out to be quite different, in fact. First, the "social contract" that solidified migrants' cooperation in the Casa Sankara project thrived on unpaid work, not unwaged labor. The difference is not trivial in my view. While unwaged labor still builds on a formal relation of privatized service delivery for the public good, unpaid volunteer work completely lacks this formal recognition, and therefore it remains open to abject abuse. Casa Sankara's workers repeatedly told me that retribution always took the form of a concession of some sorts: remunerations never figured as wage (*salario*) but rather as compensations (*rimborso, contributo*) for given services. By denying them a formal contract, furthermore, the president of the cooperative not only reproduced the boundary between those deemed to express and receive solidarity in this context, but he also denied his workers their factual citizenship rights. Their work in fact never transformed into a collective social act that transcended the specific nature of their individual tasks. Instead, Casa Sankara's volunteers remained within the bounds of the private sphere, as noncitizens who are included in the regime of citizenship but excluded from participating in its practical realm. In that sense, Casa Sankara's relation to informal labor revealed to what extent citizenship also becomes something one needs to deserve and aspire to at the same time. Hervé explained: "We needed documents, so we asked for a contract, and not the solidarity contributions [*contribute di solidarietà*] that [the director of the charity] wrote every time on his payment slips. . . . That is where the conflict started. One day in December 2014, [the director] came to Casa Sankara to change the locks and to tell us we should leave. Mbaye called the police. When they arrived, they told the director to leave us in peace. Because this place belongs to the project 'Ghetto Out' [Capo Free–Ghetto Off] and not to the cooperative."[10]

Rather than a new moral personality based on mutual solidarity, what appeared to emerge in the context of Casa Sankara was a condition of outright exclusion from being recognized as laborers and citizens at the same time. What Hervé and his fellow workers contested the most was the cultural politics of belonging and sacrifice they were asked to subscribe to, while they were actively denied a space for participation as full members of Italian society. Ironically, the name Casa Sankara had emerged in the attempt to provide a symbolic bridge between Africa and Europe in this context of mutual dialogue. In Hervé's words: "The immigrant has to be an interlocutor, protagonist of his own fate" (L'immigrant doit être un interlocuteur, protagoniste de son propre sort).[11] Even more, therefore, the culture of gifting, of sacrifice and of solidarity that the charity organization stood for, contrasted deeply with the denied political subjectivity of these workers as entrepreneurs of their own. As Hervé argued, "We are not fighting for just one thing of Africans for Africans. We want and are dreaming of an enterprise where Italians and Africans can see that things are possible if we get together. . . .

And we would be happy to hire Italians. . . . We didn't ask to give us the job, we are creating jobs."[12]

Formalizing Otherness

In hindsight, the conflict over Casa Sankara appeared to me as one of those rare moments when racialized subjects claim to be recognized not just as working bodies but as full subjects, as human beings in a context that continued to deny their equal humanity (see also Browne 2015; McKittrick 2013). During my talks with Hervé and his friends, I was reminded many times of Franz Fanon's argument about the schizophrenia of colonial identity and the way formerly colonized subjects kept being framed as subaltern Others even long after the imperial powers conceded their former colonies political independence. In his book *Black Skin, White Masks*, he speaks of the construction of a racial epidermal vision that predetermines the formerly colonized Other through the eyes of others, through "white eyes, the only real eyes," which simultaneously takes him "far off from my presence" (Fanon 1967, 112–16).

In the case of the migrant workers at Casa Sankara, this objectification had to be taken even more literally, I think, as the toiling bodies of African workers appeared to have no right to physical existence if not through the performance of a predefined presence that captured them as victims that needed to be saved, rather than human beings who had a right to exist on their own terms. This tension came abruptly to the fore during a gathering of the labor union FLAI-CGIL in Foggia in 2014, Hervé recalled, where the issue of migrant exploitation in agriculture was openly discussed. Hervé remembered he was given two minutes to speak after a long line of local party and labor union functionaries of this agricultural syndicate. In a packed hall, he stood up and said, "Behind your food lies our slavery" (Dietro il vostro cibo c'è la nostra schiavitù). Hervé recalls this as an important rupture: "Ho preso la parola," he said (literally: I have taken the word), "I've broken a convention, I speak for myself, there is no intermediary." At that point, he remembers, something of a shock wave ran through the meeting hall. Other African workers present in the room applauded and yelled while rebelling against the union representatives, telling them they should be given the word, too. Mbaye recalls that this moment shook the foundations of the way "Ghetto Off" was conceived as a project. Migrant workers were no longer going to accept to be spoken for by their white representatives but would instead be masters of their own self-proclaimed struggle.

What made this moment of public outcry and *presa di parola* unique was that, for the first time, workers took aim at the humanitarian operation they felt was keeping their claims to autonomy and self-determination deliberately suppressed. And they insisted on being recognized as active entrepreneurs, rather than passive humanitarian victims. At some point, Hervé said, "We do not want to be instrumentalized. . . . We have denounced the man who exploits us, so for us there is no going back. It is like Thomas Sankara said: 'If assistance does not form a basis for autonomy, it is no real help.' . . . Let's not be fooled: for these organizations, these charities, for me it looks as if it helps them to find us there, in the ghetto. To me they are worse than the *caporali*. At least they [the *caporali*] live among the workers." Recalling decades of humanitarian assistance in sub-Saharan Africa, Mbaye questioned, "How many billions do they gain by putting people in line like that for a sack of rice? . . . It's a real shame." Hervé added, "We are dealing with an emergency of twenty years here . . . an eternal emergency. . . . So are we really interested in closing the ghetto or rather in developing it?"

In my subsequent meetings with Casa Sankara's inhabitants, it became clear to me that a larger political and ideological shift was at stake here, or better said, a double shift. On the one hand, Hervé, Mbaye, and their fellow noncitizens were proposing an "epistemic decentering" (Sarr 2016, 107), a "bringing to matter" of Casa Sankara's denied existence (Mbembe 2017, 47) that simultaneously agitated against the Black man as an objectified, extractive body while enlightening the permanent shadows in which it kept being cast. "We were not people in need who [the director] found in the street like that," Hervé said. "We live in San Severo. This is our home." Referring to his native country, Senegal, Mbaye added, "We do not have to take any lesson in democracy from no one. . . . We are born democrats [Siamo nati démocratique]." While the recognition as citizens of a European country remained an important desire, his statement appeared to say that this should not mean having to subject one's personal dignity to a cultural template designed by others.

On the other hand, Casa Sankara proposed a rupture with the humanitarian emergency that had characterized migration politics since the "collapse" of the Libyan border. Along with the associations that declared their support for the Casa Sankara initiative (such as Libera and Legacoop), Mbaye and Hervé criticized not only the business of the *caporali* they had been contesting over the years, but also the humanitarian organizations that were operating "at the expense of immigrants"—as the regional administrator had described the situation to me in his interview. In line with this shift, a network of associations proposed to make Casa Sankara a center of economic reconversion and social integration.[13] While picking up the remnants of the dilapidated "Ghetto Off" project, the new project would employ migrant workers as waged laborers on an alternative agricultural project after their eviction from Puglia's main ghettos (Rignano, Borgo Mezzanone, and Ghana House). This project, called

Cooperativa Di Vittorio Africa (significantly referring to an important agrarian syndicalist from the area), would comprise a twenty-hectare field directed by Mbaye and an Italo-Senegalese association with technical assistance from a neighboring regional consortium. Ideally, the cooperative should have formed the foundation of an alternative, active citizenship, as the regional administrator explained to me later: "We need to erect a system of reception that is different from the common model of overassistance, because—as we have seen in the diffused reception centers (*alberghi diffusi*), this model results in a curbing of social services." The administrator used the term *assistenzialismo*, which is frequently evoked in the context of "inefficient" service delivery in Italy. The term also serves as an ideological trope to stimulate the neoliberal moral citizenship reconversion Muehlebach and others talk about in their writings. The plan of the new Casa Sankara project was instead meant to introduce a system where migrants would help each other in giving and receiving hospitality. At least on the face of it, this proposition aimed to revoke the exclusionary order that the Mediterranean refugee crisis had been constructing all along: with a formal recognition of their labor rights, migrant workers could now fully aspire to their right as future Italian citizens, or so it was said.

Interesting in this context was Casa Sankara's growing advancement of the terminology of "legality." "We have to be on the side of legality," Mbaye told me in his first interview.[14] Even if for a very brief period, therefore, Casa Sankara may have held the promise of an urban prefiguration, in a sense that the recuperation of the agency to act without the mediation of representative structures may serve to describe a distinct mode of producing urban space (Minuchin 2021; Holston 2008); the need to be recognized and seen by the state was predominant among the project's objectives. As soon as relations started to formalize, the emphasis on "legality" became more and more important. In mid-2016, Hervé told me over the phone, "Things have to be organized more formally now."[15] While insisting that they needed to take matters into their own hands, he and his coworkers continued to emphasize the operations of "criminals" in the ghetto who remained a major obstacle to making Casa Sankara a viable alternative by terrorizing the ghetto's inhabitants into submission. In his assessments, and in close concordance with the regional administration, Hervé compared the ghetto to a "lawless area" (*zona franca*) situated "outside civilization" (*fuori della civiltà*).[16]

After two years of legal limbo, the forceful eviction of the Grand Ghetto in the winter of 2017 clearly constituted another turning point, as doubts arose as to whether the proclaimed autonomy of Casa Sankara had not made place for an indirect form of border externalization. The thought that Casa Sankara was evolving into another situation of *accoglienza diffusa* effectively occurred to me when, in the winter of 2017, large groups of African workers kept arriving on its premises after the Grand Ghetto was ultimately evicted by the regional adminis-tration.[17] In the new convention that Casa Sankara signed, the government care-fully renamed the site Azienda Fortore, its original name from the years of land reform, to avoid confusion with the previous cooperative. While the directors officially took their distance from other antiracist associations and initiatives in the area, such as Pro Fuga and Campagne in Lotta,[18] they argued that any attempt to organize labor autonomously outside the formal state reception cen-ters in the end was doing a service to the criminal economy of the ghetto. Hervé told me in January 2016, "If they want to solve the problems of the ghetto, they have to start giving a decent accommodation to these people. . . . This is the first step. I told them, 'Let's take people to the facilities and go there to see them if we love them, because now only criminals live in the ghetto.'" Gradually, the system of accommodation changed as well. Inhabitants were hosted for a three-month probation period, during which they had to actively show their engagement in the concession's daily management. This meant taking turns in distributing food portions, cleaning the kitchen and the rest of the premises, and performing other quotidian tasks. The inhabitants of Casa Sankara–Azienda Fortore were promised intensive Italian classes, professional training, and—in case of a posi-tive evaluation—a residency permit at the end of the probation period. But my interlocutors in the center complained that none of the promised courses had taken place. Not long after the arrival of Rignano's evicted workers, I witnessed agents from the Italian civil protection (*protezione civile*) delivering a truck of standard field beds to the concession on which the reception center was located. The next month, Hervé and Mbaye transformed the field that was once planned for experimental agriculture into a giant tent camp. In the meantime, the gates of the concession remained firmly closed; entry to Casa Sankara's premises was possible only with a special permit or upon strict invitation of the association's directorship. For the more than five hundred inhabitants of the center, this clearly meant a return to humanitarian logics. Instead of the communal garden, food to the former ghetto dwellers came from a local cooperative, now in the form of precooked meals. During a short visit in the winter of 2017, I heard sev-eral inhabitants complain about the failed promises of the management. When I met with a group of Gambian men in their mid-to-late twenties, one of the men told me, "We only eat and sleep here." After having resided in several recep-tion centers in the north of the country, he came to the ghetto to earn a living. But the fire destroyed his belongings, so he voluntarily came to Casa Sankara to start anew. "My three months here are ending," one of them concluded. "If they don't give me my residence [papers], I will tell them they are faking me and go to Germany."[19]

Once again, therefore, the proposed "social contract" that solidified migrants' cooperation in the Casa Sankara project appeared to thrive not on unwaged, voluntary or charity labor, but on unpaid work. The directors of Azienda Fortore motivated this differentiation between their own formal role and the informal voluntary work of their clients as a form of solidarity on which the recognition of the latter depended. Significant in this respect was that to receive a territorial residency permit, migrant workers, as citizens-to-become, not only needed to show their allegiance to the laws of the Italian nation-state on which their status formally depended; they also needed to demonstrate their participation in the intimate economy of voluntary work. In this manner, therefore, the new management of Casa Sankara ironically solidified the formal/informal boundary on which their own exclusion had originally been founded. In the absence of formal labor, informal migrant workers saw the vicious cycle that kept them hostage in their condition of noncitizens organically reconfirmed. For many young Black African workers who kept arriving on the Mediterranean shorelines, the ghetto continued to represent an important infrastructure, which in the absence of a formally recognized autonomous social space where they could develop their personal life projects at least gave them a glimpse of opportunity and a possibility to relate to their peers—even if that meant subjecting themselves to yet other violent hierarchies.

Then, in 2018, positive change suddenly started to gain momentum at Casa Sankara. Thanks to the official recognition of Casa Sankara–Ghetto Out as a formal association,[20] its directors were able to build a public and private partnership with the region of Puglia for an ethical and sustainable agriculture project, the project Mbaye Ndiaye had proposed with Cooperativa Di Vittorio Africa in 2016. Other partners in the project included the agro-industrial association Le Due Palme; the labor unions CGIL, CISL, and the autonomous agricultural workers association NO CAP; and the regional government of Puglia. On the land concession that the regional authorities had already granted (a total of twenty hectares), the project planted its first tomato plants in 2020 with the support of three agricultural enterprises from the vicinity. The project directors proudly announced a fully ethical supply chain, from the field to the transformation into peeled tomatoes in the industrial plant of Conserve Italia (one of the major canning groups in Europe) and the sale to consumers through Coop Alleanza, the historical cooperative supply chain in Italy. With a production of 120,000 cans, Riaccolta, as the enterprise was named, was taking its first footsteps as an alternative supply chain to the retailers that still dominate agri-business in most of the country. Hervé proudly told me all this in his interview with me in April 2021, echoing the president of Coop Alleanza, Mario Cifiello, who in his press statement called the brand "proof that another economy, another way of understanding work and consumer purchasing choices are possible."[21] "If the inhabitants of Casa Sankara get to earn a regular wage through this project," Hervé concluded, "I think we have already reached a grand objective."[22]

In the meantime, the easing of security norms after the eviction of the Grand Ghetto of Rignano also contributed to a more relaxed atmosphere in Casa Sankara's guesthouse. The initial idea of a social contract, in which the directorship and Casa Sankara's inhabitants agree on mutual norms and support, progressively took shape in a collective management structure. In an interview with the magazine of Italy's historical encyclopedia, Treccani, Mbaye Ndiaye explained the principle of *Khelcom* that he and his associates were implementing in the project of Casa Sankara:[23]

> In the association, we are four people to take care of the administration, planning, reception, and registration of new arrivals, necessary documents, relations with institutions: prefecture, law enforcement, municipality, region. We have responsibilities with respect to the young guests, we take care of them, we meet their needs. At the same time, they themselves are actively involved with us in the daily functioning of Casa Sankara, in its management, in the maintenance of its spaces. Once a month we hold meetings with all of them to discuss, collect needs, and to sensitize them and make them understand the meaning of this community, to urge them to be active and involved, to make a path of full autonomy. Many young people who have passed through Casa Sankara now live in San Severo, pay rent, have an employment contract, the employer pays them their contributions. Here, we want this! So we want to live in Italy, which is a second mother for us!

In the same interview, Hervé repeated what he told me back in 2015: "Our strong point is that this structure is based on the full protagonism of the migrants themselves because we know what we need." Citing an interview with the former Burkinabè president Thomas Sankara, he added, "We must have the courage to invent the future." Firmly rejecting the humanitarian aid model that for decades the Italian state has been implementing (and continues to implement) to assist migrant laborers in the region, he appeared determined to take up the challenge of inventing another path, of imagining an alternative economic model that crushes the repertoire of stereotypes and clichés and instead emphasizes hospitality and assistance (Manfreda 2020). A national news service concluded, "Casa Sankara is the response of the state against the ghetto. It guarantees workers access to that what they obtain at a high cost in the ghetto from the *caporale*. . . . But Casa Sankara is a drop. Out there, there is the ocean" (*TG24*, May 15, 2020).

The Dialectics of Informal Development

The experience of the Capo Free–Ghetto Off project and its many ramifications in Puglia shows once more the intricacies of formalizing informal migrant work in the context of South Italy's rural economy. The obstinate government strategy to cyclically evict and destroy informal settlements where precarious migrant labor continues to be concentrated and segregated did not appear to produce any structural effects. On the contrary, still today, thousands of so-called seasonal workers continue to live and take care of themselves in the ghettos, which over the years have taken on more permanent features as peripheral urban infrastructures— including the Grand Ghetto of Rignano, the Pista of Borgo Mezzanone in Puglia, the Ghana House of Borgo Tre Titoli in Puglia, Boreano and Mulini Matinelle in Basilicata, San Ferdinando in Calabria, and Saluzzo in Piemonte. The main reason for this apparent development failure, I argue, lies in a generalized neglect of the fundamentally racialized and gendered organization of agricultural production and reproduction. The ghetto, as a central infrastructure of rural capitalist development, has the key function of externalizing the costs of social reproduction and using informality as a systematic subsidy to capital (see also Mezzadri 2019). In rural Italy, the overtly criminalized and illegalized space of the ghetto performs exactly that function of outsourcing and externalizing the cost, not so much of the reproduction of labor as an exchange value (which continues to be externalized to social spaces that are usually far removed from the site of production, like the household and the community), but of all kinds of other "services" that are subsequently commodified into parallel, informal economies of care, exchange, and outright exploitation. In the ghetto, it makes indeed little sense to neatly distinguish between labor as a factor of production or reproduction, as the very services that are commodified here serve also to bolster uneven relations in the agricultural production process. To put the blame for this externalization on criminal economies—as the proponents of labor formalization continue to do—is to upset the causal chain, I argue, because capitalist supply chains benefit greatly from this externalization through a cut in wages and social contributions like health care, pensions, and accommodation—not to mention the rigid labor discipline and coercion laborers are naturalized into as a result of this capitalization on their social networks. The fixation of social reproduction into such informalized economies creates a form of "gray space": an outside space where people who are not considered worth governing through the "lightness" of formal regulations are deliberately segregated and marginalized, while at the same time deprived of their ability to act autonomously.

The experience of Capo Free–Ghetto Off also confirms Roy and AlSayyad's (2004, 5) observation that the distinctions between formal and informal must be interpreted as emerging "in practice." To quote one of the first observers of "informal" economic wealth in Africa, Keith Hart: "The task is not only to find practical ways of harnessing the complementary potential of bureaucracy and informality, but also to advance thinking about their dialectical movement" (Hart 2008, 4). Indeed, the experience of Casa Sankara as a potential alternative to migrant labor informality tells us that for such alternatives to take form, it very much depends on the legal and political concessions the state is willing to grant in order to recognize and accommodate mobile workers with non-Italian roots not just as factors of production but as full citizens with complete labor rights. As one observer noted, such recognition forms in fact one drop in the ocean of submission and neglect.

Unfortunately, one of the structural effects of the Capo Free–Ghetto Off project in Puglia was that regional governments across Italy gradually became convinced that the key to eradicating "illegal" *caporale* intermediation lay in eradicating migrant settlements. In his interviews with me, the regional administrator for migration of Basilicata firmly confirmed his adherence to the *liste di prenotazione* model of formal employment that the Capo Free–Ghetto Off plan introduced.[24] Task forces from different Italian regions have taken part in exchanges and discussed strategies and plans to formalize labor, stimulate ethical consumption, and improve the living conditions of the thousands of migrant workers occupied in Italian agriculture. The shared strategy in these roundtables was always the same: eradicate illegal labor intermediation by systematically evicting migrants from the unruly space of the ghetto while at the same time submitting their right to territorial residence to a formal registration in camp infrastructures and employment lists managed by state-funded institutions. While the outcome of this formalization strategy could be described as highly problematic, its narration as a national success story undoubtedly constituted an important building block of the ideology of migrant management in the domain of industrial agriculture across the country (see also Ippolito, Perrotta, and Raeymaekers 2021). In fact, after 2016, subsequent governments on the Left and Right would adopt an increasingly aggressive strategy toward the informal ghettos that continued to emerge in Italy's horticultural districts. In 2016–2020, regional administrations evicted the Pista of Borgo Mezzanone (Puglia), the *barracopoli* (slum) of San Ferdinando (Calabria), the *tendopoli* (tent camp) of Saluzzo (Piemonte), and the ghetto of Felandina (Basilicata). Each time, these highly performative interventions were accompanied by government promises of alternative accommodation in the form of temporary camp infrastructures managed by humanitarian emergency organizations. Each time, though, governments failed to keep their promises—either because of delays or because promised residency papers did not materialize, or for whatever other reason. Each time, therefore, these makeshift camps emptied to give rise again to the same ghettos that have become so characteristic of the informal urbanization that has been going on for years in these agricultural districts. In that sense, Capo Free–Ghetto Off forms indeed an emblematic case of the convoluted politics of formalization that has characterized not a few commodity frontiers in our current era of violent globalization.

CONCLUSION

What can the Mediterranean teach us about the deep socio-ecological crisis we are experiencing today in terms of human mobility, agrarian change, and the limits to neoliberal growth? In this book, I explore the question from the perspective of West African migrant workers currently employed in the agricultural supply chain between the southern Sahel and the northern Mediterranean. Because of profound geopolitical and ecological transformations in this past decade, their lives have been radically shaken. Human and natural desertification captures the Sahel in an increasingly deadly grip. Alternative sources of livelihood seem to be progressively destroyed because of armed conflict and political instability. The figurative last straw that broke down historical patterns of South-South labor migration in Africa has been the outbreak of armed conflict in Libya, which, among other consequences, has led to a profound crisis of the EU-African border regime. But while NATO and EU interventions have been putting in place an increasingly sophisticated and repressive border regime to control Mediterranean waters and push back the undesired, these strategies have further accelerated a process that was already well under way. Under the radar of Europe's spectacular border politics, a deeply ramified and exploitative mode of production is gaining strength through its embedded roots in Black Mediterranean history. In the following sections, I will outline, first, what my perspective can possibly add to complement persistent notions of the Mediterranean. After that, I will turn to the main conceptual and methodological conclusions of this book, which concern the relation between mobile labor and extractive urbanization in this interconnected border space.

A first contribution of this book involves a shift of attention toward the history of Mediterranean capitalism as a set of layered traces. My study complements, but also partly challenges, the scholarship of Fernand Braudel (1995), who only marginally acknowledged the pivotal role of the Mediterranean in propelling enslavement as a central characteristic of European capitalism. It is indeed telling how Braudel's whitening gaze has continued to inspire a historical analysis of capitalism as a world system while remaining blind to the way the rights of free men and women have been persistently denied and destroyed in this context. Based on the insights I provide in this book I hope to contribute to a change of mind-set. But I also extend the notion of racial capitalism beyond its historical focus on Blackness and slavery, by insisting on the "multiple histories" of capitalist articulation through racial, gendered, and generational hierarchies (Federici 2020, 29). Concurring with recent feminist and critical race scholarship (e.g., Federici 2020; Pulido 2015, 2017; but also and foremost Davis 1983 and Robinson [1983] 2005), I insist that these histories must be told by weaving together the testimonies of those who are—often through prolonged violence and terror—enslaved, colonized, and turned into unpaid workers. I agree it is important to foreground how interlocking systems of domination produce new subjectivities and new configurations of forces.

More attention could indeed be paid to the intersecting racisms that continue to reproduce the peoples of the Mediterranean as those having a lesser form of modernity, and how the chromatic norm that sustains their inequality continues to pervade relations with so-called "new Italians" in the context of recent history (see also Lombardi-Diop and Romeo 2014, 372). As I hope to have shown, these intersecting discriminations have become structural components of the geography of capitalist development in the sphere of agri-food supply chains. The subjection of contemporary migrant agri-food workers to excessive labor exploitation and social and spatial segregation could not have materialized the way it did without the preexisting hierarchies of discrimination and economic differentiation on which the Mediterranean agrarian mode of production materially and ideologically thrives. In that sense, I see a logical thread of racist discrimination running through contemporary Mediterranean economic history, involving the political enactment of difference between subjects that were deemed to deserve and not deserve to take part in the "miracle" of modern national progress. In my view, this color line runs right through these racialized bodies whose labor is extracted but whose social and political participation is actively refused through the infrastructures of contemporary supply chain agriculture.

A second contribution I hope to make in this domain involves changing our understanding of the Mediterranean as a border(ed) space. Critical migration scholarship has clearly shown how the proceeding securitization of the

Mediterranean in the context of NATO and European interventions has made territorial boundaries more and more ubiquitous. To quote Vacchiano (2013, 337), the Mediterranean has become a "contact zone" for the testing of new policies concerning mobility and migration control, with often problematic consequences for basic human rights. Rather than a test zone, I would say, this border regime has become a new mode of government within which the control over life and death becomes operational. A penetrating example here has been the deliberate externalization of the European border and its materialization in North African concentration camps. Through multilateral and bilateral measures, European member states are now actively externalizing territorial borders and ports of entry: Europe's borders are not only progressively moving offshore onto African territories, but also onshore into new reception and detention infrastructures to detain, channel, and dissect differently valued humans. While within Europe sovereign territory has taken on a more fluid and dynamic profile, at its margins we are witnessing the material manifestation of an expanding migrant exclusion through the erection of new barriers, prisons, and walls.

From the perspective of Mediterranean history, there is something less unprecedented in the way territorial boundaries figure in the government of space, however. Black radical scholars make us aware of these continuities, in the sense that capitalism has been anything but a closed system since its emergence in the Mediterranean in the late medieval period. The institutionalized racism that took root then in the Mediterranean plantation economy—and from there traveled to the Caribbean and the Americas—has laid the foundations of a regime of global terror that has continued to sustain capital accumulation through the active implementation of racializing spatial divisions. *Pace* Cedric Robinson, therefore, one could argue that "capitalism was less a catastrophic revolution (negation) of feudal social order than the extension of these social relations into the larger tapestry of the modern world's political and economic relations" (Robinson [1983] 2005, 42–43). Rather than a state of exception, it makes in fact more sense to regard the spectacular border politics we are witnessing in the Mediterranean as a "state of repetition" (Lombardi-Diop 2021), a kind of superborder that has determined the lives of subaltern subjects in this geographic space since a very long time ago and continues to divide humanity along racial lines (Ticktin 2007).

To account for these racial divisions, I use the terminology of natural racialization. As I said, this term refers to the specific ways in which racism effectively "naturalizes" a group into a permanent form of nonbelonging. More specifically, I analyze the "naturalizing" of the space of Blackness in the Mediterranean as part of a social, discursive, and material deployment of forces that divide humanity through explicitly racial categories and distinctions. These categories and distinctions are in turn made intelligible through an overlaid spatial and cultural grid of racial differentiation, and of "managing difference [through] spatial dispersal" (Hawthorne 2021a, 5). The emblematic example of this "natural racialization" is of course the Black African migrant ghetto, which in today's development planning and discourse has assumed the identity of a lawless "outside" space that should be redeemed and sanitized (*bonificata*) in order to restore its humanity. The term *bonifica* can be directly associated to the historical attempts of the Italian state to capture and channel the peasantry toward the type of capital-oriented monoculture agriculture that is so characteristic of the Mediterranean today—a history I address in chapters 1 and 2 of the book. Drawing this historical connection helps me explain how today, the material-discursive association between peasant lifeworlds and incivility has remained a constant in Italian development planning since the late 1800s. Contemporary sanitation policies, in fact, have gathered their most acute political expression in the active destruction, dispersal, and dispossession of migrant workers' habitats, a destruction that, not coincidentally, corresponds to the progressive crackdown on migrant rights along migrant trajectories in the Mediterranean over the past decade.

Yet while these politics of active ruination may raise the impression of a joint desire on the part of national governments to force migrants into formal state templates, the reality is more contorted. In chapters 2, 3, and 4, I show the functionality of the migrant workers' ghetto in contemporary supply chain agriculture in the sense that (a) ghettos fulfill the role of social reproduction, because it is there that relations of care and subsistence that the state does not provide are directly discharged on the workers and their social networks and (b) this social reproduction is functional to the illegal forms of labor intermediation that state development discourse overtly condemns but effectively serve as a subsidy to capital.

What characterizes Black African subjectivity in the contemporary Mediterranean plantation, therefore, is not so much their vertical integration (or adverse incorporation) in capitalist supply chains—after all, this condition is characteristic of all precarious work in today's capitalist society—but their permanent state of liminality. This liminality, represented by the Mediterranean middle passage, is actively reproduced and sustained by the increasingly deadly triangle between state terror, humanitarian security management, and labor coercion that places Black migrants into the grip of capital. Specific of rural capitalism in this context is the historical trope on which this liminality is founded. Like yesterday's peasants, today's migrant agri-food workers are deemed incapable of modernity, and therefore their fate needs to be molded and adapted so as to make them apt to the needs of modern, capitalist civilization. The vicissitudes of this reasoning come to the fore in the way not just African migrants, but all migrating people, are prey to increasingly inhumane subjections and repressions in the Mediterranean. What makes the experience of Black migrants specific is their natural racialization into a space that is deemed unworthy of humanity and modern civility. As I write in chapter 3, the prison complex of Libya, with its systematic torture, abuse, and exploitation, plays a central role in this dehumanization process, because it is here that African migrants are subjected to the regime of terror that will continue to haunt their existence as they travel onward to other destinations (if they indeed make it across this deadly threshold). Reconnecting this traumatic experience to the lifeworlds of African migrant workers in the fields of Southern Italy—a majority of whom today are refugees and asylum seekers who have passed through the Mediterranean death channel—indeed motivates my argument about the Mediterranean Sea as a new middle passage that is both a rupture point and generative of a new form of liminal Black existence. In this regard, my book clearly follows the line of earlier arguments about the functionality of (late) liberalism to bracket certain forms of life as "not yet" developed, civilized, and modern. Through the technologies of segmentation and segregation, such bracketed lives indeed acquire the status of a permanent limbo, "an edge of life located somewhere between given and new social positions and roles, and between the conditions of the past and the promise of the future" (Povinelli 2011, 78). Like Povinelli, I say we should regard the endurance of this "edge of life" simultaneously as a political battle and an uneven social terrain, which, next to generating the matter of exclusions, also produces a new political condition (Povinelli 2011, 17). Following this line of thought, my book proposes four main conclusions, which I will detail one by one in the following sections.

First, I argue that the distinction between free and unfree, waged and unwaged labor, slavery and freedom in modern (or late) capitalism is always the result of a political process, of the active *making* of capitalist subjectivities (Kasmir and Carbonella 2014; Thompson 1963). I regard the political subjectivities that emerge in the context of Mediterranean supply chain agriculture as the result of a process of social differentiation and spatial stratification—a process that is ontologically grounded in the politics of race that underpins the history of capitalist alienation. This (call it) cultural reading of racial capitalism forms a critique against orthodox Marxism, which took less seriously the importance of race as a key component of this alienation process.

Second, I regard the temporary labor camps, informal ghettos, and their continuous unsettlement and destruction in the Italian context as key infrastructures that serve to discipline and control rural labor in Black Mediterranean agri-food chains. These infrastructures give rise to a specific kind of logic of separation, or a "plantation logic," which, to paraphrase Katherine McKittrick (2013, 3), produces differential modes of living and spaces of Otherness. This logic in turn finds its expression in a widespread racialized surveillance that pins down toiling bodies in such segregated sites, while deliberately delegating the responsibility over labor reproduction to the sphere of informality and unwaged work.

Third, the cyclical pattern of neglect and destruction that has characterized state intervention in the domain of migrant agri-food labor shows at once a logic of racial cruelty and sovereign withdrawal. In line with critical race scholars, I see state institutions not as all-seeing and all-encompassing, but rather part of a relational geography in which the terms of controlling the means of production are heavily contested and constantly renegotiated (Pulido 2015, 525). Racial cruelty in the tomato fields expresses itself through the ambivalent performance of (regional and national) state institutions, as these seek to establish themselves as the protector of freedom and citizen rights while simultaneously effecting excessive physical violence on migrant workers (see also Melamed 2015, 77). At the same time, I argue, relationality is key to the expression of human difference. Therefore, it is important to also emphasize the active production of race in the context of agrarian society and the way racial categories and distinctions take shape through everyday interactions, because it is exactly through this uneven jigsaw of differentiated networks that racialized social hierarchies are being bolstered and reproduced (Gilmore 2002a, 16).

Fourth, the moral economy of personalized relations that transfuses the fields of migrant accommodation, of humanitarian assistance, and of rural employment cyclically reproduces the migrant ghetto as a permanent rural infrastructure, a city on the edge, which—though actively forged through racial cruelty—also expresses an important relational geography in support of rural capitalism. In contrast to the ideal-type notion of the polis as a self-contained unit, I insist, with others, on a variable, multiscalar, and processual conceptualization of urbanization in this context (Brenner 2013; Brenner and Katsikis 2013). The term I choose for this urban form is that of a city on the edge, a liminal city or *eschatopolis*: from *polis* (city, state, city-state) and *eschatia* (confines, border, edge). In this context, it is worth emphasizing that in the historical Greek city-state, the *eschatia* was exactly that area along the city's confines that served as a buffer between the city and its territorial outside, a marginal and not fully incorporated land only partially integrated into the productive system (Horden and Purcell 2000, 80; Constantakopoulou 2018). Inspired by this historical reference, I insist on the contemporaneous emergence of this type of marginal urbanity in the interstitial area between rural and urban lifeworlds. It is a form of life that persists on the boundary between the formal and the informal and in the margins of nation-state territoriality that separate the white, national citizenry from the black forms of life that are permanently exiled from its sovereign body. *Eschatopolis*, therefore, is distinct from both the urban slums and from the make-shift forms of urbanity that characterize the middle passage of migrant mobility because of its outspoken relation to rural capitalism. The traces of this liminal space, however intermittent and ephemeral they may appear, in my view signify a persistent peripheralization of the rural lifeworlds that sustain agrarian capitalism in our contemporary era. As I argue, we need to imagine this peripheralization not so much as a fixed border in the landscape but rather as a stratified compartmentalization of space that lodges the power of the capitalist relations of rural production and reproduction at every geographic scale. Thus, and returning to my earlier quotation of Neil Smith, we need to think of the production of this peripheral space as an active process that is both driven and reinforced by the interaction of different forces—and not as the automated outcome of capitalist expansion. In the following sections, I will further specify these points one by one before highlighting the potential methodological ramifications of my work.

Before Labor

"Under capitalism, the only thing worse than being exploited is not being exploited," Michael Denning writes in his provocative essay (2010, 79). Referring to Karl Marx's classical distinction between the relative surplus population and the virtual pauper, or wageless being, he highlights how it is capitalist accumulation itself that constantly produces a relatively redundant working population— a population that is superfluous to capital's average requirements for its own valorization and is, therefore, a surplus population. The classic example Marx invokes is the industrial reserve army: the precarious collection of unemployed individuals whose labor power exists only at the mercy of capital's requirements. With a little imagination, and as many scholars indeed have done before me, one could apply this definition to the contemporary masses of exploited workers active in the agricultural industry, whose commodified value, indeed whose value as human beings, appears to depend entirely on capital's demands (for a discussion see Pradella and Cillo 2021). Often euphemistically referred to as "harvesters" or "day laborers," they appear to be a reflection of what orthodox Marxism calls the paradox of "free" labor. Marx in fact insists that the very concept of the "free" laborer already contains within it the sentence of its denial: because "if the capitalist has no use for his surplus labor, then the worker may not perform his necessary labor" (Marx [1885] 1973, 604).[1]

In this book, I try to move beyond a materialist interpretation of the capitalist value of labor by using Orlando Patterson's (1982) insight that, in essence, the unfree worker, stripped from recognition and deliberately placed in the margins, forms the specter against which *all* abstract labor is ideologically and materially placed: her or his adverse incorporation into the formal domain of capitalist production is literally inherent in the way capitalism thrives and survives as a system (see also Douglass [1845] 1999). To analytically differentiate between the unfree laborer and the slave in the context of supply chain capitalism, I argue, one needs to place the body of the waged worker ontologically after, and not before, the toiling, dehumanized flesh that constitutes the site of original capital accumulation since its very inception. As Patterson writes, slavery cannot be uniquely circumscribed through the imposition of force upon the dispossessed, but it entails an incorporating of working bodies into the dominant normative order while excluding their human presence. In that sense, slaves are the extreme expression of human unfreedom, a form of bare life that can be killed but not sacrificed, Ziarek (2008, 95) writes; they represent the institutional destruction of the very possibility of political and symbolic subjectivity: "[The figure of the slave] creates the anomaly of the socially dead but biologically alive and economically exploited being. Because the expropriation of a slave's life constitutes him or her as a nonperson or a socially dead person, it produces another instance of bare life, violently stripped of genealogy, cultural memory, social distinction, name, and native language, that is, of all the elements of Aristotle's *bios*."[2]

While Michael Denning is of course being provocative, what he means by the statement cited at the beginning of this section is that the modern preoccupation—or shall we say obsession—with formal, industrial labor not only goes paired with a normalization of unemployment as a condition of "temporary impermanence" (Denning 2010, 84), but consequently this hegemony also actively produces an antisubject, a human zombie if you will, whose unwaged, informal, or "nonstandard" efforts deliberately stand excluded from formal citizen recognition. The result of this paradigm is the equation of wage labor with the good life—in short, with formal, state citizenship, and the exclusion of such nonrecognized forms with a political marginality that is not (yet) fully incorporated within this realm. Rather than diametrically opposing these categories, therefore, it becomes important to understand the wider symbolic apparatus that isolates unwaged workers into a permanent state of impermanence, as Patterson foresaw.

Particularly in today's post-Fordist era, where the relation between formal and informal labor is highly destabilized and subject to renegotiation, the specter of slavery—rather than slavery itself—becomes a useful perspective to understand the process of social and cultural differentiation on which the permanent exclusion of informal workers continues to be founded. In critical sociology, the inclination is high to associate this exclusion with a form of redundancy, a wasted life, which furthermore expresses itself into the "filthy" marginalized conditions in which informal laborers try to make a life despite all odds. But as Patterson shows, the fetishization of the slave as a "strange" and "uncivilized" being is significative of a symbolic process through which the incorporation of living labor gains its cultural meaning. It highlights a ritual incorporation of marginalized bodies, which, after being stripped of their cultural identity, are framed as political nonbeings, as noncitizens contained in a space of institutionalized marginality. What distinguishes the condition of slaves from that of "unfree" workers in this context is not so much the forced nature of their labor, but rather their *social death*, a condemnation to life on the margin between community and chaos, life and death, the sacred and the secular (Patterson 1982, 51; see also van Gennep [1909] 1960; Turner 1967, 1969).

In the context of the Black Mediterranean plantations, I find Patterson's terminology of social death a fruitful way to reopen the discussion about labor exploitation. As I said before, I regard the liminality of contemporary Black agri-food workers to be representative not just of a process of alienation and social differentiation, but of a permanent state of nonbelonging. Social death, Patterson writes, represents the way slaves are cast into a figure of nonbelonging, or rather of belonging to a hostile, alien culture, which at the same time represents the antithesis of a social order that needs to be maintained and defended at all costs. As other scholars have repeated after him, this historical figure should inspire us to awareness of the active politicization of humanity that is produced through the commodification of humans as laboring subjects. One could argue, therefore, that the political liminality of unfree Black migrant workers, stripped of recognition and deliberately placed in the margins, is inherent in the way contemporary rural capitalism thrives and survives as a system because it renders their nonbelonging functional to the way the social relations of production are reproduced in specific times and places. Based on my ethnographic research among Black African migrant workers in Basilicata, I propose three types of liminality that characterize the status of unfree workers in the Mediterranean.

The first of these I call *detached liminality*: the alienation from all formal, legally enforceable ties as a consequence of the permanent detachment from territory (as the poem on the wall in one of Basilicata's ghettos goes: the person who leaves the beloved land behind is a ruined person: see chapter 4). This alienation may result from a spatial segregation into a camp form—like the prison camps of Libya, or the migrant detention camps in Europe. But it could also signify a more diffused detachment, a permanent refoulement of migrants' political rights from what are considered the foundations of modern humanity: the access to territory and national belonging. One of the major consequences of the securitization of

Mediterranean migration, I write, has been in fact that authority over such rights has become more diffused, and thus less accountable, less visible, and frequently also more overtly violent. This withdrawal results in the emergence of an expanding gray space in which migrant rights are deliberately trespassed upon, denied, and violated.

A second form of liminality I would call *embedded liminality*. It highlights the impossibility of maintaining social ties other than those of the closed community or social group. Again, the question is one of proportionality, as Patterson highlights. Embedded liminality (or "human parasitism," as he calls it: 1982, 336–37) involves a continuum ranging from minor dependence or exploitation to an exclusive dependence on the dominant master. While the master feeds on the slave to gain the very direct satisfactions of power and authority, the slave, intended as a socially dead person, loses all claims to autonomous power and in the process is degraded and reduced to a state of liminality. This embeddedness finds its expression in the dominance of the labor intermediary, or *caporale*, over all aspects of workers' lives. To the extent that unfree workers demonstrate an exclusive dependence on this kind of authority, the unfree workers can be regarded as fully embedded, and the *caporale* fully parasitic on the workers' bodily presence.

A final form of liminality I would call *political liminality*: it represents a state of permanent nonbelonging that can be overcome only by unconditionally accepting the hegemonic social order upon which one's life is premised. This condition is representative of the diffuse social disintegration characteristic of many Black African workers' lives. I witnessed such disintegration clearly in the context of formal migrant labor infrastructures, which serve to incorporate racialized bodies within the dominant mode of production while denying their rights to any form of political subjectivity outside the strict confines of nation-state territoriality. While I want to make clear that none of these three stages or conditions form a historical necessity (see also Cunningham 2020), I think they represent quite well the politicide that looms as a specter over the lives of contemporary Black African migrant workers in the south of Europe, and Italy in particular. This political death forms the backbone of a symbolic and political incorporation of human bodies whose force fundamentally supports the survival of an economic system, but which system, in the process, undercuts and destroys the very foundations of life that sustains it.

Before the Urban

My second argument, then, is to reevaluate what, in recent years, has come to be termed as the "dark side" of global capitalism, or the largely informalized, invisibilized, and marginalized underground economies that keep capital accumulation going as a wider societal project. In their book *States, Borders, and the Other Side of Globalization*, Itty Abraham and Willem van Schendel observe the persistent trend in public culture to depict illegal or informal economic activity as a "specter" haunting globalization: "the specter of international organized crime networks, coterminous with underworld mafias, snakeheads, coyotes, traffickers, and other transnational jetsam" (2005, 2). Such networks, we are told, are taking advantage of the unprecedented ease of communication and global flows to create an alternative, if only partly visible, global system that exists in parallel to legitimate international transactions of corporations, individuals, and states. As such, Abraham and van Schendel write, these networks fill the darkest dreams of policy makers and average citizens of industrialized countries, whose desire for protection motivates the rise of ever more muscular and intrusive forms of law enforcement against such unlawful exceptions. In contrast, the authors propose a radically different way of conceptualizing the distinction between "illegal" and "legal" transactions, by extending it toward what participants in global economic networks consider (il)licit and (il)legitimate. What they find out is that, quite often, these conceptions stand in sharp contrast to the norms and rules of formal legality. So, while legal standards may very well be the official form of legitimate political authority, they are not always the licit, accepted norm in the eyes of participants in global flows.

In recent years, economic geographers have tended to echo this observation about the blurred boundaries between formal and informal centers of capitalist growth, while being careful to delineate the spatial arrangements through which this spectral division is actively maintained. So, for example Nicola Phillips (2011, 2013) and others indicate the "adverse incorporation" of informal workers whose included exclusion from formal capitalist growth is actively planned, implemented, and built into industrial supply chains. Their active informalization thus becomes part and parcel of a superexploitation (Selwyn 2019), a form of depletion, debt, and disposability (Lawreniuk 2020) that exploits workers at levels far beyond their social reproduction costs. Some scholars deliberately evoke a terminology of death here, a necro-capitalism that is at once a denial of life outside capital's needs and a form of accumulation that involves "dispossession and the subjugation of life to the power of death" (Banerjee 2008, 1541). After having sucked out all productive energy, industrial supply chains willfully expel from the production network those bodies that are no longer deemed necessary for accumulation, abandoning them without the means of subsistence (Tyner 2019; Phelps, Atienza, and Arias 2018).

By using the terminology of social and political death as a proxy for migrant unfreedom, I insist on the fundamentally racial differentiation of value in capitalist production and reproduction. To put it bluntly: there can be no capitalism without race. It is not enough to study the outcomes of capitalist differentiation without also analyzing the active racial production upon which such differentiation is based (Pulido 2017, 527). Following also Gilmore (2002a and b, 2007), I insist here on the instrumentalization of race as an abstraction of human difference that simultaneously displaces and reconnects humanity in existentially unequal terms that feed capital. But while all workers in this context suffer some form of labor exploitation, territorial stigmatization and ghettoization is inflicted most drastically on people who, because of an *inherent* ascription of inferiority, are deemed unworthy of the fruits of modern civilization. In that sense, the ghetto—as an emblematic zone of racialized exclusion—fulfills a central role in maintaining the racial hierarchies necessary to sustain uneven capitalist expansion. Márquez (2013, 44) calls this sort of devaluation a "racial state of expendability," which he describes as "a fundamental and existential life devaluation, a perpetual susceptibility to obliteration with legal impunity." So, while labor exploitation and unfreedom may appear to have the same origin in capitalist alienation, this ontological devaluation explains why there is an important qualitative difference. It explains why laboring bodies may be overexploited in the "dark" corners of capitalist supply chains, but racialized bodies may be made expendable, expelled, and killed with legal impunity. Furthermore, it explains that, today as in the past, racism is never an abstract force, but it thrives on the active implementation of technologies of surveillance and recognition, of stigmatization and exclusion, of devaluation and unequal incorporation.

In the context of the Black Mediterranean, therefore, I think it is important to understand how racism has been a driving force of an agrarian mode of production that continues to expand through such articulations of difference. My study must be read as an attempt to speak back to the history of the so-called industrialized North from the perspective of those (former) colonial places and peoples who have been adversely incorporated into the project of modern capitalist development over the last century and a half. At the same time, I also insist on the wider ecological implications of this differentiation—in the sense of its active production of geographic scales. If uneven development is the systematic geographic expression of the differentiated distribution of levels and conditions of capitalist production, as Neil Smith argues, then we need to imagine the geography of capitalism as the active production of spaces and scales that give such uneven development its coherence. The history of the Black Mediterranean plantation shows how important it is to understand how such scales take shape at different spatial conjunctions. In other words, it reveals the close connections, interactions, and mutual reinforcement of social factors of production that are situated both inside and outside formal industrial development as they bring together labor and capital at different spatial scales. The reproduction of racialized marginality in this context in fact brings me back to the *political* question Neil Smith asked some time ago, of how geographic configurations of the land and those who cultivate it contribute to the survival of capitalism as a hegemonic economic system (Smith [1984] 2008, 4).

My contribution specifically accentuates two dimensions of this question. First, it foregrounds the importance of territory as an active agent in drawing and maintaining spatial conjunctions in the unfolding of capitalist frontiers. As a technology that upholds the geographic relation between the state and sovereign authority over the national citizenry, territory remains a crucial parameter to conceive, perceive, perpetuate, and shape our political identities within the sovereign domain of the territorial nation-state (Newman 2003, 15). Territory, according to Elden (2010, 760), is indeed a "political technology" through which the "spatial order of things" comes to be normalized and perpetuated. This involves not only techniques in the narrower sense (like maps, measurements, land surveys, and population censuses) but also the broader notion of *techne* as a "way of grasping and conceiving of the world" (as in the application of normative systems, moral discourse, and narratives: Elden 2013a, 16). In their analysis of urban informality, Roy and Crane (2015) highlight the implications of such a territorial understanding of uneven capitalist development because it advances a relational perspective of marginality through the analysis of concrete practices and connections that "make" the territories of uneven development.

Building on these insights, I highlight the importance of territorial residence as a technique of racial discrimination in the context of Southern Italy's agrifood economy. Territorial residence is exactly the switchboard agent capitalism needs to exploit differently valued laboring subjects. In chapters 2 and 3 of this book I uncover this administrative mechanism of exclusion as an instrument of citizen stratification and differential inclusion of migrant workers—from the peasant families forced from their homes to counter the national "shame" of underdevelopment in postwar Basilicata, to the overpopulated urban peripheries during the Northern economic "miracle" years, to contemporary migrant ghettos. What unites these marginalized places analytically is that it is exactly in these sites, at the edge of the officially planned towns and labor compounds, that the dark scales of capitalism's geography are maintained and reproduced. But territory is more than a physically contained space. Next to its being an active border technology that serves to stratify and exclude populations beyond the territorial boundary lines of the modern nation-state, a kind of invisible border (Gargiulo 2021), I also insist on the normative dimension of territory, as a "way of grasping and conceiving of the world" (Elden 2013a, 16). As I argue, territorial residence figures as an important frame of recognition for distinguishing between those who do and who do not belong within the boundaries of national or local citizenship.

The politics of humanitarian securitization imposed by Europe's response to South-North migration has generated a multiplication of territorial borders to control "unruly" migrant populations. This response has in turn contributed to a transformation of the way migrant workers acquire their territorial residence papers. Through the obligation to subject one's labor power to capitalist employers (which has been the historical tendency in Italy, from Fascism to the Bossi-Fini law), for migrant seasonal workers labor is now something that needs to be actively deserved, often through stages of unwaged or voluntary work. In the context of rapid political reconfigurations in Puglia and Basilicata, I describe how migrant workers are often trapped between the desire to regularize their status and the open suspicion of bureaucrats and humanitarian workers who in fact deny migrants a territorial place of belonging. From the perspective of the growing refugeeization of the agricultural workforce—meaning the gradual replacement of agri-food workers by refugees and asylum seekers (Dines and Rigo 2015; Ippolito, Perrotta, and Raeymaekers 2021)—since the so-called migration emergency in the Mediterranean, such denial is particularly important, as it can become another tool of the wider surveillance techniques of European nation-states to enforce sovereign control over migrant mobility. At the same time, I insist that the denial of territorial residence to migrant workers is not an exception but in fact runs as a logical thread through Italian economic history. It forms part of exactly that existential life devaluation that has underpinned the convoluted history of Italian and, by extension, Mediterranean market growth (Lombardi-Diop and Romeo 2014; Palmi 2021).

To show that the outcome of territorial seclusion is not at all predetermined, I have referenced the contested materiality of segregated migrant spaces in the context of Italy's agrarian economy. Invoking James Holston's (2008) terminology of "insurgent citizenship" and Faranak Miraftab's (2009) notion of "insurgent planning," in which citizens actively challenge the state's allocation of public resources, I depict migrant ghettos as places where the relational dimension of the state-society contract is fundamentally being contested but also partly renegotiated. Situated at the edge of the citizens' polis, ghetto infrastructures also function as the dynamic embodiment of the struggle over citizenship rights. I describe how their expression of liminality, as the boundary between formality and informality, legality and illegality, of public and private realms of citizen-state interaction, forms an integral part of the racial naturalization of its inhabitants as not (yet) developed and not (yet) civilized. I also show how the contested citizenship of the ghetto reflects a struggle over membership in a society that continues to spatially exclude a considerable section of its productive population in marginal and segregated sites. In that sense ghettos can be regarded as sites of infrastructural renewal, or of concessions of some sorts, where the terms of citizenship and its relation to formal, capitalist labor are actively mediated and transformed.

Finally, I invite the reader to look through the layered materiality of frontier settlements like the ones I describe in this book. In my work with MIC|C, but also more broadly, in my adoption of a geographic-archaeological method, I have tried to unveil the layered memory of these places. Characterized by consecutive cycles of occupation and abandonment, they become repositories of accumulated traces in the form of utensils, objects, documents, and other artifacts we can visibly detect, like the ashes of a smoldering fire, or the traces of a caravan after it has taken off to other destinations. These traces—or fragments, as I call them—highlight quite visibly the continuous transformation of sites that are deemed absent of order but in fact reproduce a relational space that is both conditioned by and a reacting against this abandonment. As such, they provide additional evidence of the continuous renewal of urban infrastructures in a context where borders, bodies, and territories are caught in a vortex of rapid change. I invite readers to experience these traces as an archaeology of future forms of *eschatopolis*, in the sense that the detailed exposure of ruined fragments has the potential to trace the trajectories of a layered history of emergent, peripheral forms of life at the time of their recurrent and deliberate dissolution. A more pronounced emphasis on the materiality of such rural frontiers in the context of capitalist extraction, in my view, has the potential for unwrapping the multiple temporalities of often untold and marginalized histories in today's agrarian frontier (DeSilvey and Edensor 2012). It also has the potential to highlight the political ecology of ruination as a continuous process, in which the convergence of material and personal memory, and the capacity for alternative engagements with the past and the present, may effectively take root. I hope that my provocation may invite others to investigate the transformation of capitalist extraction by actively looking for the traces of abandonment and ruination. These traces teach us how people readily construct the foundations of an emergent and transient form of life on the edge of a system that exploits their bodies yet refuses their presence as fully recognized human beings.

An Archaeology of Future Urbanisms

My work finally invites readers to analyze the morphologies of human life under capitalism beyond its modern ideal types of the city and the periphery, the core and the margin. Inspired by recent scholarship in the domain of planetary urbanization (Merrifield 2013; Brenner 2013; Brenner and Katsikis 2013), I opt for a more territorially differentiated, morphologically variable, multiscalar and processual conceptualization. In other words, the call is out to study future urban morphologies not as a science of cities but as "a liminal process that expands as a kind of 'dispersal of fragments'" (Wilson and Jonas 2018, 1577) and to pick up the invitation to study urbanization as a palimpsest, "a composite landscape made up of different built forms superimposed upon each other with the passing of time" (Harvey 2013, 61; Harvey 1985; see also Graham and Marvin 2001; McFarlane and Rutherford 2008).

I connect with planetary urbanization scholarship by showing how layers of migrant occupancy generate the seeds of increasingly solid urban roots: through the locus of collective memory, of political identity, and of powerful symbolic meanings embodied in what first appear as abandoned sites but which are effectively full of life, we can see the bundling of important resources that constitute possibilities as well as barriers in the built environment—very much depending on the way these resources are incorporated or expelled in official state planning efforts. Rather than seeing only tabula rasa and reconstruction, therefore, I indeed invite future scholars to concentrate on the liminality of contemporary urbanization—particularly through the barracks, the ghettos, and camp infrastructures that facilitate the material flow of capitalist urbanization.

But also methodologically, I open a few new questions: What are, for example, remnants of segregated life in the frontier? What can we regard as its traces, and how can we connect these to a wider relational geography of racial capitalism? What positive objectives does one reach, furthermore, with the curation and documentation of such invisibilized traces? And what negative consequences can such research instead generate? In sum, who could effectively be harmed through such research practice? As Hamilakis (2016, 133) reminds us, our research practice always inherently rides an uncomfortable balance between the necessity to document displacement while respecting impermanence. That said, I think a more distinct archaeological focus and methodology may simultaneously help to enrich and interconnect ongoing research in the broader domain of border studies in two important respects. First, it may complement the analysis of camps as sites of transformative urbanization. Although they historically have been, and still are, purposively imagined, built, and employed as material infrastructures of exception to displace and confine colonized and racialized subjects outside the space of metropolitan legality and political order, Picker and Pasquetti (2018, 681–82) write, camps may indeed turn into "durable socio-spatial formations whose logics of functioning and effects are articulated at the intersection of global, state and urban scales." I particularly agree with their conclusion that "a fuller understanding of the conditions under which and the forms in which camps become incubators of urban processes and camp inhabitants think and act politically requires bringing together top-down forms of management, ranging from securitized humanitarianism to neoliberal governance and the formation of everyday practices, claims and relationships. It also requires situating camps within broader historical and contemporary racial formations in their various permutations, thus linking spatial and racial processes as they unfold at the level of both governance and everyday life" (2018, 683). I find it useful to reiterate Merrifield (2013, 389) here when he warns about one-sided readings of socio-spatial transformation; for him, the urban is not only "bricks and mortar, high-rise buildings and autoroutes"; it is also a process that manifests itself in unpaved streets, back roads, by-waters, and marginal zones that feel the wrath of the world market.

A focus on the liminal and the emergent may also help us move away from a doomsday anthropocentric interpretation of urban forms as the expression of cyclical trajectories of construction and destruction. The Black Mediterranean scholarship on which my study builds instead calls forth an investigation of emergent urban borderlands underpinned by contradictory yet interwoven processes of homogenization and fragmentation. Integrating the partly justified critiques of the Western-centric and totalizing gesture of planetary urbanization scholarship (Wilson and Jonas 2018), I particularly take to heart the political perception that Brian Jefferson's research agenda proposes. "From the perspective of the political," Jefferson (2018, 1582) writes,

> it is incumbent to understand the extent to which dividing social groups and social spaces are necessary preconditions for new rounds of urban agglomeration. It is also necessary to foreground who is included and excluded from emerging city-settlement spaces and their nonurban "operational landscapes" . . ., who is visibilized and invisibilized, and what extra-economic means . . . are deployed to link new areas into agglomerative processes while simultaneously delinking others. In short, coming to terms with emergent forms of urbanization requires analysis on the hidden terrain of the political. It is only by probing this dark side of urbanization—where people and places are not only subsumed by agglomerative processes but also brutally divided and discarded by them—in conjunction with geographies of accumulation, that critical theory of contemporary urbanization can be substantively deepened.

What is political about the liminal city of the Black Mediterranean is precisely the way categorical distinctions between formal and informal, desired and undesired, white bodies and black flesh are inscribed into the landscape and onto the body as inherent features of planetary urban forms. I take it that marginal urbanization is best looked at through the lens of populations and places that are unevenly categorized, constituted, and positioned with respect to the forces of uneven capitalist development. And I invite scholars to direct their attention to populations and places that are deliberately placed into the gray zone in which modernity feeds off its own strategies of discharge, seclusion, and adverse incorporation.

Notes

INTRODUCTION

1. The reader may note that I define "racism" and "racialization" in one breath, as the mechanisms of ontological exceptionalism that underpin society's categorization of Self and Other along strictly defined, racial boundaries—as Du Bois ([1903] 2007) so sharply defined it.

2. I can mention the works of Gregory and Pred (2007), Kobayashi (2009), Sheppard and Tyner (2016), and Springer and Le Billon (2016).

3. Ghana House, August 31, 2016.

4. MSF estimated the number of asylum applicants and refugees living in "informal" habitats at around ten thousand (MSF 2016). Strikingly, though, the NGO did not include in its study what it called "informal labor camps"—sites like Borgo Mezzanone and Rignano Garganico (Puglia), San Ferdinando (Calabria), and Boreano (Basilicata), where thousands of migrants continued to flock each year to harvest grapes, oranges, and tomatoes for Italian enterprises and the big distribution networks, but which increasingly took on the function of informal migrant relief sites during this period. In its next report, published in 2018, MSF noticed not only a growth but also a growing geographic and ethnic fragmentation of such informal settlements, apart from the already noticeable absence of local social and health services, water, food, and electricity (MSF 2018). Among the 1,356 migrant workers the humanitarian NGO Caritas assisted in the ghettos of Puglia and Basilicata between 2014 and 2017 in its Presidium project, 64.3 percent resulted in having some form of refugee status. For the diocese of Acerenza in Basilicata, this number was even higher: 71.1 percent (see also chapter 3).

5. The original inspiration of this citation was of course Karl Marx: "Labor is the living, form-giving fire; it is the transitoriness of things, their temporality" ([1885] 1973, 361).

6. The displayed billboards and recordings of this public intervention are shared on the projects page of www.mic-c.org.

7. "The aim is to create here in Britain a really hostile environment," Theresa May, then the UK home secretary, said in 2012, and the Immigration Acts of 2014 and 2016 were designed to make it easier to deport people from the UK (Hicks and Mallet 2019, 7).

8. The notion of abstract space can be traced back to the French geographer Henri Lefebvre, who argued that capitalism generates an abstraction in space because the commodification of life reduces the sensory, multifaceted texture of places to quantifiable, homogeneous abstractions to be sold and bought (Lefebvre [1974] 1992; for a discussion see Gordillo 2014; Stoler 2008).

9. Of course, this is not an entirely new thought, Massey admits, as Henri Lefebvre, writing in 1974, was beginning to argue a very similar position (Lefebvre [1974] 1992; Gregory and Urry 1985; Soja 1989).

10. In a similar manner, this is also what Walter Benjamin observed through his analysis of capitalism as a repetitive cycle of ruin and devastation. In his elaboration of Paul Klee's emblematic engraving *Angel of History* he writes: "Where we perceive a chain of events, he sees one single catastrophe which keeps piling wreckage upon wreckage and hurls it in front of his feet" (Benjamin 1999, 249; see also Gordillo 2014).

11. My main source of inspiration here is Angela Davis's analysis of the apartheid regime in South Africa, the architects of which had bolstered this division in the crudest manner. The logic of separation that lay beneath the spatial organization of apartheid in Bantustans and Black African ghettos was that the South African government viewed Black men simply as labor units whose productive potential rendered them valuable to the capitalist class, Davis argues. Their wives and children, in contrast, were regarded as "superfluous appendages"—nothing more than adjuncts to the procreative capacity of the black male labor unit (Davis 1983, 276). For Davis, this structural separation of the home economy from the social relations of capitalist production forms evidence of the total disinterest of capitalist employers in the sphere of social reproduction. This argument forms the subject of a long-standing debate in feminist scholarship (see Mezzadri 2019).

12. This observation pairs with the widespread acknowledgment of the systematic use of slavery in the Mediterranean colonies of the Italian city-states (see also Verlinden 1977; Blackburn 1997; and contrary to Fernand Braudel, who mentions slavery only in passing). Curtin (2012) later added more details to Robinson's analysis, noting, for example, how the first slaves subjected to plantation labor in the eleventh century involved a group of Black captives on a group of cane sugar estates on the Balkan peninsula—so exactly at the time and place when and where monocropping agriculture was for the first time introduced as a large-scale, export-oriented mode of production (see also Hunwick 1992).

13. Cedric Robinson originally coined the term "racial capitalism" in the context of the active destruction of black economic institutions during South Africa's apartheid (Leong 2013). Robinson's work aimed to rehistoricize and develop the concept of racial capitalism to understand the entire history of modern capitalism (Kelley 2017): "No matter the quality of local genius, apartheid South Africa did not invent itself. It was an incubus in all those racial regimes that preceded it; from ancient Greece to the modern Americas," he wrote (Robinson [1983] 2005, 10).

14. It is worth mentioning that Hall's argument developed against the backdrop of a broader discussion of how to analyze the persistence of noncapitalist relations of production in Latin America, North America, and South Africa, especially with regard to the plantation mode of production (see also Arrighi 1970; Arrighi, Aschoff, and Scully 2010). Laclau (1971, 33) enabled scholars to take as their starting point the assumption that "an economic system can include, as constitutive elements, different modes of production." With Stuart Hall (1980) and Philippe Rey (1982), Ernesto Laclau proposes that accumulation of merchant and industrial capital is compatible with a variety of relations of production, not solely the capitalist one, if their outputs are commodities that can enter into the capitalist economy through market exchange. Scholars with such a perspective typically refer to and quote Karl Marx to argue that

> The circuit of industrial capital . . . crosses the commodity circulation of the most diverse modes of social production, so far as they produce commodities. No matter whether commodities are the output of production based on slavery, of peasants . . . of state enterprise . . . or of half-savage hunting tribes . . . they come face to face with the money and commodities in which industrial capital presents itself and enter as much into its circuit. . . . The character of the process of production from which they originate is immaterial. They function as commodities in the market, and as commodities they enter the circulation of the surplus value incorporated in it. (Herrigel 2018)

15. For a discussion see du Toit (2004); Elyachar (2010, 2012); Xiang (2013); Lindquist, Xiang, and Yeoh (2012), Gammeltoft-Hansen and Sørensen (2013); Barrientos, Kothari, and Phillips (2013); N. Phillips (2011, 2013); Meagher and Lindell (2013); Meagher, Mann, and Bolt (2016); Meagher (2021).

16. The human/nonhuman distinction can be understood from a Baradian perspective as the product of an observational "cut" through which human subjects and nonhuman objects are produced out of complex intra-acting material-discursive elements. Barad's neologism "intra-action" reconfigures the concept of interaction in order to emphasize the inseparability of the various discursive and material elements that lead to particular material-discursive configurations of the world (Barad 2003). Thus, on a Baradian reading, "the human" is conceived as a product of the world in its "open-ended becoming" rather than as a pre-given category. In other words, Barad suggests that people neither simply shape the world nor are they simply shaped by it. Rather, people as well as things are made as more or less "human" through the "cuts" that they both make and are made by (Squire 2014, 11).

1. COMMODITY FRONTIERS

1. Place and personal names in this section have been changed to guarantee anonymity.

2. The Placido Rizzotto Observatory—which remains a key reference for the study of agrarian transformations in the country—observes the total agricultural surface (*superficie agricola totale*, or SAT) per agricultural firm in Italy to have expanded from 7.6 hectares in 1990 to 10.5 hectares in 2010. In the same period, the number of agricultural enterprises has dropped from 3 million to 1.6 million (Osservatorio Placido Rizzotto 2014, 45; 2012).

3. Giuseppe, interview by the author, August 23, 2016.

4. A 2023 report by Oxfam, called *Fixing Your Food*, appears to confirm this inequality crisis. According to the report, market concentration in global food production and distribution is so severe that just 1 percent of the world's farms control 65 percent of the agricultural land, and four big traders carry out 70 percent of global trade in agricultural commodities by value. This concentration, rather than a food security crisis, explains why the giants of agribusiness have seen their collective wealth increase by US$382 billion (45 percent) over the past two years (2020–2022), with sixty-two new food billionaires created in the sector since the outbreak of the COVID-19 pandemic. The Cargill family, which owns the majority of one of the world's largest food traders, saw their fortune increase by almost $20 million a day from the start of the COVID-19 pandemic. In 2021, the company made almost $5 billion in net income, the biggest profit in its history.

5. The Pwalugu Tomato Factory, for instance, founded by Ghana's first postcolonial president, Kwame Nkrumah, succeeded in boosting local production until the World Bank and the International Monetary Fund forced the Ghanaian government to open its borders to global food markets in the early 2000s (Auvillain and Liberti 2016).

6. Numbers from the Ghana Ministry of Food and Agriculture and International Food Policy Research Institute (van Asselt, Masias, and Kolavalli 2018).

7. Another relevant example for the Mediterranean context has been the production of fresh strawberries across Spain and Morocco. European retailers dominating the market simply switch the purchase of fresh products in order to meet year-round demand (Gertel and Sippel 2014). EU trade policies have stimulated this type of transboundary competition through actively displacing the EU–Morocco trade barrier southward on a seasonal basis (Boeckler and Berndt 2014).

8. That said, not all agricultural supply chains in Emilia-Romagna have managed to respond to these challenges with the same efficiency as that of industrial tomatoes, and indeed they also feel the same crisis of marginalization and capital concentration (Perrotta 2014).

9. In the Italian context, it is useful to highlight the ongoing debate about Article 1 of the Constitution, which stipulates that Italy is a republic based on work/labor (L'Italia è una Repubblica democratica, fondata sul lavoro. La sovranità appartiene al popolo, che

la esercita nelle forme e nei limiti della Costituzione). The ambiguity of this formulation (in Italian, *lavoro* means both work and labor) opens a debate as to whether to include or exclude unwaged work from its republican (and thus, citizen) rights (for a discussion see Muehlebach 2012 as well as chapter 5).

10. A crucial passage here concerns again South Africa, where, according to Arrighi, Aschoff, and Scully (2010), the partial proletarization of the agricultural workforce created conditions in which the African peasants subsidized capital accumulation, because they produced part of their own subsistence; but the more proletarized the peasantry became, the more these mechanisms began to break down. This argument reconfirms Angela Davis's and Cedric Robinson's observations that the spatial organization of South African apartheid primarily was due to the fact that the regime had to become more repressive of the African labor force because it was fully proletarized and, therefore, it could no longer subsidize capital accumulation as it had done in the past (see Al-Bulushi 2022, 63).

11. From the structural viewpoint, Patterson argues, slavery must be seen as a process involving several transitional phases. The slave is violently uprooted from his milieu. He is desocialized and depersonalized. The next phase involves the introduction of the slave into the community of his master, but it involves the paradox of introducing him as a nonbeing, as he "did not and could not belong because he was the product of a hostile, alien culture" (Patterson 1982, 38–39).

12. Curiously, the Placido Rizzotto Observatory bases its calculations on the interpretation of "hidden irregular" work by the Ministry of Labor (estimated by the National Statistics Institute ISTAT at 34.9 percent of the foreign workforce of 400,000) and the Ministry of Agriculture's estimate of "irregular" workers (estimated at 136,400). Furthermore, the institute's 2020 report adds about 60,000 workers who are registered by the National Pensions Institute (INPS) but whose working hours are clearly underreported. Between this maximum estimate of 200,000 and the 160,000 reported by the Ministry of Labour, the Osservatorio Placido Rizzotto (2020) concludes that the number of "vulnerable" agricultural workers exposed to "illegal hiring" should lie around 180,000.

13. This was during a public press conference in Rome on April 19, 2015, after an overcrowded boat carrying migrants across the Mediterranean capsized with over seven hundred people on board.

14. Significant in this regard has been the renaming of the Ministry of Agriculture under the 2022 Giorgia Meloni government as the Ministry of Agriculture and Food Sovereignty.

15. To give an idea of the speed with which this transformation took place, Rigo and Caprioglio 2021 quote numbers from the Italian Labour Ministry: in 2014–2015, the ministry reported a 61.9 percent decrease in migrant residency permits issued for employment reasons; in 2016, this number dropped by another 41 percent; in 2017 about 40 percent of migrant workers held an asylum or humanitarian permit, and just over 4 percent obtained a residency permit for work. In short, over the last half decade, asylum has rapidly replaced the historical channels of contractual employment and territorial residency papers as the main channel toward official migrant labor in the country.

16. The one and only interview with Masslo was transmitted in its entirety on the Italian television TG2 news broadcast during the state funeral on August 28, 1989:

. . . Pensavo di trovare in Italia uno spazio di vita, una ventata di civiltà, un'accoglienza che mi permettesse di vivere in pace e di coltivare il sogno di un domani senza barriere né pregiudizi. Invece sono deluso. Avere la pelle nera in questo paese è un limite alla convivenza civile. Il razzismo c'è anche qui: è fatto di prepotenze, di soprusi, di violenze quotidiane con chi non chiede altro che solidarietà e rispetto. Noi del terzo mondo stiamo contribuendo allo sviluppo del vostro paese, ma sembra che ciò non abbia alcun peso. Prima o poi qualcuno di noi verrà ammazzato, ed allora ci si accorgerà che esistiamo.

(. . . I thought I'd find in Italy a living space, a breath of civilization, a reception that would allow me to live in peace and to cultivate the dream of a future without barriers or prejudices. Instead, I am disappointed. Having black skin in this country is a limit to civil coexistence. Racism is present, too, here: it is made up of bullying, abuse, daily violence against those who ask for nothing but solidarity and respect. We in the third world are contributing to the development of your country, but it seems that this has no weight. Sooner or later some of us will be killed, and then we will realize that we exist.)

17. For a more systematic overview I refer to the website http://www.cronachedior dinariorazzismo.org.

18. Among the sustained supporters active in the area I can mention the ex-Canapificio social center from Caserta, as well as the local Caritas bureau. The protests gave rise to an autonomous association and artistic collective, Kalifoo Ground (interview with Kalifoo Ground, February 1, 2020).

19. For a systematic discussion see Perrotta (2020). The protests have been narrated in an impressive docudrama by Jonas Carpignano and Koudous Seihou, the latter a citizen of Burkina Faso who in the film plays himself with the name of Ayiva.

20. *Daily Telegraph* (London), January 9, 2010. It is in fact no coincidence that the shooting of African migrant workers occurred specifically at a time when they had modestly started to grow out of their subaltern relation to the state. During 2010–2011, representatives of different workers' communities of Burkinabè and Ghanaian origins had been actively working across institutional boundaries with local police and members of the *prefettura* to claim and implement their rights to territorial residence, and to public state support (Mangano 2010, 36).

21. Basso cites a long series of discriminatory measures that deliberately place "foreign" (non–Italian born) residents in a submissive position toward capital and the state. Since the so-called Martelli law (introduced by the then minister of justice Claudio Martelli) of February 28, 1990, stipulated for the first time the modalities of entry and rejection of immigrants at the border through the redefinition of asylum and the channeling of migratory flows (the so-called *decreti flussi*), the Turco-Napolitano law (from the names of the minister for social solidarity Livia Turco and the then minister of the interior Giorgio Napolitano) of March 6, 1998, attempted to set the limits of non-work-related entries by specifying the terminology of "clandestine migrant" as the recipient of an expulsion order from the state, and by introducing the so-called temporary centers of stay (*centro di permanenza temporanea*, a contradictory term), which, through Article 12 of the law, should host "all foreigners subjected to expulsion and refoulement measures with forced accompaniment to the border that cannot be immediately executed." The subsequent Bossi-Fini law (named after the minister for institutional reforms Umberto Bossi and the vice president of the Council of Ministers Gianfranco Fini) of July 30, 2002, not only bolstered the institution of the expulsion centers (renamed *centri per l'identificazione e l'espulsione*), but it furthermore assigned exclusive responsibility for migrant recruitment in the context of the so-called flow decrees directly to the Italian employer. *Pace* Cedric Robinson, therefore, one can confidently argue that the consolidation of these legal measures demonstrates quite well how "capitalism was less a catastrophic revolution (negation) of feudal social order than the extension of these social relations into the larger tapestry of the modern world's political and economic relations" (Robinson [1983] 2005, 42–43). Furthermore, it should be emphasized that *ius sanguinis*—the bloodline

that provides the ontological foundation of Italian citizenship—became enshrined in law 55/1912 in explicit response to the growing pressures of emigration and colonialism (legal restrictions prohibiting the acquisition of citizenship by children of white Italian men and Black African women in the Italian colonies were overturned only in the early 1950s): see Hawthorne (2021a, 35); Giordano (2008, 591).

22. Cillo and Perocco (2016) show how in the Italian context, for example, construction work, shipbuilding, and metal construction are characterized by clearly differentiated working conditions between migrant and Italian workers—reflected not only in terms of wages but also of workers' rights protection, discrimination, and intimidation (for a US-based comparison see Holmes 2013).

23. In the first six months after the Bossi-Fini law was introduced, for instance, only 2 percent of foreign workers were in such condition (Basso 2010, 203).

24. During the lockdown (March 20–May 1, 2020), Italian residents were allowed to leave their homes exclusively for sanitary reasons (going to a pharmacy or doctor), acquisitions of prime necessities, or to reach the workplace. The latter also potentially spurred a verification of the employer. The MEDU reports can be consulted at https://mediciperidirittiumani.org.

25. This deliberate manipulation of statistical data is exemplified furthermore in the statement of the Italian agriculture minister Teresa Bellanova, who at the time of the parliamentary debate on the impact of COVID-19 on the sector estimated the number of migrants without residency permits in the country at around six hundred thousand. Besides being a crude misrepresentation, these statements indicate the tendency to inflate the problem of migrant irregularity in order to justify drastic interventions (Ippolito, Perrotta, and Raeymaekers 2021).

26. The law in fact involved numerous constraints and remained restricted to a limited number of professions, including agriculture, livestock, and fishing. It established the dual objective of formalizing so-called irregular (undeclared, or only partially declared) employment while granting applicants a six-month residency permit aimed at seeking employment: Decreto legge 19 maggio 2020, n. 34 (converted into legge n. 77/2020).

2. PLANTATION ASSEMBLAGES

1. The history of Italy's brigandage falls beyond the scope of this study and has been discussed amply in the historical literature. As Angelo Del Boca (2020) writes, the violent way the newly established Italian state treated this multifaceted rebellion—which at some point involved over eighty thousand fighters and fourteen hundred villages across the South—punctuated the entire history of its future intervention in Africa as well, in the sense that it continued to treat those who resisted its attempts at rural modernization merely as backward, unworthy, and criminal subjects. Interesting to note also are Alliegro's (2019) observations about the rural resistance against the mill taxes the government imposed during the 1880s, which peasants considered a frontal attack on their moral economy.

2. One famous example of this rationalist design was the new town of Sabaudia, designed by the architect and urban planner Luigi Piccinato. In accord with his original diagram, the town emerged as a political and administrative center, which developed a series of radial relations among different rural functions: of the farmstead, the service centers (or *borghi*), and the different institutional functions. The town center hosted the Operazione Nazionale Combattenti (ONC), the national institution that was subsequently made responsible for the land reclamation of the Pontine marshes.

3. The agri-aqueduct connected the plain areas of Matera to its monumental, principal water source in the vicinity of Potenza. Completed in the summer of 1937, the

aqueduct ensured a flow of seventy-three hundred cubic meters of water per minute thus providing twenty-nine urban settlements access to clean water over a distance of three hundred kilometers.

4. About the death toll inflicted on the population of these colonial projects in the Horn of Africa see Wrong (2005).

5. According to Giorgio Rochat (1973, 22), a pioneer in the study of Italian colonialism, the colonial policy was in fact "saturated with racism and abuse of power, which are preliminary conditions for all colonial conquests, because the very idea of wanting to dispose as one wishes of the fate of a people that is militarily weaker is profoundly racist and oppressive." The introduction of systematic racial segregation in Italy's colonial cities, which both ideologically and materially preceded similar systems in other colonies, could be seen as a cornerstone in this racialization process.

6. The notion of Italian colonialism as "too benevolent" and "too liberal" an undertaking and the idea of the "Italians as good folk" (*Italiani brava gente*) continue to dominate scholastic historiography and geography in the country, a myth that Angelo Del Boca (2020) and other contemporary writers find indeed "hard to crack" (see also Burdett 2003; Atkinson 2003, 2005). One of the protagonists of colonial demystification in Italy has been the Italo-Somali writer Igiaba Scego, but other initiatives and collectives are gathering historical momentum in the decolonization of Italian colonial historiography.

7. European investors and state regulators at the time found it difficult to gain clearly delineated uncontested rights to land, which were often subject to litigation by multiple parties—including alliances of customary chiefs, lawyers, and African and European business interests. In fact, the land question already emerged in the context of the gold boom in the Gold Coast in the 1880s and 1890s, which led to increasing speculations around concessions for gold, rubber, and timber. For a discussion see Saul (1957), A. Phillips (1989), and Cowen and Shenton (1996).

8. In Italy, Fabian socialism found support in the Movimento Comunità founded by Adriano Olivetti, entrepreneur, engineer, and politician, who was one of the major promoters of the forced (but partial) eviction of Matera's *Sassi* to La Martella, in Basilicata, in the early 1950s.

9. To quote Wallerstein (1967) once more, semiperipheral states like Côte d'Ivoire, Senegal, and Ghana succeeded quite well in siphoning off labor from the "periphery's periphery" through the adverse incorporation of migrant workers in their vertically integrated export economies.

10. For a complete discussion of the liberalization of West African land markets I refer back to Amanor (2011).

11. In 1983, for example, Nigeria expelled two million West African immigrants in the onslaught of civil war (Arthur 1991, 75). In 2009, the Ivorian government engaged in massive expulsion while stepping up its rhetoric against immigrants from Burkina Faso.

12. Besides this general contribution, scholarship on African migration to Libya during the Gadhafi regime remains scarce and fragmented, except for the titles already mentioned and Bredeloup and Zongo (2004), Bensaâd (2012), Schapendonk (2017), Cepero (2018), and Achtnich (2022).

13. The derogatory terms for Black Africans in Libya evoked this historical relationship: *abdel, abdou, kahala,* or *Afriqiya* designated a "social position as a servant, certifying the violence of exclusion" from a society that both rejected its own Africanness and increasingly engaged in a "state xenophobia" against the migrants it so desperately needed for its economy and well-being: Bensaâd (2012, 100); see also Cepero (2018), Lecocq (2010).

14. The 2003, $5 billion agreement provided for Italy to train, equip, and accommodate Libya's border guards under the auspices of the European border agency Frontex. The deal included the financing of new detention facilities and technologies for the imprisonment

and repatriation of African nationals. To foster this collaboration, Libyan authorities demanded reparations for the crimes of Italian colonialism, which they achieved in 2008 with the "Treaty of Friendship, Partnership and Co-operation." With its $5 billion reparations package (to be paid over twenty-five years, mainly by ENI), the treaty favored Italian infrastructural investment in Libya and increased cooperation on migration controls, leading to joint patrolling operations in Libyan waters and pushbacks. In 2009, the same Berlusconi government passed a law that criminalized undocumented immigrants as unlawful subjects (Law 94/2009), and Italian border patrols systematically started illegally to drive migrants back to Libyan waters: Pradella and Cillo (2021); see also introduction.

15. Pierce notes two legal distinctions between human trafficking and migrant smuggling that are frequently overlooked, the most important being consent: while migrants' consent to being smuggled and their relationship with the smuggler stops once they have reached their destination, victims of human trafficking do not always consent to the result of the transaction, and even if at times they do, the initial consent becomes legally irrelevant to the crime once the trafficker has used threat, coercion, or fraud to exploit the victim. Second is the concept of movement: while smugglers always move migrants across national borders, human trafficking does not necessarily involve international movement. In fact, the UNODC estimates that approximately one-quarter of human-trafficking victims are exploited within their country of origin.

16. Equally interesting is that most agricultural laborers in the national postwar census defined themselves as "day workers" (*braccianti*)—thus highlighting the precarity to which the southern peasantry remained subjected (Rossi-Doria 1982).

17. The Gullo decrees (1944–1945), named after the minister of agriculture, constituted a first attempt at agrarian reform through the partial transformation of agrarian property structures as well as the expropriations of some (but not all) large land estates. Two additional legislative measures (the Sila e Stralcio laws of 1950) subsequently gave rise to a major land reform, which had the objective of stimulating agricultural entrepreneurship through privatization and modern technological intervention (Prinzi 1956).

18. In a famous passage in Levi's *Christ Stopped at Eboli*, his sister depicts what appeared as the antithesis of Italian rural development ideals: inside the black holes excavated in the porous sandstone from which the city was built she observes the miserable conditions of Italy's peasant families struck by poverty, marginality, and disease.

19. The design of La Martella involved, quite interestingly, a master plan from Luigi Piccinato, who picked up the diagram he had used in 1934 for the integral land reclamation of the Agro-Pontine area (Monica and Bergamaschi 2019, 9).

20. The narrative goes that Burkina Faso's migration trajectory to Italy started in the early 1980s when a Bissa from Béguedo working in Côte d'Ivoire was invited by his employer, an Italian, to work for him as a driver around Rome. Migration to Italy by men from Niaogho and Béguedo subsequently gained momentum through their employment in horticulture around Naples and, much later, as factory workers in the Italian industries of Brescia and Bergamo: Wouterse and Van den Bergh (2011, 361).

21. "If an Arab wants someone for one or two hours, he goes to the crossroads to find people. They discuss the price and if they understand each other, they go together," one Nigerian migrant explained to Catalan researcher Oriol Cepero (2018, 67).

22. Interview by the author at Kalifoo Ground, February 1, 2020.

23. The ghetto of Villa Literno consisted of two parts, situated about six to seven hundred meters apart from each other and at two sides of an asphalt road. While the smallest section was inhabited by about three hundred Bissa from Burkina Faso, the large section constituted a proper *bidonville*, consisting of several trailers and barracks between which winding streets and alleys were traced. Among the tradespeople in the ghetto were tailors, launderers, vendors of cold drinks, grocers, Islamic butchers, sellers of pirated copies of

African music tapes, transcribers, barbers, shoe sellers, and restaurant owners. The menu of the restaurants was invariably "African"—especially rice with meat or fish—and varied according to the nationality of the manager and cook, who was often a woman. Finally, at the entrance of the large ghetto, a sort of parking lot took shape in the shade of some canopies and trees, where mechanics and electricians worked on cars that mostly had northern number plates. The ghetto also hosted two cinemas equipped with television and video recorder (Schmidt di Friedberg 1996, 33–36). Apart from the Burkinabè, the largest group of inhabitants were Ivorians and *haalpulaaren* from Guinea and Mali. Interesting also was the gendered pattern of labor reproduction, as women were operating boutiques and restaurants in the ghetto's enclosure, but married couples preferred to move out as soon as they could.

3. TERRITORIALIZING LABOR

1. According to the research website Fortress Europe (founded by journalist Gabriele del Grande), since 1988 at least 27,382 people have died along the Mediterranean borders of Europe, including 4,273 in 2015 and 3,507 in 2014. In 2017, the International Organization for Migration (IOM) reported 171,635 migrants and refugees entering Europe by sea. This compares with 363,504 arrivals across the region through the same period in 2016. While this reduction of migrant flows rejoiced European policy makers in their attempts to bolster communal borders, the risk to cross increased proportionally in this period: in 2017, a total of 3,116 migrants were reported dead or missing (representing 0.018 percent of total crossings), compared to 5,143 in 2016, according to IOM estimates (representing 0.014 percent of total crossings).

2. The ENA rules stipulated that migrants who were fleeing from Northern Africa between 2011 and 2012 acquired an automatic right to a temporary permit of stay for humanitarian reasons (a *permesso umanitario*).

3. Migrant reception usually unfolded in the following manner: Upon their arrival in Italian territory, migrants were assigned to a prime reception center called CARA (Centro di Accoglienza per Richiedenti Asilo) or CAS (Centro di Accoglienza Straordinaria). There they received a first level of assistance, which varied according to the reception centers. Migrants who applied for asylum were obliged to submit their application to the territorial commission in the region of stay. In the case of a successful outcome, this resulted in the prefect assigning a place of residence where the applicant could stay. The residential permit (called *permesso di soggiorno*—literally, a right to stay) had to be renewed every three months until a territorial commission decided if the applicant would receive protection from the Italian state, and of what kind. In the case of a positive decision, the commission then granted a subsidiary, humanitarian, or refugee protection, after which the applicant was "free" to lead an independent life in Italy or any other European country. One specific refugee protection program was the SPRAR (*sistema di protezione per richiedenti d'asilo e rifugiati*). This program, which is frequently invoked as the center of excellence of the Italian asylum system, aims to assist refugees and asylum applicants for a limited period in order to be enhance their "personal autonomy". In practice, the participants' trajectories are elaborated through a close linkage between nonstate agencies responsible for the migrants' daily reception and the state bureaucracy, which remains officially responsible for the refugees' protection. In 2014, about ten thousand beneficiaries were able to access this program, which comes down to 5 percent of the total refugee population (source: Rapporto sulla protezione internazionale in Italia 2014, http://www.anci.it/Contenuti/Allegati/Rapporto_low.pdf, last consulted October 23, 2018).

4. According to official numbers, the first-level reception centers (CAS and CARA) were already working at 24 percent over their capacity in 2014 (see Novak 2019).

5. An illustrative example was a demonstration in 2015 in Lampedusa, when a group of two hundred Eritrean migrants protested while shouting "We are human beings! No fingerprints! We want freedom!"; some of them also started hunger strikes. Scholarly works in border and migration studies—especially those related to the Autonomy of Migration (AoM) thesis—saw in those acts of dissent at the border a demonstration of the political agency of migrants manifested by their capacity to devise strategies to subvert control (for a discussion see Glouftsios and Casaglia 2022).

6. Ministery of Interior, various reports; see www.interno.gov.it/it/stampa-e-comuni cazione/dati-e-statistiche/sbarchi-e-accoglienza-dei-migranti-tutti-i-dati.

7. In this intergovernmental agreement (which involved a reconfirmation of the 2008 "Treaty of Friendship, Partnership and Co-operation"), signed in February 2017, Prime Minister Paolo Gentiloni and his Libyan counterpart, Fayez al Saraj, stipulated the terms for a joint operation for the training of border staff, the provision of key infrastructure (like patrol boats), and technical assistance to the Libyan coast guard in order to restrain "illegal migration."

8. On November 6, 2016, for example, a ship from the German NGO Sea Watch, during one of its rescue operations, notably documented and denounced the violent conduct of the Libyan coast guards toward rescued migrants. During the operation, the Libyans not only deliberately dropped rescue boats containing people back into the sea, but also let several people drown while hindering the German NGO ship from intervening (Heller, Pezzani and Mann 2018).

9. Such happened for instance at the border in Ventimiglia (Liguria) and on the French-Italian border of Bardonecchio (Piemonte), where French border police were photographed while illegally accompanying migrants on Italian soil. France was condemned by the European court of Human Rights for this systematic violation of the right to asylum (Tazzioli 2020). In later years, other states followed suit in these violations. After the European readmission agreement with Turkey in 2016, Greek border guards were regularly spotted in the Aegean Sea pushing migrant vessels back from Greek territorial waters and literally waiting for Turkish and Libyan security forces to take over the management of these migrant crossings.

10. Arrivals in Italy through the central Mediterranean route increased from an average of below 40,000 in the 2000s to 62,692 in 2011 and 170,100 in 2014 (Baldwin-Edwards and Lutterbeck 2019). And since 2012, overland immigration to Libya has resumed. While East African immigrants and refugees mostly intend to transit to Europe, the majority of West and Central Africans still arrive in Libya to work, building on a long tradition of circular migration: Pradella and Cillo (2021, 5).

11. African migrants testified to having been sold from one criminal gang to another to pay ransoms. This racket also involved the military and border guards, who actively participated in the trafficking of human beings across the Libyan desert and in Mediterranean Sea crossings since 2010. That year, the Libyan government adopted a law that allowed for the detention, pending deportation, of migrants and refugees in an irregular situation. Migrants and refugees caught at sea faced criminal penalties, which included "imprisonment with labor" (UNIMSIL, UNHROHC 2018, 25–26).

12. The reverse side of this systematic dehumanization of Black Africans in Libya was their systematic racial stereotyping: the men were now more commonly referred to as dangerous criminals, and women as having "loose sexual mores." Significant was also the attitude of DCIM officials, who, when interviewed, repeatedly complained to the UN Mission about "Libya becoming black" as a justification of their actions (UNIMSIL, UNHROHC 2018, 12). The purported importance of preserving the country's demographic balance in fact provided the single most important legitimation to explain the forced labor and systematic sex work of Black African prisoners (UNIMSIL, UNHROHC 2018, 12).

13. Significantly, the minister, who was a former agricultural day laborer (*bracciante*), announced the law as a measure to integrate Italy's many "invisible" workers. In tears, she said at a press conference, "The invisible will no longer be invisible": *Repubblica*, May 14, 2020.

14. Interview by the author, July 26, 2016.

15. Interview by the author, October 10, 2016.

16. Interview by the author, February 7, 2017.

17. The single municipal tax (Imposta Municipale Propria, or IMU) is a direct property tax applied to real estate. Created to replace the municipal property tax (ICI), it also incorporates part of the personal income tax (IRPEF) and related additional taxes regarding land income on unleased assets (https://www.amministrazionicomunali.it/).

18. ASPs (*aziende pubbliche di servizi alla persona*) are public law companies that operate on a municipal level. They are set up to ensure the management and qualification of social and socio-health services. They are connected with other communal services integrated in the social, socio-health and health services, like local health centers, social councilors, and the communal administration.

19. Interview by the author, February 9, 2017.

20. NGO worker 1, interview by the author, August 22, 2016; labor union representative, interview by the author, July 5, 2016.

21. NGO worker 1 interview.

22. *Gazzetta Ufficiale* no. 257 (November 3, 2016); see also chapter 1.

23. Interview by the author, August 19, 2016.

24. "The task force deals with all issues related to immigration in the region, including by modifying the regional immigration law" (own translation: Legge regionale 13/2016, "Norme per l'accoglienza, la tutela e l'integrazione dei cittadini stranieri migranti e dei rifugiati"). Until 2019, the institution was presided over by Pietro Simonetti.

25. Interview by the author, August 28, 2017.

26. "Migranti stagionali, Simonetti: Prepararsi alla campagnìa 2017," basilicatanet, October 31, 2016.

27. NGO worker 2, interview by the author, February 27, 2017.

28. Demographic registry, interview by the author, February 19, 2017.

29. NGO worker 2, interview by the author, August 22, 2016.

30. NGO worker 2, interview by the author, February 27, 2017.

31. NGO worker 2 interview.

32. Significantly, the ghetto of San Nicola also hosted several restaurants. One of these was run by a young woman from Burkina Faso but with a long-term residence in Northern Italy, who was also an acquaintance of one of the main *capineri* but was not engaged in sex work. During my later visits to a neighboring ghetto I met several women who, during the winter months, operated bars and restaurants in order to feed and care for the male workers. All these aspects are unaccounted for in this deliberately stereotypical representation of the ghetto as a hotbed of criminality and prostitution (for a deeper discussion of these dynamics see Peano 2019).

33. The term "precarity" has aroused significant discussion in social theory recently. Personally, I follow the definition of sociological theorists Tsianos and Papadopoulos (2006), who argue that precarity is in part characterized by the continuous experience of mobility across a fractured time-space, and that precarity results in embodied experiences of exploitation in post-Fordist societies (for a discussion see Waite 2009).

34. The data reported here concern the years 2015–2016. They have been elaborated in cooperation with a local association involved in social-legal support for migrant laborers. According to the registers of the Melfi employment center, during the tomato harvesting season non-EU workers in the Alto Bradano area reached a number of 866 in 2015

and 1,192 in 2016 (representing a growth of 38 percent): a number that reflects various observations regarding the presence of foreign workers during the harvesting season in previous years. Of the thirty nationalities active in the sector during these years, most of them come from West Africa (Burkina Faso, followed by Ghana and Mali). In 2015, these workers carried out a total of 45,333 days of labor. Close to 40 percent of the workers have more contracts and therefore multiple relationships with the farming enterprises (contracts vary between one and seven per season). The total number also includes laborers who move from region to region following the cyclical harvest times.

35. Interview by the author, February 9, 2017.

36. Interview by the author, February 9, 2017.

4. IMPERMANENT TERRITORIES

1. Once again, names in this section have been changed to ensure anonymity.

2. Interview by the author, August 22, 2016.

3. The occupied building had been impounded by the police from a local organized-crime boss belonging to the Sacra Corona Unita (the Puglia-based crime syndicate) but had since remained vacant.

4. Interview by the author, February 6, 2017.

5. The *macquis*, or connection house, is a place of encounter where migrant workers come to pass time together, play *dames* (checkers) or *oware* (pit and pebbles), gather news and share information about the goings-on at "home" and in Italy. The word they used to describe this function to me was *distraction*, which, in French, means amusement, pastime. A woman came by every day to cook and serve meals and drinks for the workers. In the back rooms behind a set of curtains, she kept two sex workers working for her, but only during the summer months. Just like in the other ghettos, these women had no family or kin relations to the workers and disappeared the day the harvest was over. As my acquaintances told me, the sex workers were recruited from the networks dominated by Nigerian organized crime, but—just like the other commodified services furnished during this period—they all responded to the strict hierarchy of the Sudanese *caponero* who operated in this zone at the time.

6. As I wrote previously, the reverse side of this territorial stigma is the EURODAC fingerprint database, which, according to Glouftsios and Casaglia (2022, np), is part of a wider data infrastructure that "stigmatizes" postcolonial "others" with codes to control their mobilities (see chapter 3).

7. Conceptually, Wacquant's analysis can be related to a planetary outlook on urbanization, which, in Neil Brenner's (2013) words, advances a territorially differentiated, morphologically variable, multiscalar and processual conceptualization of urbanization under capitalism, arguing that the development, intensification, and worldwide expansion of capitalism produces a vast, variegated terrain of urban(ized) conditions that include, yet progressively extend beyond, the zones of agglomeration that have long monopolized the attention of urban researchers. I will return to this agenda in the concluding chapter.

8. A central metaphor that francophone West Africans evoke in this context is that of *la brousse* (literally: jungle), which indicates a space of opportunity but also of danger and abrupt, unexpected changes, a frontier of sorts where one's identity and social status is fundamentally shaken and up for renegotiation.

9. Despite the prevailing rhetoric against the *caporalato* mafia in Southern Italy, this politics of preserving the ghetto's premises has not been an exception: in northern Puglia, the Grand Ghetto of San Severo continued to be accessible even after its official eviction and judicial confiscation (Raeymaekers 2021). In Calabria, Puglia, Campania, and Piemonte informal dwellings of migrant workers emerge again each year in anticipation

of their labor—to be dismantled again after the end of the harvesting season (see Ippolito, Perrotta, and Raeymaekers 2021).

10. Interview by the author, January 21, 2020.

5. CITIZEN RECOGNITION

1. Francesco Materozzi, "Operazione Ghetto Out," *Corriere delle Migrazioni*, June 17, 2014.

2. AGR Basilicata, "Simonetti su lotta a caporalato," Regione Basilicata, August 10, 2017, https://www.regione.basilicata.it/giunta/site/giunta/detail.jsp?otype=1012&id=303 2142&value=regione.

3. Skype interview by the author, March 25, 2015.

4. Stefano Fumarulo, interview by the author, February 16, 2016.

5. Interview by the author, July 30, 2015.

6. Interview by the author, July 28, 2015.

7. One famous example in this case was Salvatore Buzzi, a Roman criminal who for some time administered the cooperatives of the Eriches group. At the end of 2014, Buzzi ended up in prison for Mafia-type association (a specific incrimination in Italian law), the disclosure of professional secrecy, aggravated corruption and disruption of public bidding processes, and fraud. The investigating judge Flavia Costantini wrote about Buzzi that he managed "the economic activities of the association in the sectors of waste collection and disposal, the reception of refugees and refugees, the maintenance of public parks and other sectors subject to public tenders" through his cooperatives. According to the review court (Tribunale del Riesame), Buzzi distributed the spoils of this corruption through a tight network of corrupt public officials, members of the cooperatives, and a local association of criminals around the far-Right activist Massimo Carminati. At one point, a phone tap caught Buzzi speaking to one of his collaborators: "Do you have any idea how much I earn on these migrants? Drug-trafficking pays less ("Tu c'hai idea quanto ce guadagno sugli immigrati? Il traffico di droga rende meno"): for a discussion see Abbate and Lillo 2015.

8. Stefano Fumarulo, interview by the author, August 26, 2016.

9. Quite significantly, Muehlebach clarifies the term "disarticulation" here in a historical sense, as the dismantling of Fordist society and its reliance on a national formalized, industrial waged-labor regime. Besides its promise of material stability, the Fordist state created the conditions for social belonging through the "social coagulant" of formal wage labor (Caltabiano 2002, 33). But with the dismantling of industries across the North and South of Italy, and the diffusion of ever more precarious and flexible labor regimes, this relationship of citizens to labor ended on a downward slope (Muehlebach 2011, 64; 2012).

10. Interview by the author, July 29, 2015.

11. Skype interview by the author, March 25, 2015.

12. Interview by the author, July 28, 2015.

13. For the record, what occurred was actually a long war of position between opposed networks. On the one side stood the director of the charity and his Italian cooperative members, the representative of the labor union CGIL, and some former members of the town administration; on the other side stood the Senegalese diaspora's support network, Foggia's city prefect Luisa Latella (who, quite significantly, also assisted the mayor of Riace Domenico Lucano's refugee protection program), the lawyers' collective Avvocati di Strada, the associations Libera, Legacoop, and two central political representatives, Michele Emiliano, who would later become governor of Puglia, and his close collaborator Stefano Fumarulo, who tragically died from a heart attack before he could consolidate his project at Casa Sankara.

14. Interview by the author, July 29, 2015.

15. Interview by the author, June 6, 2016

16. Fumarulo interview, August 26, 2016; interviews with Hervé, January 15, 2016, and 28 August 28, 2016.

17. The site of the Grand Ghetto had been placed under judicial investigation for almost a year. After a temporary eviction in early 2016, slightly more than three hundred of its inhabitants were arrested and brought to police headquarters. Only thirty were temporarily detained for lack of residency papers—as the local press reported. After this short intervention, the judge ordered a *perquisizione con modalità d'uso*. In practice, this meant that though some arrests took place in the context of the judicial investigation, the site continued to be accessible.

18. Individual interviews and focus group discussion on site, July 2 and 3 and August 29, 2016.

19. Interview by the author, February 5, 2017.

20. After the name change from Capo Free–Ghetto Off to Casa Sankara–Ghetto Out, the directorship changed the name of the association to Casa Sankara–Centro Stefano Fumarulo, in memory of the regional administrator who had accompanied the initiative since the very beginning.

21. "Riaccolto," i pomodori pelati di Casa Sankara in vendita nelle Coop, Casa Sankara website (casasankara.it), February 21, 2021.

22. Interview by the author, April 22, 2021.

23. *Khelcom* is a Wolof expression composed of two words: *khel*, which means intelligence, and *com*, which means prosperity. It forms a central pillar of the Mourid philosophy. Serigne Saliou Mbacke, who is the youngest son of Serigne Touba, the founder of the Mourid brotherhood, diffused this principle of prayer and work through the establishment of numerous agricultural communities in Senegal (see Diouf 2000).

24. Interview by the author, October 5, 2016.

CONCLUSION

1. In light of this maybe a better definition of seasonal laborers is what Jan Breman (1994), in the Indian context, calls wage hunters and gatherers: casual laborers and service providers who work for others in the intricate disguises of contracted and piece-rate jobs. In a breakdown of this category, Martha Chen (2006) shows the variety of such unrecorded work, including that of agricultural laborers who are employed in this manner.

2. It is indeed strange that Giorgio Agamben, who aims to philosophically bridge the boundary between biological life (*bios*) and political life (*zoon*) in Western European thought, does not consider the slave as a prototype of bare life (life stripped from sacral meaning), preferring instead to situate it in the ritual figure of the Roman outlaw. This omission is at once an expression of Agamben's state-centric and whitening perspective that is not often acknowledged (Agamben 2003; see also Ziarek 2008; Fiskesjö 2012).

References

Abbate, Lirio, and Marco Lillo. 2015. *Destra e sinistra agli ordini di mafia capitale*. Rome: Chiarelettere.

Abraham, Itty, and Willem van Schendel. 2005. *Illicit Flows and Criminal Things: States, Borders, and the Other Side of Globalization*. Bloomington: Indiana University Press.

Achtnich, Marthe. 2022. "Waiting to Move On: Migration, Borderwork and Mobility Economies in Libya." *Geopolitics* 27, no. 5: 1376–89. https://doi.org/10.1080/146 50045.2021.1919626.

Adepoju, A. 2007. *Migration in Sub-Saharan Africa*. Uppsala: Nordiska Afrika Institutet.

Adjovi, Laeila. 2015. "The Town of Women: A Place Where Wives Don't See Their Husbands for Years." BBC, December 2. https://www.bbc.co.uk/news/resources/ idt-b186fe91-ffb3-4418-a29a-a981b8b1faf4.

Agamben, Giorgio. 2003. *Stato di eccezione*. Turin: Bollati Boringhieri.

AGCM (Autorità Garante della Concorrenza e del Mercato). 2013. *Indagine conoscitiva sul settore della GDO*. Rome: AGCM.

Agnew, John. 2002. *Place and Politics in Modern Italy*. Chicago: University of Chicago Press.

Alasia, Franco, and Danilo Montaldi. (1960) 2010. *Milano, Corea: Inchiesta sugli immigrati negli anni del "miracolo."* Rome: Donzelli.

Al-Bulushi, Yousuf. 2022. "Thinking Racial Capitalism and Black Radicalism from Africa: An Intellectual Geography of Cedric Robinson's World-System." *Geoforum* 132:252–62. https://doi.org/10.1016/j.geoforum.2020.01.018.

Alliegro, Enzo Vinicio. 2019. *Terraferma. Un' "Altra Basilicata" tra stereotipi, identità e [sotto]sviluppo*. Soveria Mannelli: Rubbettino Editore.

Amanor, Kojo Sebastian. 2011. *Global Landgrabs, Agribusiness and the Commercial Smallholder: A West African Perspective*. The Hague: LDPI.

Amira, Saad. 2021. "The Slow Violence of Israeli Settler-Colonialism and the Political Ecology of Ethnic Cleansing in the West Bank." Settler Colonial Studies. https:// doi.org/10.1080/2201473X.2021.2007747.

Amnesty International. 2016. *Hotspot Italy: Abuses of Refugees and Migrants*. Rome: Amnesty International.

Anand, Nikhi, Akhil Gupta, and Hannah Appel. 2018. *The Promise of Infrastructure*. Durham, NC: Duke University Press.

Andersson, Ruben. 2014. "Time and the Migrant Other: European Border Controls and the Temporal Economics of Illegality." *American Anthropologist* 116, no. 4: 795–809. https://doi:10.1111/aman.12148.

Antonsich, Marco. 2009. "Geopolitica: The 'Geographical and Imperial Consciousness' of Fascist Italy." *Geopolitics* 14, no. 2: 256–77. https://doi:10.1080/146500408 02578708.

Arboleda, Martin. 2020. *Planetary Mine: Territories of Extraction under Late Capitalism*. London: Verso.

Armiero, Marco, and Massimo De Angelis. 2017. "Anthropocene: Victims, Narrators, and Revolutionaries." *South Atlantic Quarterly* 116, no. 2 (April): 345–62. https://doi.org/10.1215/00382876-3829445.

Arrighi, Giovanni. 1970. "Labour Supplies in Historical Perspective: A Study of the Proletarianization of the African Peasantry in Rhodesia." *Journal of Development Studies* 6, no. 3: 197–234. https:doi: 10.1080/00220387008421322.

Arrighi, Giovanni, Nicole Aschoff, and Ben Scully. 2010. "Accumulation by Dispossession and Its Limits: The Southern Africa Paradigm Revisited." *Studies of Comparative International Devevelopment* 45:410–38. https://doi.org/10.1007/s12116-010-9075-7.

Arthur, John. 1991. "International Labor Migration Patterns in West Africa." *African Studies Review* 34, no. 3 (December): 65–87.

ASGI. 2017. "Accordo Italia-Libia, ASGI all'Italia e all'UE: Così si tradisce lo spirito europeo." https://www.asgi.it/asilo-e-protezione-internazionale/italia-libia-accordo-ue/.

Atkinson, David. 2003. "Geographical Knowledge and Scientific Survey in the Construction of Italian Libya." *Modern Italy* 8:9–29.

Atkinson, David. 2005. "Creating Colonial Space with Geographies and Geopolitics." In *Italian Colonialism*, edited by Ruth Ben-Ghiat and Mia Fuller, 15–26. New York: Palgrave Macmillan.

Auvillain, Mathilde, and Stefano Liberti. 2016. "The Dark Side of the Italian Tomato." Internazionale. https://www.internazionale.it/webdoc/tomato/.

Avallone, Gennaro. 2017. *Sfruttamento e resistenze. Migrazioni e agricoltura in Europa: Italia, Piana del Sele*. Verona: Ombre Corte.

Axelsson, Linn, Charlotta Hedberg, Nils Pettersson, and Qian Zhang. 2022. "Re-visiting the 'Black Box' of Migration: State-Intermediary Co-production of Regulatory Spaces of Labour Migration." *Journal of Ethnic and Migration Studies* 48, no. 3: 594–612.

Bair, Jennifer, and Marion Werner. 2011. "Commodity Chains and the Uneven Geographies of Global Capitalism: A Disarticulations Perspective." *Environment and Planning A* 43, no. 5: 988–97. https://doi.org/10.1068/a43505.

Baldwin-Edwards, Martin, and Derek Lutterbeck. 2019. "Coping with the Libyan Migration Crisis." *Journal of Ethnic and Migration Studies* 45, no. 12: 2241–57. https://doi.org/10.1080/1369183X.2018.

Ballvé, Teo. 2020. "Investigative Ethnography: A Spatial Approach to Economies of Violence." *Geographical Review* 110, no. 1–2: 238–51. https://doi.org/10.1111/gere.12347.

Banerjee, Bobby. 2008. "Necrocapitalism." *Organization Studies* 29, no. 12: 1541–63. https://doi.org/10.1177/0170840607096386.

Barad, Karen. 2003. "Posthumanist Performativity: Towards an Understanding of How Matter Comes to Matter." *Signs: Journal of Women in Culture and Society* 28, no. 3: 801–31. https://doi.org/10.1086/345321.

Barca, Stefania. 2020. *Forces of Reproduction: Notes for a Counter-hegemonic Anthropocene*. Cambridge: Cambridge University Press.

Barrientos, Sergio, Uma Kothari, and Nicola Phillips. 2013. "Dynamics of Unfree Labour in the Contemporary Global Economy." *Journal of Development Studies* 49, no. 8: 1037–41. https://doi.org/10.1080/00220388.2013.780043.

Basso, Pietro, ed. 2010. *Razzismo di stato: Stati Uniti, Europa, Italia*. Milan: FrancoAngeli.

Basso, Pietro, and Fabio Perocco. 2003. *Gli immigrati in Europa. Diseguaglianze, razzismo, lotte*. Milan: FrancoAngeli.

Bear, Laura, Karen Ho, Anna Tsing, and Sylvia Yanagisako. 2015. "Gens: A Feminist Manifesto for the Study of Capitalism." *Cultural Anthropology*, March 30. https://culanth.org/ eldsights/652-gens-a-feminist -manifesto-for-the-study-of-capitalism.

Bello, Walden. 2020. "'Never Let a Good Crisis Go to Waste.' The Covid-19 Pandemic and the Opportunity for Food Sovereignty." Transnational Institute. April 29. https://www.tni.org/en/publication/never-let-a-good-crisis-go-to-waste.

Benjamin, Walter. 1999. *Illuminations*. New York: Schocken Books.

Bensaâd, Ali. 2012. "La Libya révolutionnaire." *Politique africaine* 125 (March): special issue.

Berndt, Christian, and Mark Boeckler. 2009. "Geographies of Exchange and Circulation I: Constructions of Markets." *Progress in Human Geography* 33, no. 4: 535–51. https://doi.org/10.1177/0309132509104805.

Bernstein, Henry. 2010. *Class Dynamics of Agrarian Change*. Halifax: Fernwood.

Best, Lloyd, and Kari Levitt. 2009. *Essays on the Theory of Plantation Economy: A Historical and Institutional Approach to Caribbean Economic Development*. Mona, Jamaica: University of the West Indies Press.

Bhattacharya, Tithi, ed. 2017. *Social Reproduction Theory: Remapping Class, Recentering Oppression*. London: Pluto.

Bhattacharyya, Gargi. 2018. *Rethinking Racial Capitalism: Questions of Reproduction and Survival*. London: Rowman & Littlefield International.

Billo, Emily, and Nancy Hiemstra. 2013. "Mediating Messiness: Expanding Ideas of Flexibility, Reflexivity, and Embodiment in Fieldwork." *Gender, Place & Culture* 20, no. 3: 313–28. https://doi.org/10.1080/0966369X.2012.674929.

Bjarnesen, Jens, and Simon Turner, eds. 2018. *Invisibility in African Displacements: From Structural Marginalization to Strategies of Avoidance*. London: Nordiska Africa Insitutet and Zed Books.

Blackburn, Robin. 1997. "The Old World Background to European Colonial Slavery." *William and Mary Quarterly* 54, no. 1, *Constructing Race* (January): 65–102.

Black Mediterranean Collective. 2021. *The Black Mediterranean: Bodies, Borders and Citizenship*. Cham, Switzerland: SpringerLink.

Blanco Brotons, Francisco. 2021. "On the Discourse of Exclusion in a Globalizing World." In *Rethinking Vulnerability and Exclusion*, edited by Rodríguez Lopez Blanca, Nuria Sánchez Madrid, and Adriana Zaharijević, 161–84. Cham, Switzerland: Palgrave Macmillan. https://doi.org/10.1007/978-3-030-60519-3_9.

Blion, Reynald. 1996. "De la Côte-d'Ivoire à l'Italie. Pratiques migratoires des Burkinabè et logiques d'états." *Studi Emigrazione / Études Migrations* 33, no. 121: 47–70.

Blion, Reynald, and Sylvie Bredeloup. 1996. "La Côte-d'Ivoire dans les stratégies migratoires des Burkinabè et des Sénégalais." In *Le modèle ivoirien en crise*, edited by Bernard Contamin, 707–37. Paris: Karthala; Abidjan: GIDIS.

Blomley, Nicholas. 2010. "Cuts, Flows, and the Geographies of Property." *Law, Culture and the Humanities* 7, no. 2: 203–16. https://doi.org/10.1177/1743872109355.

Boeckler, M., and C. Berndt. 2014. "B/ordering the Mediterranean: Free Trade, Fresh Fruits and Fluid Fixity." In *Seasonal Workers in Mediterranean Agriculture: The Social Costs of Eating Fresh*, edited by Jörg Gertel and Sarah Ruth Sippel, 23–35. London: Routledge.

Bonifazi, Corrado, and Massimo Livi Bacci. 2014. *Le migrazioni internazionali ai tempi della crisi*. Florence: Neodemos.

Borrettti, Biagio. 2010. "Da Castel Volturno a Rosarno. Il lavoro vivo degli immigrati tra stragi, pogrom, rivolte e razzismo di stato." In *Razzismo di Stato: Stati Uniti, Europa, Italia*, edited by Pietro Basso, 493–524. Milan: FrancoAngeli.

Brachet, Julien. 2018. "Manufacturing Smugglers: From Irregular to Clandestine Mobility in the Sahara." *AAPSS Annals* 676 (March): 16–35. https://doi.org/10.1177/0002716217744529.

Brass, Tom. 2014. "Debating Capitalist Dynamics and Unfree Labour: A Missing Link?" *Journal of Development Studies* 50, no. 4: 570–82. https://doi: 10.1080/00220388.2013.872775.

Brass, Tom, and Henry Bernstein. 1992. "Introduction: Proletarianisation and Deproletarianisation on the Colonial Plantation." *Journal of Peasant Studies* 19, no. 3–4: 1–40. https:// doi: 10.1080/03066159208438486.

Brasselle, Anne-Sophie, Frédéric Gaspart, and Jean-Philippe Platteau. 2002. "Land Tenure Security and Investment Incentives: Puzzling Evidence from Burkina Faso." *Journal of Development Economics* 67:373–418. https://doi.org/10.1016/S0304-3878(01)00190-0.

Braudel, Fernand. 1995. *The Mediterranean and the Mediterranean World in the Age of Philip II*. Vols. 1 and 2. Translated from the French by Siân Reynolds. Berkeley: University of California Press.

Braverman, Irus. 2011. "Civilized Borders: A Study of Israel's New Crossing Administration." *Antipode* 43, no. 2: 264–95. https://doi.org/10.1111/j.1467-8330.2010.00773.x.

Bredeloup, Sylvie, and Olivier Pliez. 2005. *Migrations entre les deux rives du Sahara*. Paris: IRD Éditions.

Bredeloup, Sylvie, and Mahamadou Zongo. 2004. "Quand les frères burkinabè de la petite Jamahiriyya s'arrêtent à Tripoli." *Autrepart* 4, no. 36: 23–147. https://doi:10.3917/autr.036.0123.

Breman, Jan. 1994. *Wage Hunters and Gatherers: Search for Work in the Urban and Rural Economy of South Gujarat*. Delhi: Cambridge University Press.

Brenner, Neil, ed. 2013. *Implosions/Explosions: Towards a Study of Planetary Urbanization*. Berlin: Jovis Verlag.

Brenner, Neil, and Nikos Katsikis. 2013. "Is the Mediterranean Urban?" In *Implosions/Explosions: Towards a Study of Planetary Urbanization*, 428–59. Berlin: Jovis Verlag.

Breusers, M. 1998. "On the Move: Mobility, Land Use and Livelihood Practices on the Central Plateau in Burkina Faso." PhD diss., Wageningen University.

Broeck, Sabine. 2018. *Gender and the Abjection of Blackness*. Albany: SUNY Press.

Browne, Simone. 2015. *Dark Matters: On the Surveillance of Blackness*. Durham, NC: Duke University Press.

Burdett, Charles. 2003. "Italian Fascism and Utopia." *History of the Human Sciences* 16:93–108. https://doi.org/10.1177/0952695103016001008.

Byrne, Denis. 2011. "Archaeological Heritage and Cultural Intimacy: An Interview with Michael Herzfeld." *Journal of Social Archaeology* 11, no. 2: 144–57. https://doi.org/10.1177/1469605311402571.

Çalışkan, Koray. 2010. *Market Threads: How Cotton Farmers and Traders Create a Global Commodity*. Princeton, NJ: Princeton University Press.

Çalışkan, Koray, and Michel Callon. 2009. "Economization, Part 1: Shifting Attention from the Economy towards Processes of Economization." *Economy and Society* 38, no. 3: 369–98. https://doi.org/10.1080/03085140903020580.

Callon, Michel. 1998. *The Laws of the Market*. Oxford: Blackwell.

Caltabiano, Franco. 2002. *Lombardia solidale. Terzo settore e civismo in una regione in transizione*. Milan: FrancoAngeli.

Caprotti, Federico. 2007. "Destructive Creation: Fascist Urban Planning, Architecture and New Towns." *Journal of Historical Geography* 33, no. 3: 651–79. https://doi.org/10.1016/j.jhg.2006.08.002.

Carbado, Devon W. 2005. "Racial Naturalization." *American Quarterly* 57, no. 3: 633–58. https://www.jstor.org/stable/40068310.

Caruso, Francesco. 2015. *La politica dei subalterni. Organizzazione e lotte del bracciantato migrante nel Sud Europa*. Rome: DeriveApprodi.

Caruso, Francesco, and Alessandra Corrado. 2022. *Essenziali ma invisibili. Analisi delle politiche e delle iniziative di contrasto allo sfruttamento e per l'inclusione dei lavoratori migranti in agricoltura nel sud Italia*. Turin: Rosenberg and Sellier.

Cepero, Oriol Puig. 2018. "The Nigerien Migrants in Kaddafi's Libya: Between Visibility and Invisibility." In *Invisibility in African Displacements: From Structural Marginalization to Strategies of Avoidance*, edited by Jens Bjarnesen and Simon Turner, 160–77. London: Nordiska Africainsitutet and Zed Books.

Chakrabarty, Dipesh. 2009. "The Climate of History: Four Theses." *Critical Inquiry* 35, no. 2 (Winter): 197–222. https://doi.org/10.1086/596640.

Chambers, Iain. 2008. *Mediterranean Crossings: The Politics of Interrupted Modernity*. Durham, NC: Duke University Press.

Chauveau, Jean-Pierre, and Jean-Pierre Dozon. 1985. "Colonisation, économie de plantation et société civile en Côte d'Ivoire." *Cahiers ORSTOM des Sciences Humaines* 21, no. 1: 68–80. https://horizon.documentation.ird.fr/exl-doc/pleins_textes/pleins_textes_4/sci_hum/19895.pdf.

Chen, Martha Alter. 2006. *Self-Employed Women: A Profile of SEWA's Membership*. Ahmedabad, India: SEWA.

Cillo, Rossana. 2010. "Economia sommersa e lavoro degli immigrati." *Economia e Società Regionale* 3:25–34.

Coddington, Kate. 2017. "Voice under Scrutiny: Feminist Methods, Anticolonial Responses, and New Methodological Tools." *Professional Geographer* 69, no. 2: 314–20. https://doi.org/10.1080/00330124.2016.1208512.

Colloca, Carlo, and Alessandra Corrado. 2013. *La globalizzazione delle campagne*. Rome: FrancoAngeli.

Colloca, Carlo, and Alessandra Corrado, eds. 2015. *La globalizzazione delle campagne. Migranti e società rurali nel sud Italia*. Milan: FrancoAngeli.

Connolly, William. 2004. "The Complexity of Sovereignty." In *Sovereign Lives: Power in Global Politics*, edited by Jenny Edkins, Veronique Pin-Fat, and Michael J. Shapiro, 23–40. New York: Routledge.

Constantakopoulou, Christy. 2018. "Landscape and Hunting: The Economy of the Eschatia," *Land* 7, no. 3: 1–12.

Cook, Benjamin I., Kevin J. Anchukaitis, Ramzi Touchan, David M. Meko, and Edward R. Cook. 2016. "Spatiotemporal Drought Variability in the Mediterranean over the Last 900 Years." *Journal of Geophysical Research: Atmospheres* 121:2060–74. https://doi.org/10.1002/2015JD023929.

Corrado, Alessandra, Carlo De Castro, and Domenico Perrotta, eds. 2016. *Migration and Agriculture: Mobility and Change in the Mediterranean Area*. London: Routledge.

Corrado, Alessandra, Martina Lo Cascio, and Domenico Perrotta. 2018. "Agricolture e cibo." *Meridiana*, no. 93.

Côte, M., and B. Korf. 2018. "Making Concessions: Extractive Enclaves, Entangled Capitalism and Regulative Pluralism at the Gold Mining Frontier in Burkina Faso." *World Development* 101:466–76. https://doi.org/10.1016/j.worlddev.2016.11.002.

Cotula, Lorenzo. 2013. *The Great African Land Grab? Agricultural Investments and the Global Food System*. London: Zed Books.

Cowen, Michael, and Robert Shenton. 1991. "The Origins and Course of Fabian Colonialism in Africa." *Journal of Historical Sociology* 4, no. 2: 143–74. https://doi.org/10.1111/j.1467-6443.1991.tb00101.x.

Cowen, Michael, and Robert Shenton. 1996. *Doctrines of Development*. London: Routledge.

Crainz, Guido. (1960) 2010. Introduction to *Milano, Corea: Inchiesta sugli immigrati negli anni del "miracolo"* by Franco Alasia and Danilo Montaldi, vii–xv. Rome: Donzelli.

CREA (Consiglio per la ricerca in agricoltura e l'analisi dell'economia agraria). 2019. *Il contributo dei lavoratori stranieri all'agricoltura italiana*. Rome: CREA. www.crea.gov.it/web/politiche-e-bioeconomia/-/on-line-il-contributo-dei-lavoratori-stranieri-all-economia-italiana.

Cross, Hannah, and Lionel Cliffe. 2017. "A Comparative Political Economy of Regional Migration and Labour Mobility in West and Southern Africa." *Review of African Political Economy* 44, no. 153: 381–98. https://doi.org/10.1080/03056244.2017.1333411.

Cunningham, Vinson. 2020. "The Argument of Afropessimism." *New Yorker*, July 13.

Cuppini, Niccolo, and Irene Peano. 2019. *Un mondo logistico: Sgardi su lavoro, migrazioni, politica e globalizzazione*. Milan: Ledizioni.

Curtin, Philip D. 2012. *The Rise and Fall of the Plantation Complex: Essays in Atlantic History*. Cambridge: Cambridge University Press. https://doi:10.1017/CBO9780511819414.

Dal Lago, Alessandro. 1999. *Non-persone. L'esclusione dei migranti in una società globale*. Rome: Feltrinelli.

Das, Veena, and Deborah Poole. 2004. *Anthropology in the Margins of the State*. Santa Fe: School of American Research.

Davis, Angela. 1983. *Women, Race and Class*. New York: Vintage Books.

Davis, Janae, Alex A. Moulton, Levi Van Sant, and Brian Williams. 2019. "Anthropocene, Capitalocene, . . . Plantationocene? A Manifesto for Ecological Justice in an Age of Global Crises." *Geography Compass* 13, no. 5: e12438. https://doi.org/10.1111/gec3.12438.

De Dominicis, Filippo. 2019. "Regionalism at All Costs: Nallo Mazzocchi Alemanni and the Bradano Valley Land Reclamation Project, 1955." *MODSCAPES SHS Web of Conferences* 63, 02001. https://doi.org/10.1051/shsconf/20196302001.

Del Boca, Angelo. 2020. *Italiani brava gente? Un mito duro da morire*. Padua: BEAT.

De Léon, Jason. 2015. *The Land of Open Graves: Living and Dying on the Migrant Trail*. Berkeley: University of California Press.

Deleuze, Gilles, and Félix Guattari. (1987) 2014. *A Thousand Plateaus*. New York: Bloomsbury.

Deleuze, Gilles, and Claire Parnet. 1987. *Dialogues*. New York: Columbia University Press.

Denning, Michael. 2010. "Wageless Life." *New Left Review* 66 (November–December): 79–97.

DeSilvey, Caitlin, and Tim Edensor. 2012. "Reckoning with Ruins." *Progress in Human Geography* 37, no. 4: 465–85. https://doi.org/10.1177/0309132512462271.

Devillard, A., A. Bacchi, and M. Noack. 2015. *A Survey on Migration Policies in West Africa*. Austria: International Centre for Migration Policy Development. Vienna and Dakar: IOM.

Deyo, L. B., and David Leibowitz. 2003. *Invisible Frontier: Exploring the Tunnels, Ruins, and Rooftops of Hidden New York*. New York: Three Rivers.

Dickie, John. 1999. *Darkest Italy: The Nation and Stereotypes of the Mezzogiorno*. Basingstoke, UK: Palgrave Macmillan.

Dijstelbloem, Huub. 2021. *Borders as Infrastructures: The Technopolitics of Border Control*. Cambridge, MA: MIT Press.

Dines, Nick, and Enrica Rigo. 2015. "Postcolonial Citizenships and the 'Refugeeization' of the Workforce: Migrant Agricultural Labor in the Italian Mezzogiorno." In *Postcolonial Transitions in Europe: Contexts, Practices and Politics*, edited by Sandra Ponzanesi and Gianmaria Colpani, 151–72. Lanham, MD: Rowman & Littlefield International.

Diouf, Mamadou. 2000. "The Senegalese Murid Trade: Diaspora and the Making of a Vernacular Cosmopolitanism." *Public Culture* 12, no. 3: 679–702.

Dixon, Jane. 2007. "Supermarkets as New Food Authorities." In *Supermarkets and Agri-food Supply Chains: Transformations in the Production and Consumption of Foods*, edited by David Burch and Geoffrey Lawrence, 29–50. Cheltenham, UK: Edward Elgar.

Dolan, Catherine, and John Humphrey. 2000. "Governance and Trade in Fresh Vegetables: The Impact of UK Supermarkets on the African Horticulture Industry." *Journal of Development Studies* 37, no. 2: 147–76. https://doi.org/10.1080/713600072.

Dorries, Heather, David Hugill, and Julie Tomiak. 2022. "Racial Capitalism and the Production of Settler Colonial Cities." *Geoforum* 132 (June): 263–70. https://doi.org/10.1016/j.geoforum.2019.07.016.

Douglass, Frederick. (1845) 1999. *Narrative of the Life of Frederick Douglass, an American Slave, Written by Himself*. Electronic ed. Chapel Hill: University of North Carolina Press.

Douwe Van der Ploeg, Jan. 2008. *The New Peasantries: Struggles for Autonomy and Sustainability in an Era of Empire and Globalization*. London: Earthscan.

Du Bois, W. E. B. (1903) 2007. *The Souls of Black Folk*. Oxford: Oxford University Press.

du Toit, Andries. 2004. *Forgotten by the Highway: Globalization, Adverse Incorporation and Chronic Poverty in a Commercial Farming District of South Africa*. Cape Town: PLAAS. http://dx.doi.org/10.2139/ssrn.1753702.

Edwards, Zophia. 2021. "Racial Capitalism and COVID-19." *Monthly Review* 72, no. 10: 21–32.

Eichen, Joshua R. 2020. "Cheapness and (Labor-)Power: The Role of Early Modern Brazilian Sugar Plantations in the Racializing Capitalocene." *Environment and Planning D: Society and Space* 38, no. 1: 35–52. https://doi.org/10.1177/0263775818798035.

Eilenberg, Michael, and Jason Cons, eds. 2019. *Frontier Assemblages: The Emergent Politics of Resource Frontiers in Asia*. Basingstoke, UK: Wiley-Blackwell.

Elden, Stuart. 2010. "Land, Terrain, Territory." *Progress in Human Geography* 34, no. 6: 799–817. https://doi.org/10.1177/0309132510362603.

Elden, Stuart. 2013a. *The Birth of Territory*. Chicago: University of Chicago Press.

Elden, Stuart. 2013b. "Secure the Volume: Vertical Geopolitics and the Depth of Power." *Political Geography* 34 (May): 35–51. https://doi.org/10.1016/j.polgeo.2012.12.009.

Elyachar, Julia. 2010. "Phatic Labor, Infrastructure, and the Question of Empowerment in Cairo." *American Ethnologist* 37, no. 3: 452–64. https://doi.org/10.1111/j.1548-1425.2010.01265.x.

Elyachar, Julia. 2012. "Next Practices: Knowledge, Infrastructure, and Public Goods at the Bottom of the Pyramid." *Public Culture* 24, no. 66: 109–29. https://doi.org/10.1215/08992363-1443583.

Emmenegger, Rony. 2021. "Unsettling Sovereignty: Violence, Myths and the Politics of History in the Ethiopian Somali Metropolis." *Political Geography* 90 (October): 102476. https://doi.org/10.1016/j.polgeo.2021.102476.

Fairhead, James, and Melissa Leach. 1996. *Misreading the African Landscape: Society and Ecology in a Forest-Savanna Mosaic*. Cambridge: Cambridge University Press.

Fanon, Franz. 1967. *Black Skin, White Masks*. New York: Grove.

FAO (Food and Agricultural Organization). 2020. *Climate Change: Unpacking the Burden on Food Safety*. Rome: FAO.

Fassin, Didier, ed. 2015. *At the Heart of the State: The Moral World of Institutions*. London: Pluto.

Federici, Silvia. 2004. *Caliban and the Witch: Women, the Body and Primitive Accumulation*. New York: Autonomedia.

Federici, Silvia. 2018. "Marx and Feminism." *TripleC* 16, no. 2: 468–75. https://doi.org/10.31269/triplec.v16i2.1004.

Federici, Silvia. 2020. *Beyond the Periphery of the Skin: Rethinking, Remaking, and Reclaiming the Body in Contemporary Capitalism*. Oakland, CA: PM.

Ferguson, James, and Akhil Gupta. 2002. "Spatializing States: Toward an Ethnography of Neoliberal Governmentality." *American Ethnologist* 29:981–1002. https://doi.org/10.1525/ae.2002.29.4.981.

Ferguson, James, and Tania Li. 2018. *Beyond the "Proper Job": Political-Economic Analysis after the Century of Labouring Man*. Cape Town: PLAAS.

Findley, S. E. 1997. "Migration and Family Interactions in Africa." In *Family, Population and Development in Africa*, edited by A. Adepoju, 109–38A. London: Zed Books.

Fiskesjö, Magnus. 2012. "Outlaws, Barbarians, Slaves: Critical Reflections on Agamben's Homo Sacer." *HAU: Journal of Ethnographic Theory* 2, no. 1: 161–80. https://doi.org/10.14318/hau2.1.009.

Flahaux, Marie-Laurence, and Hein De Haas. 2016. "African Migration: Trends, Patterns, Drivers." *Comparative Migration Studies* 4, no. 1. https://doi.org/10.1186/s40878-015-0015-6.

Fontanari, Elena. 2017. "It's My Life: The Temporalities of Refugees and Asylum-Seekers within the European Border Regime." *ERQ* 1 (January–April): 25–54.

Foot, John. 2005. "Dentro la città irregolare: Une rivisitazione delle Coree Milanesi, 1950–2000." *Storia Urbana* 108: 139–56.

Franchetti, Leopoldo. 1875. *Condizioni economiche ed amministrative delle province Napoletane: Abruzzi e Molise-Calabrie e Basilicata / appunti di viaggio di Leopoldo Franchetti per Sidney Sonnino*. Florence: Tipografia della Gazzetta d'Italia (available online at http://bd.fondazionegramsci.org/; last accessed March 2021).

Frébutte, Jean-Marc. 2021. *La tarentelle noire*. Paris: Éditions de la Rémanence.

Friedmann, Harriet. 1993. "The Political Economy of Food: A Global Crisis." *New Left Review* 197, no. 1: 29–57.

Friedmann, Harriet. 1987. "International Regimes of Food and Agriculture since 1870." In *Peasants and Peasant Societies*, edited by Theodor Shanin, 258–76. Oxford: Basil Blackwell.

Frisina, Annalisa, and Camilla Hawthorne. 2018. "Italians with Veils and Afros: Gender, Beauty, and the Everyday Anti-racism of the Daughters of Immigrants in Italy." *Journal of Ethnic and Migration Studies* 44, no. 5: 718–35. https://doi.org/10.1080/1369183X.2017.1359510.

Gammeltoft-Hansen, Thomas, and Ninna Nyberg Sørensen, eds. 2013. *The Migration Industry and the Commercialization of International Migration*. London: Routledge.

Garelli, Glenda, and Martina Tazzioli. 2016. "Warfare on the Logistics of Migrant Movements: EU and NATO Military Operations in the Mediterranean." *Open Democracy*, June 16.

Gargiulo, Enrico. 2021. *Invisible Borders: Administrative Barriers and Citizenship in the Italian Municipalities*. Basingstoke, UK: Palgrave Macmillan.

Gertel, Jörg, and Sarah Ruth Sippel, eds. 2014. *Seasonal Workers in Mediterranean Agriculture: The Social Costs of Eating Fresh*. London: Routledge.

Gibbon, Peter, and Stefano Ponte. 2005. *Trading Down: Africa, Value Chains, and the Global Economy*. Philadelphia: Temple University Press.

Giglioli, Ilaria, and Eric Swyngedouw. 2008. "Let's Drink to the Great Thirst! Water and the Politics of Fractured Techno-natures in Sicily." *International Journal of Urban and Regional Research* 32, no. 2: 292–414. https://doi.org/10.1111/j.1468-2427.2008.00789.x.

Gilmore, Ruth Wilson. 2002a. "Fatal Couplings of Power and Difference: Notes on Racism and Geography." *Professional Geographer* 54, no. 1: 15–24. https://doi.org/10.1111/0033-0124.00310.

Gilmore, Ruth Wilson. 2002b. "Race and Globalization." In *Geographies of Global Change: Remapping the World*, edited by R. J. Johnston, Peter J. Taylor, and Michael J. Watts. New York: Wiley-Blackwell.

Gilmore, Ruth Wilson. 2007. *Golden Gulag: Prisons, Surplus, Crisis, and Opposition in Globalizing California*. Berkeley: University of California Press.

Gilroy, Paul. 1993. *The Black Atlantic: Modernity and Double Consciousness*. London: Verso.

Gilroy, Paul. 2021. Antiracism, Blue Humanism and the Black Mediterranean." *Transition* 132:108–22. https://www.muse.jhu.edu/article/856593.

Giuliani, Gaia, and Cristina Lombardi-Diop. 2013. *Bianco e nero: Storia dell'identita razziale degli Italiani*. Florence: La Monnier.

Gledhill, John. 2000. *Power and Its Disguises: Anthropological Perspectives on Politics*. London: Pluto.

Glouftsios, Giorgios, and Anna Casaglia. 2022. "Epidermal Politics: Control, Violence and Dissent at the Biometric Border." *Environment and Planning C: Politics and Space* 41, no. 3. https://doi.org/10.1177/23996544221144872.

Godio, Giovanni. 2014. "Casa occupata, residenza sfumata? L'incredultà, gli spazi di rincorso." *Vie di Fuga* 12 (June). http://viedifuga.org/page/128/?lang=en. Last accessed March 2021.

Goldberg, David Theo. 2002. *The Racial State*. Basingstoke, UK: Wiley-Blackwell.

Gordillo, Gastón R. 2014. *Rubble: The Afterlife of Destruction*. Durham, NC: Duke University Press.

Graham, Stephen, and Simon Marvin. 2001. *Splintering Urbanism: Networked Infrastructures, Technological Mobilities and the Urban Condition*. New York: Routledge.

GRAIN. 2008. *SEIZED! The 2008 Land Grab for Food and Financial Security*. Barcelona: GRAIN.

Gray, Leslie, and Brian Dowd-Uribe. 2013. "A Political Ecology of Socio-economic Differentiation: Debt, Inputs and Liberalization Reforms in Southwestern Burkina Faso." *Journal of Peasant Studies* 40, no. 4: 683–702. https://doi.org/10.1080/03066150.2013.824425.

Grechi, Giulia. 2021. "Colonial Cultural Heritage and Embodied Representations." In *The Black Mediterranean: Bodies, Borders and Citizenship*, edited by Black Mediterranean Collective, 83–98. Cham, Switzerland: SpringerLink.

Gregory, Derek, and Allan Pred, eds. 2007. *Violent Geographies: Fear, Terror, and Political Violence*. New York: Routledge.

Gregory, Derek, and John Urry, eds. 1985. *Social Relations and Spatial Structures*. Basingstoke, UK: Palgrave Macmillan.

Grischow, Jeff D. 2006. *Shaping Tradition: Civil Society, Community and Development in Colonial Northern Ghana, 1899–1957*. Leiden: Brill.

Hall, Derek, Paul Hirsch, and Tania Murray Li, eds. 2011. *Powers of Exclusion: Land Dilemmas in Southeast Asia*. Kolowalu: University of Hawai'i Press.

Hall, Stuart. 1980. "Race, Articulation, and Societies Structured in Dominance." In *Sociological Theories: Race and Colonialism*, 305–45. Paris: UNESCO.

Hamilakis, Yannis. 2016. "Archaeologies of Forced and Undocumented Migration." *Journal of Contemporary Archaeology* 3, no. 2: 121–39. https://doi.org/10.1558/jca.32409.

Haraway, Dona. 2015. "Anthropocene, Capitalocene, Plantationocene, Chthulucene: Making Kin." *Environmental Humanities* 6:159–65. https://doi.org/10.1215/22011919-3615934.

Harney, Stefano, and Fred Moten. 2013. *The Undercommons: Fugitive Planning and Black Study*. New York: Autonomedia.

Harsch, Ernest. 2014. *Thomas Sankara: An African Revolutionary*. Athens: Ohio University Press.

Hart, Keith. 2008. *Between Bureaucracy and the People: A Political History of Informality*. Copenhagen: Danish Institute for International Studies.

Harvey, David. 1985. *The Urbanization of Capital: Studies in the History and Theory of Capitalist Urbanization*. Baltimore: Johns Hopkins University Press.

Harvey, David. 2013. "Cities or Urbanization?" In *Implosions/Explosions: Towards a Study of Planetary Urbanization*, edited by Neil Brenner, 52–66. Berlin: Jovis Verlag.

Hawthorne, Camilla. 2021a. *Contesting Race and Citizenship: Youth Politics in the Black Mediterranean*. Ithaca, NY: Cornell University Press.

Hawthorne, Camilla. 2021b. "L'Italia meticcia? The Black Mediterranean and the Racial Cartographies of Citizenship." In *The Black Mediterranean: Bodies, Borders and Citizenship*, edited by Black Mediterranean Collective. Cham, Switzerland: SpringerLink.

Hazard, Benoit. 2004. "Entre le pays et l'outre-pays." *Journal des africanistes* 74, no. 1–2: 2–15.

Hazard, Benoit. 2010. "Réeinventer les ruralités." *Cahiers d'Études Africaines* 198–200:507–28.

Heller, Charles, and Lorenzo Pezzani. 2016. "Mourning the Dead While Violating the Living." *Open Democracy* 30 (June).

Heller, Charles, Lorenzo Pezzani, and Itamar Mann. 2018. "'It's an Act of Murder': How Europe Outsources Suffering as Migrants Drown." *New York Times*, December 26.

Hennings, Anne. 2018. "Plantation Assemblages and Spaces of Contested Development in Sierra Leone and Cambodia." *Conflict, Security and Development* 18, no. 6: 521–46. https://doi.org/10.1080/14678802.2018.1532640.

Herrigel, Johanna. 2018. "Shifting Global Market Frontiers: Performing Global Fresh Vegetable Commodity Chains in Tanzania." PhD diss., University of Zurich.

Herzfeld, Michael. 1984. "The Horns of the Mediterraneanist Dilemma." *American Ethnologist* 11, no. 3: 439–54. https://doi.org/10.1525/ae.1984.11.3.02a00020.

Herzfeld, Michael. 1985. "Of Horns and History: The Mediterraneanist Dilemma Again." *American Ethnologist* 12, no. 4: 778–80. https://www.jstor.org/stable/644185.

Herzfeld, Michael. 2005. "Practical Mediterraneanism: Excuses for Everything, from Epistemology to Eating." In *Rethinking the Mediterranean*, edited by William Vernon Harris, 45–63. Oxford: Oxford University Press.

Hicks, Dan, and Sarah Mallet. 2019. *Lande: The Calais "Jungle" and Beyond*. Bristol: Bristol University Press.

Hoerling, Martin, Jon Enscheid, Judith Perlwitz, Xiaowei Quan, Toa Zhang, and Philip Pegeon. 2012. "On the Increased Frequency of Mediterranean Drought." *Journal of Climate* 25, no. 6: 2146–61. https://doi.org/10.1175/JCLI-D-11-00296.1.

Hoffman, Danny. 2007. "The City as Barracks: Freetown, Monrovia, and the Organization of Violence in Postcolonial African Cities." *Cultural Anthropology* 22, no. 3: 400–428. https://doi.org/10.1525/can.2007.22.3.400.

Holland, Sharon Patricia. 2000. *Raising the Dead: Readings of Death and (Black) Subjectivity*. Durham, NC: Duke University Press.

Holmes, Seth. 2013. *Fresh Fruit, Broken Bodies: Migrant Farmworkers in the United States*. Berkeley: University of California Press.

Holston, James. 2008. *Insurgent Citizenship: Disjunctions of Democracy and Modernity in Brazil*. Princeton, NJ: Princeton University Press.

Horden, Peregrine, and Nicholas Purcell. 2000. *The Corrupting Sea: A Study of Mediterranean History*. Oxford: Wiley-Blackwell.

Howard, Neil, and Roberto Forin. 2019. "Migrant Workers, 'Modern Slavery' and the Politics of Representation in Italian Tomato Production." *Economy and Society* 48, no. 4: 579–601. https://doi.org/10.1080/03085147.2019.1672426.

Humphrey, Caroline. 2004. "Sovereignty." In *A Companion to the Anthropology of Politics*, edited by David Nugent and Joan Vincent, 418–36. Malden: Blackwell Publishing.

Hunter, J. M. 1963. "Cocoa Migrations and Patterns of Ownership in the Densu Valley near Suhum, Ghana." *Transactions and Papers of the Institute of British Geographers* 33:161–86.

Hunwick, J. O. 1992. "Black Slaves in the Mediterranean World: Introduction to a Neglected Aspect of the African Diaspora." *Slavery & Abolition* 13, no. 1: 5–38. https://doi.org/10.1080/01440399208575049.

ILO (International Labour Organization). 2001. *Decent Work and the Informal Economy*. Geneva: ILO.

ILO (International Labour Organization). 2018. *Women and Men in the Informal Economy: A Statistical Picture*. 3rd ed. Geneva: ILO.

Iocco, Giulio, Martina Lo Cascio, and Domenico Perrotta. 2020. "'Close the Ports to African Migrants and Asian Rice!': The Politics of Agriculture and Migration and the Rise of a 'New' Right-Wing Populism in Italy." *Sociologia Ruralis* 60, no. 4: 732–53. https://doi.org/10.1111/soru.12304.

Ippolito, Ilaria, Mimmo Perrotta, and Timothy Raeymaekers, eds. 2021. *Braccia rubate dall'agricoltura: Pratiche di sfruttamento del lavoro migrante*. Turin: SEB27.

Ipsen, Carl. 1996. *Dictating Demography: The Problem of Population in Fascist Italy*. Cambridge: Cambridge University Press.

Jefferson, Brian Jordan. 2018. "Dark Side of the Planet: Hidden Dimensions of Urban Agglomeration." *Urban Geography* 39, no. 10: 1581–88. https://doi.org/10.1080/02723638.2018.1450464.

Jessop, Bob. 2002. *The Future of the Capitalist State*. Cambridge: Polity.

Kaag, Mayke, Gerard Baltissen, Griet Steel, and Anouk Lodder. 2019. "Migration, Youth, and Land in West Africa: Making the Connections Work for Inclusive Development." *Land* 8:60–71. https://doi.org/10.3390/land8040060.

Kaika, Maria, and Eric Swyngedouw. 2000. "Fetishising the Modern City: The Phantasmagoria of Urban Technological Networks." *International Journal of Urban and Regional Research* 24:120–38. https://doi.org/10.1111/1468-2427.00239.

Kasmir, Sharryn, and August Carbonella. 2014. *Blood and Fire: Toward a Global Anthropology of Labor*. New York: Berghahn Books.

Kelley, Robin D. G. 2017. "What Did Cedric Robinson Mean by Racial Capitalism?" *Boston Review*, January 12. http://bostonreview.net/race/robin-d-g-kelley-what-did-cedric-robinson-mean-racial-capitalism.

Kevane, Michael, and Pierre Englebert. 1998. "A Developmental State without Growth? Explaining the Paradox of Burkina Faso in a Comparative Perspective." *African Development Yearbook* 6:259–85.

Kilomba, Grada. 2008. *Plantation Memories: Episodes of Everyday Racism*. Berlin: Unrast Verlag.

Klute, Georg, and Trutz von Trotha. 2004. "Roads to Peace: From Small War to Parasovereign Peace in the North of Mali." In *Healing the Wounds: Essays on the Reconstruction of Societies after War*, edited by Marie-Claire Foblets and Trutz von Trotha, 109–44. Oxford: Oñati International Series in Law and Society.

Kobayashi, Audrey. 2009. "Geographies of Peace and Armed Conflict: Introduction." *Annals of the Association of American Geographers* 99, no. 5: 819–26. https://doi.org/10.1080/00045600903279358.

Kohl, Ines. 2015. "Tuareg Transborder Business: Afrod Will Never End, Afrod Is Our Work!" *Broker*, October 16.

Kurtz, Hilda. 2009. "Acknowledging the Racial State: An Agenda for Environmental Justice Research." *Antipode* 41:684–704. https://doi.org/10.1111/j.1467-8330.2009.00694.x.

Labanca, Nicola. 2018. "Exceptional Italy? The Many Ends of the Italian Colonial Empire." In *The Oxford Handbook of the Ends of Empire*, edited by Martin Thomas and Andrew S. Thompson, 123–43. Oxford: Oxford University Press.

Laclau, Ernesto. 1971. "Feudalism and Capitalism in Latin America." *New Left Review* 67:19–38.

Larkin, Brian. 2013. "The Politics and Poetics of Infrastructure." *Annual Review of Anthropology* 42:327–43. https://doi.org/10.1146/annurev-anthro-092412-155522.

Latour, Bruno. 2014. "Agency at the Time of the Anthropocene." *New Literary History* 45, no. 1 (Winter): 1–18. https://doi.org/10.1353/nlh.2014.0003.

Lawrence, Geoffrey, and David Burch. 2007. *Supermarkets and Agri-food Supply Chains*. Cheltenham, UK: Edward Elgar.

Lawreniuk, Sabina. 2020. "Necrocapitalist Networks: COVID-19 and the 'Dark Side' of Economic Geography." *Dialogues in Human Geography* 10, no. 2 (July): 199–202. https://doi.org/10.1177/2043820620934927.

Lecoq, Baz. 2010. *Disputed Desert: Decolonization, Competing Nationalisms and Tuareg Rebellions in Northern Mali*. Boston: Brill, 2010.

Lefebvre, Henri. (1974) 1992. *The Production of Space*. Hoboken, NJ: Wiley.

Lemanski, Charlotte. 2020. "Infrastructural Citizenship: The Everyday Citizenships of Adapting and/or Destroying Public Infrastructure in Cape Town, South Africa." *Transactions of the Institute of British Geographers* 45, no. 3 (September): 589–605. https://doi.org/10.1111/tran.12370.

Lentin, Ronit. 2007. "Ireland: Racial State and Crisis Racism." *Ethnic and Racial Studies* 30, no. 4: 610–27. https://doi.org/10.1080/01419870701356023.

Leong, Nancy. 2013. "Racial Capitalism." *Harvard Law Review* 126, no. 8: 2151–226

Li, Fabiana. 2013. "Relating Divergent Worlds: Mines, Aquifers and Sacred Mountains in Peru." *Anthropologica* 55:399–411. https://www.jstor.org/stable/24467345.

Li, Tania Murray. 2005. "Beyond 'the State' and Failed Schemes." *American Anthropologist* 107, no. 3: 383–94. https://doi.org/10.1525/aa.2005.107.3.383.

Li, Tania Murray. 2014. *Land's End: Capitalist Relations on an Indigenous Frontier.* Durham, NC: Duke University Press.

Lin, Weiqiang, Johan Lindquist, Biao Xiang, and Brenda S. A. Yeoh. 2017. "Migration Infrastructures and the Production of Migrant Mobilities." *Mobilities* 12, no. 2: 167–74. https://doi.org/10.1080/17450101.2017.1292770.

Lindquist, J., Biao Xiang, and Brenda Yeoh. 2012. "Opening the Black Box of Migration: Brokers, the Organization of Transnational Mobility and the Changing Political Economy in Asia." *Pacific Affairs* 85, no. 1: 7–19. https://doi.org/10.5509/20128517.

Lodovici, M. S., S. Ferrari, E. Paladino, F. Pesce, N. Torchio, and A. Crippa. 2020. *Revaluation of Working Conditions and Wages for Essential Workers.* Brussels: Policy Department for Economic, Scientific and Quality of Life Policies Directorate-General for Internal Policies, EU Parliament.

Lombardi-Diop, Cristina. 2021. "After 'the Mediterranean.'" In *The Black Mediterranean: Bodies, Borders and Citizenship*, edited by Black Mediterranean Collective, 1–8. Cham, Switzerland: SpringerLink.

Lombardi-Diop, Cristina, and Caterina Romeo. 2014. "The Italian Postcolonial: A Manifesto." *Italian Studies* 69, no. 3: 425–33. https://doi.org/10.1179/0075163 414Z.00000000081.

Losch, Bruno. 2002. "Global Restructuring and Liberalization: Côte d'Ivoire and the End of the Cocoa Market?" *Journal of Agrarian Change* 2, no. 2: 206–27. https://doi.org/10.1111/1471-0366.00031.

Lucht, Hans. 2012. *Darkness before Daybreak: African Migrants Living on the Margins in Southern Italy Today.* Berkeley: University of California Press.

Luxemburg, Rosa. (1951) 2003. *The Accumulation of Capital.* London: Routledge.

Mah, Alice. 2010. "Memory, Uncertainty and Industrial Ruination: Walker Riverside, Newcastle upon Tyne." *International Journal of Urban and Regional Research* 34, no. 2: 398–413. https://doi.org/10.1111/j.1468-2427.2010.00898.x.

Manfreda, Ada. 2020. "*Khelcom* a San Severo, un percorso per la dignità." Atlante, September 2. https://www.treccani.it/magazine/atlante/societa/cartello_ Khelcom_a_San_Severo.html.

Mann, Michael. 1984. "The Autonomous Power of the State: Its Origins, Mechanisms and Results." *European Journal of Sociology / Archives Européennes de Sociologie / Europäisches Archiv für Soziologie* 25, no. 2: 185–213.

Marks, Susan. 2010. "Exploitation as an International Legal Concept." In *Contemporary Perspective on Justice*, edited by Wenzel Matiaske, Sergio Costa, and Hauke Brunkhorst, 137–50. Munich-Mering: Hampp.

Márquez, John D. 2013. *Black-Brown Solidarity: Racial Politics in the New Gulf South.* Austin: University of Texas Press.

Martin, Philip. 2017. *Merchants of Labor: Agents of the Evolving Migration Infrastructure*. Geneva: International Institute for Labor Studies.

Marx, Karl. (1885) 1973. *Grundrisse*. Translated by Martin Nicolaus. New York: Vintage Books.

Massey, Doreen. 1992. "Politics and Space/Time." *New Left Review* 196:65–84. https://newleftreview.org/issues/i196/articles/doreen-massey-politics-and-space-time.pdf.

Mbembe, Achille. 2017. *Critique of Black Reason*. Translated by Lauren Dubois. Durham, NC: Duke University Press.

McFarlane, Colin, and Jonathan Rutherford. 2008. "Political Infrastructures: Governing and Experiencing the Fabric of the City." *International Journal of Urban and Regional Research* 32, no. 2 (June): 363–74. https://doi.org/10.1111/j.1468-2427.2008.00792.x.

McKay, Ben M. 2017. "Agrarian Extractivism in Bolivia." *World Development* 97 (September): 199–211. https://doi.org/10.1016/j.worlddev.2017.04.007.

McKittrick, Katherine. 2013. "Plantation Futures." *Small Axe* 17, no. 3 (November): 1–15. https://doi.org/10.1215/07990537-2378892.

McMichael, Philip. 2005. "Global Development and the Corporate Food Regime." *Research in Rural Sociology and Development* 11:265–99. https://doi.org/10.1016/S1057-1922(05)11010-5.

Meagher, Kate. 2021. "Informality and the Infrastructures of Inclusion: An Introduction." *Development and Change* 52 no. 4 (July): 729–55. https://doi.org/10.1111/dech.12672.

Meagher, Kate, and Ilda Lindell. 2013. "ASR Forum: Engaging with African Informal Economies: Social Inclusion or Adverse Incorporation?" *African Studies Review* 56, no. 3 (December): 57–76. https://doi.org/10.1017/asr.2013.79.

Meagher, Kate, Laura Mann, and Maxim Bolt. 2016. "Introduction: Global Economic Inclusion and African Workers." *Journal of Development Studies* 52, no. 4: 471–82. https://doi.org/10.1080/00220388.2015.1126256.

MEDU (Medici per i Diritti Umani). 2017. *Terraingiusta. Rapporto 2017*. Rome: MEDU.

MEDU (Medici per i Diritti Umani). 2022. *Ritorno alla Terraingiusta: Sfruttamento, ghetti e incerte prospettive*. Rome: MEDU.

Meillassoux, Claude. 1973. "The Social Organisation of the Peasantry: The Economic Basis of Kinship." *Journal of Peasant Studies* 1, no. 1: 81–90. https://doi.org/10.1080/03066157308437873.

Melamed, Jodi. 2015. "Racial Capitalism." *Critical Ethnic Studies* 1, no. 1 (Spring): 76–85. https://doi.org/10.5749/jcritethnstud.1.1.0076.

Merrifield, Andy. 2013. "The Urban Question under Planetary Urbanization." *International Journal for Urban and Regional Research* 37:909–22. https://doi.org/10.1111/j.1468-2427.2012.01189.x.

Merrill, Heather. 2018. *Black Spaces: African Diaspora in Italy*. London: Routledge.

Mezzadra, Sandro, and Brett Neilson. 2011. "Borderscapes of Differential Inclusion: Subjectivity and Struggles on the Threshold of Justice's Excess." In *The Borders of Justice*, edited by Étienne Balibar, Sandro Mezzadra, and R. Samaddar, 181–203. Philadelphia: Temple University Press.

Mezzadra, Sandro, and Brett Neilson. 2013. *Borders as Method, or, the Multiplication of Labor*. Durham, NC: Duke University Press.

Mezzadra, Sandro, and Brett Neilson. 2019. *The Politics of Operations: Excavating Contemporary Capitalism*. Durham, NC: Duke University Press.

Mezzadri, Alessandra. 2019. "On the Value of Social Reproduction: Informal Labour, the Majority World and the Need for Inclusive Theories and Politics." *Radical*

Philosophy 2, no. 4 (Spring): 33–41. https://www.radicalphilosophy.com/article/on-the-value-of-social-reproduction.

Miapyen, Buhari Shehu, and Umut Bozkurt. 2022. "Racial Capitalism and Capitalism in Africa: The Utility and Limits of Cedric Robinson's Perspective." *Review of African Political Economy.* https://doi.org/10.1080/03056244.2022.2075722.

Minuchin, Leandro. 2021. "Prefigurative Urbanization: Politics through Infrastructural Repertoires in Guayaquil." *Political Geography* 85 (March): 102316. https://doi.org/10.1016/j.polgeo.2020.102316.

Miraftab, Faranak. 2009. "Insurgent Planning: Situating Radical Planning in the Global South." *Planning Theory* 8, no. 1 (February): 32–50. https://doi.org/10.1177/1473095208099297.

Molinero Gerbeau, Yoan, and Gennaro Avallone. 2016. "Producing Cheap Food and Labour: Migrations and Agriculture in the Capitalistic World-Ecology." *Social Change Review* 14, no. 2: 122–40.

Molinero Gerbeau, Yoan, and Audrey Leonel. 2018. "West African Migration to Mediterranean Countries and Agricultural Work." In *Mediterra: Migration and Inclusive Rural Development in the Mediterranean,* 59–80. Paris: CIHEAM.

Monica, Luca, and Luca Bergamaschi. 2019. "From the Thirties to Post-war Reconstruction: The Land Reclamation Consortia and Rural Architecture in Italy." *MODSCAPES SHS Web of Conferences* 63, 03001. https://doi.org/10.1051/shsconf/20196303001.

Moore, Jason W. 2015. *Capitalism in the Web of Life.* London: Verso.

Moore, Jason W., ed. 2016. *Anthropocene or Capitalocene? Nature, History and the Crisis of Capitalism.* Oakland, CA: PM.

Mould, Oli. 2018. "The Not-So-Concrete Jungle: Material Precarity in the Calais Refugee Camp." *Cultural Geographies* 25, no. 3: 393–409. https://doi.org/10.1177/1474474017697457.

MSF (Médecins sans Frontières). 2016. *Out of Sight: Asylum Seekers and Refugees in Italy; Informal Settlements and Social Marginalization.* Brussels: Médecins sans Frontières.

MSF (Médecins sans Frontières). 2018. *Out of Sight: Social Marginality, Obstacles to Access to Healthcare and Basic Needs for Migrants, Asylum Seekers and Refugees.* Brussels: Médecins sans Frontières.

Muehlebach, Andrea. 2011. "On Affective Labour in Post-Fordist Italy." *Cultural Anthropology* 26, no. 1: 59–81. https://doi.org/10.1111/j.1548-1360.2010.01080.x.

Muehlebach, Andrea. 2012. *The Moral Neoliberal: Welfare and Citizenship in Italy.* Chicago: University of Chicago Press.

Müller, Martin. 2015. "Assemblages and Actor-Networks: Rethinking Socio-material Power, Politics and Space." *Geography Compass* 9, no. 1: 27–41. http://doi.org/10.1111/gec3.12192.

Nail, Thomas. 2017. "What Is an Assemblage?" *SubStance* 46, no. 1: 21–37.

Nelson, Gerald C., Mark W. Rosgrant, Jawoo Koo, Richard Robertson, Timothy Sulsr, Tingju Zhu, Claude Ringler, et al. 2009. *Climate Change: Impact on Agriculture and Costs of Adaptation.* Washington, DC: International Food Policy Research Institute.

Newman, David. 2003. "On Borders and Power: A Theoretical Framework." *Journal of Borderlands Studies* 18, no. 1: 13–25.

Nitti, Francesco Saverio. 1888. *L'emigrazione italiana e i suoi avversari.* Turin and Naples: L. Roux. Available at https://archive.org/details/lemigrazioneital00nitt; last accessed March 2021.

Nixon, Rob. 2011. *Slow Violence and the Environmentalism of the Poor*. Cambridge, MA: Harvard University Press.

Novak, Paolo. 2019. "The Neoliberal Location of Asylum." *Political Geography* 70:1–13.

Oriji, Chinwe Ezinna. 2020. "From Biafra to Police Brutality: Challenging Localized Blackness toward Globally Racialized Ethnicities of Nigerians in the US." *Ethnic and Racial Studies* 43, no. 9: 1600–1617.

Osservatorio Placido Rizzotto. 2012. *Agromafie e caporalato, primo rapporto*. Rome: CGIL-FLAI.

Osservatorio Placido Rizzotto. 2014. *Agromafie e caporalato, secondo rapporto*. Rome: CGIL-FLAI.

Osservatorio Placido Rizzotto. 2020. *Agromafie e caporalato, quinto rapporto*. Rome: CGIL-FLAI.

Pallister-Wilkins, Polly. 2022. "Whitescapes: A Posthumanist Political Ecology of Alpine Migrant (Im)mobility." *Political Geography* 92. https://doi.org/10.1016/j.polgeo.2021.102517.

Palmi, Tommaso. 2021. *Decolonizzare l'antirazzismo. Per una critica della cattiva coscienza bianca*. Rome: Derive Approdi.

Patel, Raj, and Jason W. Moore. 2017. *A History of the World in Seven Cheap Things*. Berkeley: University of California Press.

Patterson, Orlando. 1982. *Slavery and Social Death: A Comparative Study*. Cambridge, MA: Harvard University Press.

Peano, Irene. 2019. "Supply chain affettive tra agro-industria e migrazioni, contenimento e rifugio." In *Un mondo logistico: Sgardi su lavoro, migrazioni, politica e globalizzazione*, edited by Niccolò Cuppini and Irene Peano, 63–76. Milan: Ledizioni.

Peck, Jamie, and Nik Theodore. 2001. "Contingent Chicago: Restrucuring the Spaces of Temporary Labor." *International Journal of Urban and Regional Research* 25, no. 3 (September): 471–96. https://doi.org/10.1111/1468-2427.00325.

Pelek, Deniz. 2020. "Ethnic Residential Segregation among Seasonal Migrant Workers: From Temporary Tents to New Rural Ghettos in Southern Turkey." *Journal of Peasant Studies* 49, no. 1: 54–77. https://doi.org/10.1080/03066150.2020.1767077.

Peluso, Nancy L., and Christian Lund. 2011. "New Frontiers of Land Control: Introduction." *Journal of Peasant Studies* 38, no. 4: 667–81. https://doi.org/10.1080/03066150.2011.607692.

Percoco, Marco. 2018. "Wealth Inequality, Redistribution and Local Development: The Case of Land Reform in Italy." *Environment and Planning C: Politics and Space* 36, no. 2: 181–200. https://doi.org/10.1177/2399654417691282.

Perrotta, Domenico. 2014. "Behind the Cheap Tomato: Migrant Workers in Southern Italy." *Global Dialogue* 11, no. 1. https://globaldialogue.isa-sociology.org/articles/behind-the-cheap-tomato-migrant-workers-in-southern-italy.

Perrotta, Domenico. 2020. *Rosarno, la rivolta e dopo. Cosa è successo nelle campagne del sud*. Rome: Edizioni dell'Asino.

Perrotta, Domenico, and Timothy Raeymaekers. 2022. "Caporalato Capitalism: Labour Brokerage and Agrarian Change in a Mediterranean Society." *Journal of Peasant Studies* (July). https://doi.org/10.1080/03066150.2022.2072213.

Perrotta, Domenico, and Devi Sacchetto. 2014. "Migrant Farmworkers in Southern Italy: Ghettoes, *Caporalato* and Collective Action." *International Journal of Strikes and Social Conflicts* 1, no. 5: 75–98.

Pesarini, Angelica, and Guido Tintori. 2020. "Mixed Identities in Italy: A Country in Denial." In *The Palgrave International Handbook of Mixed Racial and Ethnic*

Classification, edited by Zarine L. Rocha and Peter J. Aspinall, 349–65. Cham, Switzerland: SpringerLink.

Phelps, Nicholas A., Miguel Atienza, and Martin Arias. 2018. "An Invitation to the Dark Side of Economic Geography." *Environment and Planning A: Economy and Space* 50, no. 1 (February): 236–44. https://doi.org/10.1177/0308518X17739007.

Phillips, Anne. 1989. *The Enigma of Colonialism: British Policy in West Africa*. London: James Currey; and Bloomington: Indiana University Press.

Phillips, Nicola. 2011. "Informality, Global Production Networks and the Dynamics of 'Adverse Incorporation.'" *Global Networks* 11, no. 3 (July): 380–97. https://doi.org/10.1111/j.1471-0374.2011.00331.x.

Phillips, Nicola. 2013. "Unfree Labour and Adverse Incorporation in the Global Economy: Comparative Perspectives on Brazil and India." *Economy and Society* 42, no. 2: 171–96. https://doi.org/10.1080/03085147.2012.718630.

Picker, Giovanni, and Silvia Pasquetti. 2018. "Durable Camps: The State, the Urban, the Everyday." *City* 19, no. 5: 681–88. https://doi.org/10.1080/13604813.2015.1071122.

Pierce, Sarah. 2014. "The Vital Difference between Human Trafficking and Migrant Smuggling." *Open Democracy* 12 (November). https://www.opendemocracy.net/en/beyond-trafficking-and-slavery/vital-difference-between-human-trafficking-and-migrant-smuggling.

Pierre, Jemima. 2013. *The Predicament of Blackness: Postcolonial Ghana and the Politics of Race*. Chicago: University of Chicago Press.

Pinelli, Barbara. 2017. "Borders, Politics and Subjects: Introductory Notes on Refugee Research in Europe." *ERQ* 1 (January–April): 5–24.

Pontrandolfi, Alfonso. 2002. *La vergogna cancellata: Matera negli anni dello sfollamento dei Sassi*. Matera: Altrimedia.

Povinelli, Elizabeth. 2011. *Economies of Abandonment: Social Belonging and Endurance in Late Liberalism*. Durham, NC: Duke University Press.

Pradella, Lucia, and Rossana Cillo. 2021. "Bordering the Surplus Population across the Mediterranean: Imperialism and Unfree Labour in Libya and the Italian Countryside." *Geoforum* 126 (November). https://doi.org/10.1016/j.geoforum.2020.06.019.

Prinzi, Daniele. 1956. *La riforma agraria in Puglia, Lucania, Molise nei primi cinque anni*. Bari: Laterza.

Proglio, Gabriele. 2016. *Memorie oltre confine. La letteratura postcoloniale italiana in prospettiva storica*. Verona: Ombre Corte.

Pulido, Laura. 2015. "Geographies of Race and Ethnicity 1: White Supremacy vs White Privilege in Environmental Racism Research." *Progress in Human Geography* 39, no. 6: 809–17. https://doi.org/10.1177/0309132514563008.

Pulido, Laura. 2017. "Geographies of Race and Ethnicity II: Environmental Racism, Racial Capitalism and State-Sanctioned Violence." *Progress in Human Geography* 41, no. 4: 524–33. https://doi.org/10.1177/0309132516646495.

Quiligotti, Jeff. (1960) 2010. "Postfazione." In *Milano, Corea: Inchiesta sugli immigrati negli anni del "miracolo,"* edited by Franco Alasi and Danilo Montaldi, 315–35. Rome: Donzelli.

Quintano, Claudio, Paolo Mazzocchi, and Antonella Rocca. 2018. "The Determinants of Italian NEETs and the Effects of the Economic Crisis." *Genus* 74, no. 5. https://doi.org/10.1186/s41118-018-0031-0.

Raeymaekers, Timothy. 2014. *Violent Capitalism and Hybrid Identity in the Eastern Congo: Power to the Margins*. Cambridge: Cambridge University Press.

Raeymaekers, Timothy. 2021. "Impermanent Territories: The Mediterranean Crisis and the (Re-)production of the Black Subject." In *The Black Mediterranean: Bodies, Borders and Citizenship*, edited by Black Mediterranean Collective, 117–44. Cham, Switzerland: SpringerLink.

Ralph, Michael, and Maya Singhal. 2019. "Racial Capitalism." *Theory & Society* 48, no. 6: 851–81. https://doi.org/10.1007/s11186-019-09367-z.

Reeves, Madeleine. 2014. *Border Work: Spatial Lives of the State in Rural Central Asia.* Ithaca, NY: Cornell University Press.

Regassa, Asebe, Yetebarek Hizekiel, and Benedikt Korf. 2019. "'Civilizing' the Pastoral Frontier: Land Grabbing, Dispossession and Coercive Agrarian Development in Ethiopia." *Journal of Peasant Studies* 46, no. 5: 935–55. https://doi.org/10.1080/03066150.2017.1420060.

Rey, Pierre-Philippe. 1982. "Class Alliances." *International Journal of Sociology* 12, no. 2: 1–120.

Reyna, S. P. 1987. "The Emergence of Land Concentration in the West African Savanna." *American Ethnologist* 14:523–41. https://doi.org/10.1525/ae.1987.14.3.02a00070.

Richards, Paul, and Jean-Pierre Chauveau. 2007. *Land, Agricultural Change and Conflict in West Africa: Regional Issues from Sierra Leone, Liberia and Côte d'Ivoire.* Issy-les-Moulineaux: CSAO/SWAC.

Rigo, Enrica. 2015. *Leggi, migranti e caporali: Prospettive critiche e di ricerca sullo sfruttamento del lavoro in agricoltura.* Pisa: Pacini.

Rigo, Enrica. 2022. *La straniera. Migrazioni, asilo, sfruttamento in una prospettiva di genere.* Milan: Carocci.

Rigo, Enrica, and Carlo Caprioglio. 2021. "Diritto, migrazioni e sfruttamento nell'agricoltura italiana." In *Braccia rubate dall'agricoltura: Pratiche di sfruttamento del lavoro migrante*, edited by Ilaria Ippolito, Mimmo Perrotta, and Timothy Raeymaekers, 39–64. Turin: SEB27.

Robinson, Cedric J. (1983) 2005. *Black Marxism: The Making of the Black Radical Tradition.* Chapel Hill: University of North Carolina Press.

Rochat, Giorgio. 1973. *Il colonialismo italiano.* Turin: Loescher.

Rodogno, Davide. 2003. *Il nuovo ordine mediterraneo.* Turin: Bollati Boringhieri.

Roitman, Janet. 2005. *Fiscal Disobedience: An Anthropology of Economic Regulation in Central Africa.* Princeton, NJ: Princeton University Press.

Rossi-Doria, Manlio. 1982. *Scritti sul Mezzogiorno.* Turin: Einaudi.

Roy, Anyanya, and Nezar AlSayyad. 2004. *Urban Informality: Transnational Perspectives from the Middle East, Latin America, and South Asia.* New York: Lexington Books.

Roy, Anyanya, and Emma Crane. 2015. *Territories of Poverty: Rethinking North and South.* Athens: University of Georgia Press.

Rye, Johan Fredrik, and Sam Scott. 2018. "International Labour Migration and Food Production in Rural Europe: A Review of the Evidence." *Sociologia Ruralis* 58, no. 4: 928–52. https://doi.org/10.1111/soru.12208.

Saitta, Armando. 1967. *Dal fascismo alla resistenza.* Rome: La Nuova Italia.

Saldanha, Arun. 2019. "A Date with Destiny: Racial Capitalism and the Beginnings of the Anthropocene." *Environment and Planning D: Society and Space* 38, no. 1 (September): 12–34. https://doi.org/10.1177/0263775819871964.

Santoianni, Vittorio. 2008. "Il razionalismo nelle colonie italiane 1928–1943: La 'nuova architettura' delle terre d'Oltremare." Doctoral thesis, Naples.

Sanyal, Kalyan. 2013. *Rethinking Capitalist Development: Primitive Accumulation, Governmentality and Post-colonial Capitalism.* Delhi: Routledge.

Sarr, Felwine. 2016. *Afrotopia.* Paris: Philippe Rey.

Saucier, Khalil. 2021. "Carne nera." In *The Black Mediterranean: Bodies, Borders and Citizenship*, edited by Black Mediterranean Collective, 101–16. Cham, Switzerland: SpringerLink.

Saul, S. B. 1957. "The Economic Significance of 'Constructive Imperialism.'" *Journal of Economic History* 17, no. 2 (June): 173–92. https://doi.org/10.1017/S0022050700080396.

Schapendonk, Joris. 2017. "Navigating the Migration Industry: Migrants Moving through an African-European Web of Facilitation/Control." *Journal of Ethnic and Migration Studies* 44, no. 4: 663–79. https://doi.org/10.1080/1369183X.2017.1315522.

Schmidt di Friedberg, Olivia. 1996. "Strategie migratorie e reti etniche a confronto: I burkinabè e i senegalesi in Italia." *Studi Emigrazione* 33, no. 121: 25–46.

Scoones, Ian, Marc Edelman, Saturnino Borras, Ruth Hall, Wendy Wolford, and Ben White. 2019. "Emancipatory Rural Politics: Confronting Authoritarian Populism." *Journal of Peasant Studies* 45, no. 1: 1–20. https://doi.org/10.1080/03066150.2017.1339693.

Scott, James. 1998. *Seeing Like a State: How Certain Schemes to Improve the Human Condition Have Failed*. New Haven, CT: Yale University Press.

Scott, James. 2009. *The Art of Not Being Governed: An Anarchist History of Upland Southeast Asia*. New Haven, CT: Yale University Press.

Selwyn, Benjamin. 2019. "Poverty Chains and Global Capitalism." *Competition & Change* 23, no. 1: 71–97. https://doi.org/10.1177/1024529418809067.

Sheppard, Eric, and James Tyner. 2016. "Forum on Geography and Militarism: An Introduction." *Annals of the American Association of Geographers* 106, no. 3, 52016: 503–5. https://doi.org/10.1080/24694452.2015.1131141.

Simone, AbdouMaliq. 2001. "On the Worlding of African Cities." *African Studies Review* 44, no. 2: 15–41.

Simone, AbdouMaliq. 2004. "People as Infrastructure: Intersecting Fragments in Johannesburg." *Public Culture* 16, no. 3: 407–29. https://www.muse.jhu.edu/article/173743.

Skrivankova, Klara. 2010. *Between Decent Work and Forced Labour: Examining the Continuum of Exploitation*. York: Joseph Rowntree Foundation.

Smith, Neil. (1984) 2008. *Uneven Development: Nature, Capital, and the Production of Space*. Athens: University of Georgia Press.

Soja, Edward. 1989. *Postmodern Geographies: The Reassertion of Space in Critical Social Theory*. London: Verso Books.

Springer, Simon, and Philippe Le Billon. 2016. "Violence and Space: An Introduction to the Geographies of Violence." *Political Geography* 52:1–3. https://doi.org/10.1016/j.polgeo.2016.03.003.

Squire, Vicky. 2014. "Desert 'Trash': Posthumanism, Border Struggles, and Humanitarian Politics." *Political Geography* 39:11–21. https://doi.org/10.1016/j.polgeo.2013.12.003.

Stallabrass, Julian. 1996. *Gargantua: Manufactured Mass Culture*. London: Verso.

Steffen, Will, Paul J. Crutzen, and John R. McNeill. 2007. "The Anthropocene: Are Humans Now Overwhelming the Great Forces of Nature?" *Ambio* 36, no. 8 (December): 614–21. https://doi.org/10.1579/0044-7447(2007)36[614:TAAHNO]2.0.CO;2.

Stoler, Ann L. 2008. "Imperial Debris: Reflections on Ruins and Ruination." *Cultural Anthropology* 23:191–219. https://doi.org/10.1111/j.1548-1360.2008.00007.x.

Svampa, Maristella. 2012. "Resource Extractivism and Alternatives: Latin American Perspectives on Development." *Journal fur Entwicklungspolitik* 28, no. 3: 43–73.

Swyngedouw, Eric. 2004. *Social Power and the Urbanization of Water Flows of Power*. Oxford: Oxford University Press.

Swyngedouw, Eric, and Henrik Ernstson. 2018. "Interrupting the Anthropo-obScene: Immuno-biopolitics and Depoliticizing Ontologies in the Anthropocene." *Theory, Culture & Society* 35, no. 6: 3–30. https://doi.org/10.1177/0263276418757314.

Tazzioli, Martina. 2020. "Governing Migrant Mobility through Mobility: Containment and Dispersal at the Internal Frontiers of Europe." *Environment and Planning C: Politics and Space* 38, no. 1 (February): 3–19. https://doi.org/10.1177/2399654419839065.

Tenzon, Michele. 2018. "Rural Modernity in Post-war Southern Italy: The La Martella Village in Matera." *Journal of Architecture* 23, no. 3: 498–522. https://doi.org/10.1080/13602365.2018.1460731.

Teti, Vito. 2004. *Il senso dei luoghi. Memoria e storia dei paesi abbandonati*. Rome: Donzelli.

Teti, Vito. 2017. *Quel che resta. L'Italia dei paesi, tra abbandoni e ritorni*. Rome: Donzelli.

Thaler, Gregory M., Cecila Viana, and Fabiano Toni. 2019. "From Frontier Governance to Governance Frontier: The Political Geography of Brazil's Amazon Transition." *World Development* 114 (February): 59–72. https://doi.org/10.1016/j.worlddev.2018.09.022.

Thomas, Darryl C. 2013. "Cedric J. Robinson and Racial Capitalism: Africana Liberation Resistance Structures and Black Internationalism in the Twenty-First Century." *African Identities* 11, no. 2: 133–47.

Thomas, K. A. 2021. "International Rivers as Border Infrastructures: En/forcing Borders in South Asia." *Political Geography* 89, 102448. https://doi.org/10.1016/j.polgeo.2021.102448.

Thompson, Edward Palmer. 1963. *The Making of the English Working Class*. New York: Vintage Books.

Ticktin, Miriam. 2007. "The Offshore Camps of the European Union: At the Border of Humanity." Paper presented at the American Anthropological Association Annual Meetings, November/December. https://www.files.ethz.ch/isn/106535/Ticktin_2009-03.pdf.

Ticktin, Miriam. 2017. "A World without Innocence." *American Ethnologist* 44, no. 4 (November): 577–90. https://doi.org/10.1111/amet.12558.

Timera, Mahamet. 2011. "Les migrations des jeunes Sahéliens: Affirmation de soi et émancipation." *Autrepart* 18:37–49.

Tinti, Peter, and Taylor Reitano. 2017. *Migrant, Refugee, Smuggler, Saviour*. New York: Oxford University Press.

Tsianos, Vassilis, and Dimitris Papadopoulos. 2006. "Precarity: A Savage Journey to the Heart of Embodied Capitalism." *Machines and Subjectivation* 10. https://transversal.at/transversal/1106/tsianos-papadopoulos/en.

Tsing, A. 2005. *Friction: An Ethnography of Global Connection*. Princeton, NJ: Princeton University Press.

Turner, Victor. 1967. *The Forest of Symbols*. Ithaca, NY: Cornell University Press.

Turner, Victor. 1969. *The Ritual Process*. Chicago: Aldine.

Tyner, James. 2019. *Dead Labor: Toward a Political Economy of Premature Death*. Minneapolis: University of Minnesota Press.

UNIMSIL, UNHROHC (United Nations Support Mission in Libya, United Nations Human Rights Office of the High Commissioner). 2018. *Desperate and*

Dangerous: Report on the Human Rights Situation of Migrants and Refugees in Libya. New York: United Nations.

Vacchiano, Francesco. 2013. "Fencing in the South: The Strait of Gibraltar as a Paradigm of the New Border Regime in the Mediterranean." *Journal of Mediterranean Studies* 22, no. 2: 337–64. https:// muse.jhu.edu/article/671627.

Vammen, Ida Marie Savio, Signe Cold-Ravnkilde, and Hans Lucht. 2022. "Borderwork in the Expanded EU-African Borderlands." *Geopolitics* 27:1317–30. https://doi.org/10.1080/14650045.2022.2008734.

Van Beusekom, Monika M. 1997. "Colonisation Indigène: French Rural Development Ideology at the Office du Niger, 1920–1940." *International Journal of African Historical Studies* 30, no. 2: 299–323.

Van Der Ploeg, Irma. 1999. "The Illegal Body: Eurodac and the Politics of Biometric Identification." *Ethics and Information Technology* 1:295–302.

van Gennep, Arnold. (1909) 1960. *The Rites of Passage*. Chicago: University of Chicago Press.

Verlinden, Charles. 1977. *L'esclavage dans l'Europe médiévale*. 2 vols. Bruges: de Tempel.

Vigh, Henrik. 2009. "Motion Squared: A Second Look at the Concept of Social Navigation." *Anthropological Theory* 9, no. 4 (December): 419–38. https://doi.org/10.1177/1463499609356044.

Wacquant, Loïc, Tom Slater, and Virgilio Borges Pereira. 2014. "Territorial Stigmatization in Action." *Environment and Planning A: Economy and Space* 46, no. 6: 1270–80. https://doi.org/10.1068/a4606ge.

Waite, Louise. 2009. "A Place and Space for a Critical Geography of Precarity?" *Geography Compass* 3:412–33. https://doi.org/10.1111/j.1749-8198.2008.00184.x.

Wallace, Rob, Alex Liebman, Luis Fernando Chaves, and Rodrick Wallace. 2020. "COVID and Circuits of Capital." *Monthly Review* 72, no. 1 (May). https://monthlyreview.org/2020/05/01/covid-19-and-circuits-of-capital/.

Wallerstein, Immanuel. 1967. *Urbanization and Migration in West Africa*. Berkeley: University of California Press.

Warren, Calvin L. 2018. *Ontological Terror: Blackness, Nihilism, and Emancipation*. Durham, NC: Duke University Press.

Weeks, Kathi. 2016. "Introduction: The Problem with Work." In *Global Histories of Work*, edited by Andreas Eckert, 1–36. Berlin: de Gruyter.

Weheliye, Alexander G. 2014. *Habeas viscus: Racializing Assemblages, Biopolitics, and Black Feminist Theories of the Human*. Durham, NC: Duke University Press.

Wiley, Danielle. 2010. "A Walk about Rome: Tactics for Mapping the Urban Periphery." *Architectural Theory Review* 15, no. 1: 9–29. https://doi.org/10.1080/13264821003629220.

Wilson, David, and Andrew E. G. Jonas. 2018. "Planetary Urbanization: New Perspectives on the Debate." *Urban Geography* 39, no. 10: 1576–80. https://doi.org/10.1080/02723638.2018.1481603.

World Bank. 2019. *World Development Report 2019: The Changing Nature of Work*. Washington, DC: World Bank.

Wouterse, Fleur, and Marrit Van den Bergh. 2011. "Heterogeneous Migration Flows from the Central Plateau of Burkina Faso: The Role of Natural and Social Capital." *Geographical Journal* 177, no. 4 (December): 357–66. https://doi.org/10.1111/j.1475-4959.2011.00423.x.

Wrong, Michela. 2005. *It Didn't Do It for You: How the World Betrayed a Small African Nation*. New York: Harper.

Young, William. 2004. *Sold Out: The True Cost of Supermarket Shopping*. London: Vision Paperbacks.

Yiftachel, Oren. 2009. "Critical Theory and 'Gray Space': Mobilization of the Colonized." *City* 13, no. 2–3: 240–57. https://doi.org/10.1080/13604810902982227.

Xiang, Biao. 2013. "Multi-scalar Ethnography: An Approach for Critical Engagement with Migration and Social Change." *Ethnography* 14, no. 3: 282–99. https://doi.org/10.1177/1466138113491669.

Ziarek, Ewa Płonowska. 2008. "Bare Life on Strike: Notes on the Biopolitics of Race and Gender." *South Atlantic Quarterly* 107, no. 1: 89–105. https://doi.org/10.1215/00382876-2007-057.

Zoomers, Annelies. 2018. "Plantations Are Everywhere! Between Infrastructural Violence and Inclusive Development." *Geoforum* 96:341–44. https://doi.org/10.1016/j.geoforum.2018.04.006.

Index

Note: References followed by "n" refer to endnotes.

www.ingramcontent.com/pod-product-compliance
Lightning Source LLC
Chambersburg PA
CBHW051728260326
41914CB00040B/2019/J